G000054164

An *Intentional Life*

An Intentional Life

Musings of a Secular Monastic

Andrew Fitz-Gibbon

Copyright © 2012 by Andrew Fitz-Gibbon.

Cover photo Cape Henlopen State Park, DE. © 2011, Andrew Fitz-Gibbon.

Library of Congress Control Number: 2012918085
ISBN: Hardcover   978-1-4797-2369-0
               Softcover   978-1-4797-2368-3
               Ebook   978-1-4797-2370-6

All rights reserved. No part of this book may be reproduced or transmitted in any form or by any means, electronic or mechanical, including photocopying, recording, or by any information storage and retrieval system, without permission in writing from the copyright owner.

This book was printed in the United States of America.

To order additional copies of this book, contact:
Xlibris Corporation
1-888-795-4274
www.Xlibris.com
Orders@Xlibris.com
116423

CONTENTS

PART TWO: SEASONAL REFLECTIONS

Dedication

For all those who dare to take the inner journey

FOREWORD

I did not intend to write this book. It began as a series of reflections I recorded for members of the Lindisfarne Community and sent to our community mailing list. Later, the reflections were posted to *The Abbot's Blog* on the Internet. Over the six years or so that these musings were composed, they have become something of a window on my spiritual and philosophical journey. But the journey did not begin six years ago, nor does it end with the last of these reflections. These serve as but a glimpse into my personal odyssey. Though these reflections are not in any way polished philosophy nor systematic theology, the careful reader will be able to piece together what I think about metaphysics (what is the case), epistemology (how we know what we think we know), ethics (how we ought to live) and aesthetics (what is beautiful and why). I comment also on understandings of God, Christ, Christianity, the Buddha, Daoism, and interfaith dialogue.

A few words about the title. Intention has a long tradition in spirituality. Conscious choice rather than mere wishes, or hopes, or happenstances is a foundation of spirituality. It is closely linked with mindfulness. For example, in Chinese philosophy, *yi* (wisdom mind) directs *qi* (life energy) and moves the body in *jin* (expressed energy). *Yi* is intention. Perhaps the greatest of all philosophers, Socrates of Athens—often compared with Jesus of Nazareth—said in the *Apology* "the life which is unexamined is not worth living" (38a).

Intention, closely associated with self examination—self-reflection—is a practice in which I have tried to engage over many years. To become more aware, more intentional, more centered, seems a worthy endeavor. One afternoon, searching for a title, it seemed obvious that this volume is quite simply that—a glimpse of an intentional life. In part, I hope it serves as a spur to others to make a similar, though unique to them, inner journey.

And the subtitle? These are the musings of a secular monastic. Besides being a philosophy teacher at a state university, I am abbot of a religious order of the sort we have begun to call the "secular monasticism." We derived the name from two ideas that Dietrich Bonhoeffer, Lutheran pastor and martyr, had in the 1930s and 1940s. The first was that Christianity needed to be renewed by a new kind of monasticism, for monasticism in its many expressions has always been a renewal movement. The second was that in a religionless world what is needed is a religionless Christianity—a secular Christianity. We have combined the two thoughts and have begun the practice of "secular monasticism."

It is secular because it is a life lived fully "in the world." Often, religious impulse is thought to involve withdrawal from the world. The "world" has often been seen in opposition to the "religious life." The world is conceived as the enemy to fight against or to flea from. The world corrupts the pure. Yet, another stream of thought suggests that if spirituality is to be of any use at all, then it must be a spirituality lived in the world and for the world. It is that current that we have tapped into.

For nineteen years, I was a pastor in a traditional congregational setting. For the last twelve years, I have taught undergraduates as a philosophy professor. When I was a traditional pastor, I rarely met anyone "in the world." If I did, it would more often than not be to meet them in the context of how they might be of use "in the church." Much of a traditional pastor's life concerns bringing more people into the sphere of the church, to continue the institution of the church. Spirituality is measured by the number of church meetings you can squash into the average week. The church exists for itself. In time, this began to bother me. It began as a niggle that things were not quite right. On reflection, the "not quite right" feeling came from a perception that a spiritual life is a life lived for the Other. Of course, many folks in the Church do live for the Other as far as they can. But it is the nature of bureaucracies that they become self-perpetuating, self-serving. When a religious organization becomes a bureaucracy, it has no other choice open to it. Bureaucracy stifles spirit, routinizes charisma.

It was with intention then that I left the paid pastorate to find a living "in the world." The intention was not to leave the spiritual life, but to "lose the self" in the world, in order to truly "find the self"—a conscious attempt to explore Bonhoeffer's religionless, secular spirituality.

Monasticism, in its Christian, Buddhist, and Daoist expressions, has always been a way of regulating spiritual life according to a particular Rule of Life. Spirituality does not "just happen." Doubtless, all people are spiritual, for in part, to be human is to be a spiritual being. But spirituality, as an intentional practice of life requires habit and guidance. Monasticism has sought to provide a framework for that in its Rule (the habits, injunctions, and commitments of the spiritual life) and in its community (where guidance is found through friendships and spiritual direction).

Secular monastics are those who are intentional about the spiritual life (derived from the habits of monasticism) and intentional about living fully in and for the world. To a certain degree, I embody the notion of secularity and spirituality in my own day-to-day life. I am a professor and chair of philosophy at a state university as well as abbot of a religious order. I receive interrogation from both "camps." Students who sometimes become aware of my spiritual commitments ask, "How can you possibly be a philosophy professor and religious!" For having heard me debunk all that can be debunked, in the great tradition of modern philosophy post-Descartes, it is inconceivable to them that I could remain committed to spirituality.

Religious folk, who far too often have been socialized in their churches to think that the academy is the enemy ask, "How could you possibly challenge everything in the way philosophers do? Doesn't it spoil you spiritually?"

My usual response to both questions is a wry smile, for I see no ultimate irreconcilability. For me, truth is truth from whatever source it is derived.

However, making sense of truth claims is another matter. Our secular and religious myths are ways of helping us make sense of Reality. Sometimes they are helpful, sometimes not. To live fully in and for the world, while at the same time pursuing a deep and authentic spirituality, is the task of the secular monastic.

Secular monasticism is, then, full of joys, challenges, and struggles. Some of these you will find discussed in these musings. By nature, they are personal musings, though they arose in the context of a scattered community of monastics.

A word about voice. These musings are written often in the first person. Occasionally, the voice of the reflection is "we." Context will show whether the "we" is the Lindisfarne Community, secular monasticism, or Western society. Rather than create a unified voice, I have left the musings in the voice in which they were originally written.

This book is not intended to be read from beginning to end. Rather, it is to be dipped into, flipped through, picking a reflection here or there and staying with it for a while. For those who use the Lindisfarne Community's *Way of Living* (2006), a reflection may be used as part of the *Daily Office*, as a meditation for the day. A reflection may be read in the morning, or in the evening as part of a spiritual discipline. Be imaginative!

I am grateful to my wife Jane, abbess of our community. These musings were mostly shared with her before anyone else and refined in the sharing. The members of the Lindisfarne Community, whom I count as friends, and among whom I serve as abbot, have listened to and dialoged with me. I am grateful to colleagues, friends, and students in the academy for keeping me rooted in the world. Special thanks to Elizabeth Boepple, my copy-editor and friend who always goes the extra mile.

PART ONE

GENERAL REFLECTIONS

ONE

THE LINDISFARNE RULE OF LIFE
HABITS AND PRACTICES

1. The New Monasticism, Religionless Christianity

This week I had a couple of opportunities to reflect on one of the foundational ideas of the Lindisfarne Community: the new monasticism as suggested by Ditriech Bonhoeffer in a letter to his brother Karl-Friedrich in 1935. It is found in the Biography of Bonhoeffer by Ebehard Bethge (1970).

The two opportunities to reflect on this came my way: first, in an interview I gave to a graduate student from an Ivy League University doing a dissertation on the new monasticism. The other occasion was a panel discussion about Al Staggs's one-person play on Bonhoeffer's reflections before his death; I was invited on stage to dialogue with him at the end of the play.

Both opportunities gave me time to reflect on what the new monasticism might be, and to link it with another idea in Bonhoeffer, that of religionless Christianity. This idea is found in his letter from prison dated April 30, 1944. Bonhoeffer does not elaborate therein, and he was executed before he could enlighten us. But he did raise interesting questions.

His view was that religion in the so-called civilized world had come to an end. The Nazi period, Holocaust, and World War demonstrated that religion in any real sense had come to an end. That was the way it seemed to him as he sat in his prison cell.

In this religionless world, what would happen to Christianity? Well, it would need to be a religionless Christianity: something new, something that would fit into a religionless world.

Whether his view of the end of religion was true is beside the point. I suspect it has proved very true of Western Europe, and is somewhat true of North America. But much of the rest of the world remains very religious.

The interesting issue is that of religionless Christianity.

I want to link it to his earlier view of the new kind of monasticism that is rooted in the Sermon on the Mount, but has nothing in common with earlier versions of monasticism.

Religionless Christianity is a Christianity that has lost itself in the world. It is the "leaven in the lump." It is a hidden way of following the Christ that does not trumpet its arrival. It does not seek to proselytize. It simply is. It is being and becoming. It is Christ in the midst of God's world. It requires new expressions of faith and new ways of praying. It is willing to discard much of the clutter of the centuries. It dies to self that others may live. It is solitary and communal. But I suspect it is never big, never the crowd. The group psychology of the crowd (witness Nazi Germany) is a fearful thing.

In the Lindisfarne Community, we have tried to practice this. It is why, in the end, both Jane and I chose to work "in the world": to be among the people; to be "little Christs." To lose ourselves. It is why we encourage our deacons and priests to do the same.

I do not think this is an easy way at all. The great danger is that you really do lose yourself. The old securities of religion fade. Religious language becomes a foreign language. When you meet the pious who speak the "language of Zion" there is a disconnect. Secular monasticism requires a different spirituality.

At this point, it seems that not many want to join such a movement, though early I had hopes. Part of the reason, I suspect, is that religion provides security. The world is often uncertain. Religion, of any kind, tries to provide the certainties of life. That is how fundamentalisms grow quickly. However absurd the certainties may be, folk like to be sure.

Religionless Christianity has no certainties. It provides only uncertainties. It is not about saving yourself, but losing yourself—and who wants to be lost! The old question of religion: "Brother, are you saved?" becomes the new question of the religionless, "Sister, have you yet lost yourself amongst those who also are lost?" In losing self is salvation. In dying is life. In the loss of religion we find the Christ. In losing the church we gain the world.

2. Simplicity of the Rule

The simplicity of the Rule of the Lindisfarne Community is to live a balanced life of prayer, work, study, and rest (some wish to add play).

Reflecting on a balanced life, toward which most of us are probably working, I came across a quote by Newman in Moss's *The Birth of the Middle Ages* (1998). Newman says that the thrust of the Rule of St. Benedict was in "having neither hope nor fear of anything below; in daily prayer, daily bread and daily work, one day being just like another, except that it was one step nearer than the day before it to that great Day which would swallow up all days, the day of everlasting rest."

3. The Daily Office

The Lindisfarne Community is part of a grass-roots movement of renewal in the church. Renewal is an interesting word. To renew is to repair something, to replace something worn-out or broken, or to return something to its former state. In the secular monasticism we have looked again to ancient practices of Christians. Monastic practices have been instruments of renewal since the desert mothers and fathers. The six practices that we encourage in Lindisfarne are: Eucharist, the Daily Office, Meditation, Mindfulness, Study, and Service. If you examine monasticism in East and West you will find these kinds of practice—at times some more prominent than others. These are the essence of anything we might call monastic. Where the secular monasticism differs is that we seek to practice in our everyday lives, immersed in the world, rather than in separate, closed communities. It is spiritual practice in the saeculum. To be in the world is important—"To be lost in the world," to summarize Dietrich Bonhoeffer.

I have been thinking about the Daily Office and its importance in our spirituality—that is, the daily rhythm of prayers, psalms, and readings. Here is my journey with the office.

I was first introduced to the Office in 1981 when I became a student at Northern Baptist College in Manchester, England. The college was very ecumenical and had begun the practice of the office, morning and evening, based on a publication of the Daily Office by the Joint Liturgical Group in the UK (1978). That office book was based to some degree on the Anglican Book of Common Prayer, though rather simplified. Of significance was that it was a product of representatives of all the main churches and all "churchmanships,"—Episcopalian, Presbyterian and Congregational. I used the Daily Office in that form for a number of years. I did not then know that its roots were monastic.

My next Daily Office was "The Minister's Prayer Book," a Lutheran publication. It was again a simplified prayer book, based around the church calendar with a daily lectionary, and full of readings of particular interest to ministers. I continued with that book until the Northumbria Community produced its Daily Office in 1990. The first edition was a loose-leaf "Filofax" binder and new months of readings were added as the community produced them. In 1994, Marshall Pickering picked up the book and it was published first in two volumes (*Celtic Daily Prayer* and *Celtic Night Prayer*), and then in one volume.

We made our first office for the Lindisfarne Community in 1998, with a flavor of our own to reflect our particular emphases (including Celtic emphases, and inclusivity). The basis of daily prayer in our Office is the Daily Prayer of the Church of England with our own peculiarities. Our current version was published in 2006, by Xlibris, and is still available.

Other versions of the Office that I use are these:

> *Celebrating Common Prayer*, the Society of St. Francis, 1992. This was the first major office book for Anglicans since the Book of Common Prayer. It became the basis for the Church of England's Daily Prayer published in 2002.

> *The Book of Common Prayer*, 1979. This the version of the Anglican Book of Common Prayer used in the Episcopal Church USA. We have based our ordination rites around services here.

> *Contemporary Office Book* 1995. This contains in full the two-year daily lectionary found in our *Way of Living* (Fitz-Gibbon and Fitz-Gibbon, 2006). As such, it is the most useful addition to our office and complements it perfectly.

> *A New Zealand Prayer Book*, 1989. The Anglican Church of New Zealand.

Liturgy of the Hours, four volumes, the official Offices of the Roman Catholic Church.

Christian Prayer, the one volume official daily prayers of the Roman Catholic Church. This is the same material as the larger work but excludes a number of services. It contains, morning and evening prayers, daytime prayers, and night prayer. The great advantage of this volume over others is that all the texts are in full. There is no need to have a second book because it has 2070 pages. Yet, it is quite compact!

For the computer literate, online versions of the office can be found in a number of places (just "Google" it). For those with iPhones, there is a very fine reading of the Liturgy of the Hours, morning prayer, evening prayer, and night prayer called the Divine Office. It is free for clergy (search Apps). Our *Way of Living* is available as an EBook on Kindle, Nook, and Sony.

There is a remarkable similarity in these office books. All have their roots in an ancient practice that goes back to sixth century Benedict. It is thought that the Christian office had its roots in Jewish prayer hours.

Besides shaping spirituality, there is a sense of connectedness in the saying of the office—connectedness with the long centuries of Christian practice, and connectedness with people all over the world today who have the office as bedrock of spiritual practice.

4. Deeper Call to Prayer

I sense a deeper call to prayer. Neither the prayer of worry turned to pleading, nor the prayer of barely concealed activity: "Oh God, we are doing such and such, please come to bless us."

It is the rhythm of prayer that turns along the axis of "being, listening, and loving."

Being—in the presence of God, Father-Mother. To recognize the presence of the divine is to pray truly. To be still. To cease from striving.

Listening—to the Spirit. Gentle promptings. Scarcely heard utterance. A profound silence. Listening instead of talking, chattering.

Loving—in response—as Jesus loved. To love God, neighbor, and enemy is to continue the cycle of prayer.

5. Eucharist as Gratefulness

Today was the third week this year that Jane and I have celebrated Eucharist outdoors, in the back garden of the motherhouse. For two weeks, Brother Larry was with us (a great treat). Today we were alone. That is not quite true. Four pugs frolicked the whole time, weaving their way as a playful pack between the ferns and the flowers—rolling over again and again on the moist grass. For three weeks the sun has kindly shone upon us.

I am filled with gratefulness. Early this morning (like, 3:00 am) we drove Cadi and James (our son and his wife) to the airport. We have had a wonderful four days, not doing much at all. Conversing, walking, eating, drinking, a little exercise, and eating and drinking again.

Eucharist is simple thanksgiving. It is the often reminder that life is good. *¡La vida es buena!* Eucharist is close to mindfulness, awareness—an "in-tuneness" with creation, with the divine in all that is.

My social and political commitments make me what some people call a progressive. Progressive types tend toward guilt. It is often guilt for the many good things we enjoy while many in the world do not. Most of my progressive friends face a frequent inner conflict. We work on our conflicted *Existenz* through some kind of activism or social concern or worthy project—trying to put something back for all we have taken out. That is not a bad thing to do.

Yet, Eucharist recalls us to gratefulness. Simple, profound thanksgiving for life, for Goodness, for all.

6. Fourfold Rhythm of Prayer, Study, Service, and Rest

Marketers are clever in their use of "jingles." When I was a boy, growing up in the northwest of England, a favorite jingle was "A Mars a day helps you work, rest, and play." The catchy little tune still pops into my head from time to time. Sadly, the days have long gone when so much chocolate, sugar, and other good stuff could be indulged on a daily basis! (A British "Mars bar" is much the same as an American "Milky Way," I think.)

But there was something profound in the sentiment. A good life is a balanced life . . . work, rest, and play.

The Lindisfarne Community, of which I am abbot, is a secular religious order, somewhat akin to a Franciscan Third Order. In Lindisfarne we are committed to live a balanced life of prayer, study, service, and rest. It is to be our daily rhythm. Rhythm need not be monotony. Rhythm is change.

There may be an emphasis on the first beat, or the fourth, or the first and third, or the second and fourth. In some rhythms, a beat is left silent for effect. Try clapping the rhythms. There are endless possibilities.

The new monasticism is like that. There will be times when there is much emphasis on prayer. At other times, more emphasis on study, or prayer and service, or simply rest. At times, one or more elements of the balance will be "silent."

The secret is to find the balance of the Spirit, to listen to the rhythm of God for you each day.

7. Why Secular Monasticism?

Aldous Huxley, in his 1944 *The Perennial Philosophy* (2009) speaks of knowing God in two ways: the heights of the inner life, and the fullness of God in the world. He says:

> Where there is exclusive concentration on the heights within, temptations and distractions are avoided and there is a general denial and suppression. But when the hope is to know God inclusively—to realize the divine Ground in the world as well as in the soul, temptations and distractions must not be avoided, but submitted to and used as opportunities for advance; there must be no suppression of outward-turning activities, but a transformation of them so that they become sacramental (61-62).

He calls this "spiritual Knowledge in its fullness . . . in and through the world as well as in and through the soul" (62). Yet, Huxley acknowledges the dangers of seeking God in the world. Without a disciplined spiritual practice life in the world either becomes antinomianistic (a kind of anything goes life) or else merely formally spiritual, with no depth (70).

Secular monasticism, as we are trying to practice it in the Lindisfarne Community, is to embrace both ways. We live fearlessly, fully and delightfully in the world, and seek to maintain our integrity in a disciplined and healthy spirituality.

Huxley says:

> As always, the path of spirituality is a knife-edge between abysses. On the one side is the danger of mere rejection and escape, on the other the danger of mere acceptance and the enjoyment of things which should only be used as instruments or symbols (72).

Quite a challenging life. Enjoy the journey!

8. On Habits

A distinctive characteristic of the monastic spirit is that it is a life based on the practices of the spiritual life—prayer, meditation, contemplation, mindfulness, and study, amongst others. Traditionally, at least in the enclosed communities and for solitaries, the monastic withdrew from "the world" into a life of quiet, reflection, and sacred space to learn the disciplines.

Yet most of us who are engaged in the way we are calling the "new monasticism" do not have that facility of withdrawal (at least not for any length of time). Our monastic practice is what we might call a "secular monasticism." We are seeking to practice the monastic disciplines within the context of everyday life, work, and family commitments.

There is a great challenge. The practices do need, well, practice! There is no easy road, no instant maturity, no "microwave" fix.

I have been a guitar player for over forty years. I now have some facility. The movement of hands, the position of notes on the fret board, the "instinctive" sense of rhythm, harmony, melody—to know which mixolydian mode to play over a song in a particular major key. All of this has become, for me, somewhat of a "second nature."

The secret has been practice—to develop the skills, to train the hands and ears. And yet, to be truthful, there are times when I feel I have only just begun to learn the instrument.

It amazes me that in the matters of the Spirit, we often experience an impatience to reach the goal. There is an unspoken understanding that all of us awakened to the Spirit of God ought to be mature, to be adept at the spiritual life.

Our forbears in the monastic spirit knew otherwise. To be monastic is to be one who engages in the practices of the monastic. It is more than about words. It is about being.

9. Practicing Deeply

I recently came across this passage:

> If we want to go deep spiritually, we can't go around and dig lots
> of little holes. We need to find one place and dig a deep hole.
> And so, as contemplatives, we need to find in our own experience
> what it is—what practice it is, what approach it is—that takes us
> deep in this way. So when I talk about commitment, I'm talking
> about commitment to practice, to engaging in direct experience.
> (Simmer-Brown, 1999, 103).

We have a simple Rule in Lindisfarne: to live a balanced life of prayer, study, work, and rest. Each element is, in itself, a practice; each practice has "sub-practices," which define the whole. It is at this level that we need to find the approach that is valuable to each of us and to "dig deep."

Here is a suggestion for practice. Our community prayer is, "that I may be as Christ to those I meet, that I might find Christ within them." It is a simple prayer and may be repeated often during the day: on the way to work, during meditation, using prayer beads, during a difficult conversation, before sleep, while jogging. In its simplicity it is a profoundly deep well and encapsulates what is, for us, the purpose of life.

To dig deep takes time and patience. It is not a quick fix, a scratching the surface. Over time—measured in years, not days—there is a profoundly transforming effect. In the immediate, there is a deep sense of inner peace, of connection and of beauty. Practice deeply.

10. The Mundane—To Be as Christ

Most of life is ordinary. It seems that the Celtic Christians discovered the knack of finding God in the ordinary: that the everyday was infused with a sense of the divine, of wonder and mystery. I am beginning to rediscover this lost truth. It might be called a "second naivite." It takes some practice, for we have come to a place in our culture where everything can be technically explained. We yawn at creation. In God's goodness, I am being brought back again to a place of discovery—to take small steps into mystery.

The ordinary is mundane. The mundane is day-to-day worldly life. There are occasional windows on the Reality that infuses all things. Yet, mostly our experience is of the mundane. Our community prayer is: "To be as Christ to those we meet, to find Christ within them." This is the daily, mundane being there for and with the folk among whom we live.

How are we to be as Christ? As Christ is deep within each of us, as we are fully present for our friends, family and colleagues, then we are as Christ to them. We are fully present when we are centered, when we "touch the Christ within." We center through practice.

There is a beautiful centering breath practice by Buddhist monk Thich Nhat Hanh:

> In breath: "Breathing in I calm my body."
> Out breath: "Breathing out I smile."
> In breath: Dwelling in the present moment."
> Out breath: "I know this is a wonderful moment."

> Or a short form:

> Calming
> Smiling
> Present moment
> Wonderful moment

Try it! The most important and precious thing we can do is practice, to be as Christ to those we meet, to find Christ within them.

11. Listening, Silence

What can be said at all can be said clearly, and what we cannot talk about we must pass over in silence. (Wittgenstein in *Tractatus*, 1922, Introduction)

Be still and know that I am God (Psalms 46:10.)

Today it snowed hard. The snow brought a profound silence. My morning dip in the hot tub was lovely. After it had finished its cycle, I relaxed and listened. Occasional bird cries. The odd car engine as a driver braved the roads. Mostly a heavy silence. Little pricks of ice as the snow touched my exposed skin. I listened.

It has been a day of listening. We walked the pugs. The new snow crunched deliciously under our boots. It was the only sound. Deer sheltering under a tree. Squirrels dashing from branch to branch sending showers of snow.

Meditation with beads.

Still listening now.

12. Deepening Our Practice

Aristotle thought that all things move toward a natural goal (*telos* in Greek). Acorns grow into oak trees. The oak tree is the *telos* of the acorn. He assumed that the world works like that. He applied it to human beings and asked the question, "What is the natural *telos* of being human?" His answer was happiness (*eudaimonia* in Greek). He meant not merely feeling happy, but a well-rounded life of well-being. We might say, "flourishing."

I think that is a noble goal to pursue. Yet, there is nothing "natural" about it. It is very difficult to move from "acorns and oak trees," to "human beings and a eudemonic life." Oak trees follow naturally from acorns, other things being equal. Flourishing does not flow from being human. Many people experience lives far from Aristotle's *telos*.

The difference seems to be that human beings have choice. Admittedly our choices are often limited by circumstances, social structures, even our biological makeup. Yet, unlike the acorn, we can choose a *telos*. Elsewhere I have called this an "elective *telos*" (*Love as a Guide to Morals*, 2012, 32, 91). We are not bound, as the acorn is, to become an oak tree. We can choose the goal we wish to pursue.

So what do we choose to become? What do we aim for?

Over the centuries, Aristotle's *telos* of happiness has been a firm favorite. Its main competitor has been pleasure. There is a difference—I'll let you work it out. A third aim has been stability—a middle way, neither too high nor too low, or to be undisturbed.

The "elective *telos*" is important. What you choose for your aim largely determines the practice you engage in. One of the most ancient questions is, "How should we live?" Many philosophers have tried to find the answer in what Immanuel Kant called a "categorical" way. What would the way to live be in every single situation, for anyone in the world, at any point in time? Kant thought you could find these "categorical imperatives" (1964). It seems to me that this is impossible!

The "should" depends on an "if." I call this the "if-then-should" principle. *If* you want to run a marathon, *then* you *should* do a course of training. *If* you want to play chess, *then* you *should* learn the rules." How should we live? It all depends on what you choose as your aim. If your aim is pleasure, then you should do those things that will bring you pleasure. If your aim is to maximize pleasure for everyone, then you should do those things that maximize pleasure and reduce pain for most concerned.

The practice in which you engage is determined by the aim you choose.

This might seem a long way round to get to the idea of deepening our practice. Here's the reason: To deepen our practice requires that we first determine what our aim is. *Telos* determines practice. Practice relies on *telos* for direction.

It will come as no surprise that the aim I choose has something to do with love—actually has everything to do with love. To choose love as a *telos* determines the kind of practice I need to engage in.

I have been mulling over aspects of our understandings in the Lindisfarne Community. There are four ways of expressing who we aspire to be. Each of these four ways relates to practice.

The summary of our Rule: "To love, to serve, to forgive."

Our community prayer: "That I may be as Christ to those I meet; that I may find Christ within them."

Our commitment to a balanced life of prayer, study, work and rest.

Our particular practices: Eucharist, daily office, meditation, mindfulness, study, and service.

To deepen our practice would be to build the daily habits of spiritual life. It might mean to concentrate on just one aspect of the above—say, to build a more conscious meditation practice.

It might mean to adopt a new element of practice. For instance, over Advent-Christmas, I have reconnected with prayer bead meditation in a much deeper way than before.

It might mean to dust off the journal that has been languishing in the drawer. It might focus on internal thought practices: thinking the good of each person in each situation; or letting go of control; or extending love and goodness to each person you meet.

How will you know? Listen intently. You will hear. Then, deepen your practice.

13. Study as Spiritual Habit

In the Lindisfarne Community, we have tried to marry the head and the heart. Study is important for us . . . but study that is more about personal growth and the experience of God than merely "knowing stuff." In this way study is a spiritual discipline. Two delightful books which help immensely in this area are: Kenneth Leech's *Soul Friend* (rev. 2001) and W.R. Inge's *Mysticism in Religion* (1947). Sadly both books are out of print, but if you can track down used copies, it will be well worth the effort. A careful reading will stimulate your spirit as you seek more of the goodness of God.

14. To Love, to Serve, to Forgive

When we were putting together the founding documents for the Lindisfarne Community (this would be in the 1990s), we wanted a little motto that would summarize what we are about—a short mnemonic phrase, something easily memorable. It needed to catch the flavor of what we hoped to be and become as a community.

We came up with:

> To love, to serve, to forgive

Recently, I have been pondering our motto. I was wondering whether the motto was still adequate, whether it "worked" for us, whether we have outgrown it, whether it needs to be changed—that sort of thing.

I was as pleased with it now as when we came up with it! There is a certain order, meaning, and movement in the phrase. It repays careful thought and contemplation. Love is at the center of what we are seeking to be—to move away from preoccupation with the self to focus on the the Other, to seek her best, to care for him. The movement of love is in service of the Other. I am glad that as the community has developed over the last decade; so has a spirit of service. At our annual retreat, it was so good to hear of the many and excellent ways members of Lindisfarne serve others. Love and service are noble aspirations. Yet, we know that the human condition is very mixed! We often get things wrong and mixed up. Hurts and misunderstandings occur. There is a great need to forgive, to let go, to prevent bitterness, to heal, to move on without resentment. Forgiveness is essential for those who love and serve to prevent burnout.

To love, to serve, to forgive. Not a bad motto for life, I think.

15. To Be as Christ

In the Lindisfarne Community we are currently looking at our common understandings. Our first understanding is:

> As a Christian community we seek above all else to be Christlike—to be as Christ to those we meet; to find Christ within them. Over the years we have deepened our understanding of what that means to us. Our understandings are those things we aspire toward as we follow Christ and seek to keep the community Rule. They are at the core of who we are and seek to become. They are not a list of do's and don'ts; nor are they a list of self-congratulations, "look at us we've made it!" At their heart they are our prayer. We see these understandings in the life of Jesus; shining, precious gems, winsome, lovely, drawing us out of ourselves and toward Christ.

Much of our discussion has been about what it might mean to be Christlike, and the conversation has been very fruitful. I have learned much from community members.

To be as Christ to others. To find Christ in others.

I have pondered the twin ideas of doing and being. To be Christlike is to act in a certain way, and it is to be a certain kind of person. A few years ago, it was popular, in some circles, to wear jewelry with the WWJD logo. "What would Jesus do?" The fad seems to have faded. Yet, the intent was a good one. The idea of the jewelry was to remind the wearer to try to act in the way Jesus would act. What would that be? Wearers of the jewelry were left to puzzle it out for themselves. My guess would be that WWJD is to read the life and teaching of Jesus, get a feeling for the way Jesus acted in different circumstances, and try to imitate the actions. The task is difficult in two ways.

The first difficulty is how you get to the actual actions of Jesus. The documents about Jesus we have are short, selective, and open to many interpretations. Take, for example, the story of Jesus driving the money-changes from the temple (Matthew 21:12). Was he acting violently? Should we emulate that interpretation? But what about other ways of reading the story? Check out the commentaries and you will see the problem. WWJD? It's open to interpretation!

The second difficulty is this: when you have arrived at your best interpretation, how do you actually do it? Putting WWJD into practice is another matter altogether. It is here that we arrive at conclusions such as, "This is too hard!" "I've failed again!" "It's impossible!" The WWJD jewelry becomes embarrassing to wear. It's like getting road rage while wearing a clerical collar. (Best to slip the little white insert off before you drive!) I wonder how many pieces of WWJD jewelry are languishing at the bottom of drawers under the socks or underwear?

To act in a certain way is a noble and necessary idea. It can only be done when you are a certain kind of person. That brings me from doing to being.

To "be as Christ" is an ambiguous phrase. You can read "doing" into it. You can also read "being" into it. Here it becomes a little more esoteric. To be as Christ is a form of Christ-mysticism. There are a number of ways folk have wrestled with this historically. Here is one way. There is a "spark of the divine" in all. This small beginning for many folk (most perhaps?) remains small and undeveloped. For others, the small beginning grows slowly through spiritual discipline. How we get to start on the Way is a mystery. For some, a life crisis will be the immediate cause. For others, it is a chance meeting, or reading a book that catches the imagination, or a thousand other gateways. In whatever way it begins it is always a gift. To fan the spark into a flame takes time, discipline, practice. This was the genius of monasticism and is still the heart of what we call the new monasticism.

This Christ-mysticism is to find the Christ within. When our Buddhist friends speak of the "Buddha nature" I think they are speaking of the same thing. Thich Nhat Hanh leads us this way in his wonderful *Living Buddha, Living Christ*.

The point is that we can only begin to "do as Jesus did" when we "become as Christ is" though the disciplines of the spiritual life. It's a long term project. Don't confuse religious zeal with developed inner divinity.

To find Christ in others is to look for this small beginning in them. It is in all. In some, it is very difficult to see, but it is there. It is most difficult to see when the actions of others are far from Christlike. The temptation is to write them off. A good friend of ours had a wonderful (if time consuming) habit. He wanted to bring a little happiness to each person he met, and made a point of not leaving a conversation until the other person had smiled at least once. I recall one visit to J.C. Penney's that took a while. The dour shop assistant resisted my friend's kindness for the longest time. She did smile in the end, but it was a marathon! I think this was my friend finding Christ within, a connection of spirit to spirit.

16. Breathe

Ithaca, New York, where we live, is a town for bumper stickers. (Let's call them BS for short.) All self-respecting Ithacans have a bevy of BS, mostly political. Reading BS passes the time when you are in a traffic jam. If you're lucky, you will be behind a Subaru wagon with more than a dozen. (It used to be a Volvo 240, but they don't make them anymore.) Besides being a political activist sort of town, Ithaca is also a spiritual, new-agey kind of place. It's eclectic. It suits us.

One of my favorite BSs is "Breathe." Of course, there is more than a grain of truth in many BS. In other words, not all BS is BS, so to speak! "Breathe" is profoundly true. Jesus, on the night of resurrection said so. "He breathed on the disciples and said 'Receive the Holy Spirit.'" To breathe is to live. Breath is life. God comes to us as breath.

I have been learning to breathe. That sounds a bit silly. If we don't breathe we die—quickly! I don't mean that. I mean to breathe consciously, to breathe deeply, to breathe like a baby breathes, from the abdomen. Next time you have the joy of seeing a baby, watch how it breathes. You will see its little belly goes in and out and not its chest. As we get older we begin to breathe inefficiently. We breathe from the chest. We fill only the top part of our lungs. To breathe from the abdomen, sensing the rise and fall of the diaphragm, allows the lungs to fully expand and contract. For a baby, it all comes naturally. After years of breathing shallowly, it is not natural at all.

Belly breathing takes time and much practice. But it is worth it. There are many physiological benefits. Healthier lungs. Improved oxygen circulation. Better blood flow. Lower blood pressure. More energy. (These benefits have all been medically documented.) There are deeply spiritual benefits too. Breath connects us with the divine. It is no accident that Hebrew *ruach* means breath and spirit, as does Greek *pneuma*, as does Chinese *qi* and Japanese *ki*. The ancients knew the mysterious connection of life, breath, spirit, God and all things.

Conscious breathing is mindfulness. Mindfulness is attention. Attention is being present. Being present is to touch eternity. Breathe.

17. A Secular Monasticism: What Does it Look Like?

For aspiring secular monastics: what does a new monastic do? What does it look like? Here are a few ideas.

First, secular monasticism begins with intention. This is most important. I make a commitment, I choose to be a secular monastic. This is the basis of a vowed life. It's an intention to live a certain way; to be a certain kind of person. Formally, intention is renewed periodically in ritual, witnessed by others. Informally, intention is renewed daily.

Second. Secular monasticism is a practice of life: a complex social activity, a way of living. As such, there are certain disciplines engaged in, habits that make the practice what it is.

In traditional cloistered monasticism the whole of life was ordered by the rhythms of monastic routine. In a new monasticism, we live immersed in the world. It is a secular monasticism. There are many demands from many directions. If I want to be serious about new monasticism, what exactly am I making a commitment to? Practically, how much time does this take? Here's a very rough guide.

> **Eucharist:** One to two hours each week.
> **Daily Office:** Fifteen minutes to one hour each day.
> **Meditation:** Fifteen minutes to two hours a day.
> **Mindfulness:** a discipline of the whole of life.
> **Study:** a few hours each week.
> **Service:** for many folk their full-time work will be service. For others a particular form of service for a few hours each week.

In some ways, this is quite demanding. But then, anything worthwhile is. Begin with intention.

18. Revisioning Priesthood!

Since the early 1990s, Jane and I have been exploring the idea of the home-based church, which is the practice of church without specifically designated religious buildings. It has given us great flexibility and has helped produce a closeness of fellowship—*koinonia* in the Bible. To this concept, we have added the notion of the centrality of the Eucharist, developing an understanding of sacrament in which the "interpenetration of spirit and matter" has become central to our spirituality. Home Eucharists are a joy to celebrate.

At the same time, we have adopted the centuries-old understanding of a threefold ordained ministry that includes deacons, priests, and bishops. Priests are those specifically authorized through the empowerment of ordination to represent Christ at the Eucharistic table. Those we recognize as priests are no different—no better, no holier—than other members of the church. But they are set aside and recognized as those whom the church has entrusted with great responsibility. In order for the church to practice priesthood in a meaningful way (in all the traditions), those seeking to become priest engage in a process of discernment, study, training and finally ordination. At its heart, it includes:

(1) A sense God's call.
(2) The willingness to study and be trained by other senior ministers.
(3) The church's blessing through the hands of the bishops.

During our recent vacation, it came to me that for this to be a reality—the joining of the home church and the centrality of the Eucharist—then we will need many more priests than we have at present. It will mean many more "bishop's schools" for the training of deacons and priests.

It will also mean a re-thinking of what priesthood means.

It will mean the breaking of the link of priesthood with career, with full-time salaries, with a four-year (plus) disruption of everyday life, with a certain high academic ability, and a status in society. The priest will not be one in a thousand or even one in fifty believers, but one in twelve, one in six. It will make the priesthood more accessible to women and men of all ages and academic abilities.

In other words, it is a far-reaching rethinking of church, priesthood, and training for ministry. In the Lindisfarne Community, we have begun to explore the changes needed. It will need many such communities, many such training schools, much imagination, and much courage in following the Wild Goose.

19. Finding Our Calling

I have always found the idea of a calling intriguing—intriguing because important, yet elusive. For a long time in Western history, calling was associated either with the priesthood or the monastery. In other words, calling involved activities that were necessarily religious. At the beginning of the early modern period, calling was expanded to include all walks of life. Whatever your activity in life was perceived as a calling from God. God was involved in all, not just the religious life.

More recently, calling was narrowed again to include only pastors and missionaries. "Do you have a calling?" referred to "home mission" or "foreign mission." There was still a shadow of the idea of a non-religious calling, but related to only a few professions. Medicine was a calling. Teaching was a calling, but few other professions were.

I take the broader view: that God is involved in the whole of life and that each of us has a particular responsibility to find that which God wants us to be and do. I also take an egalitarian view: that each calling is necessary and that each contributes to the whole. It is a circle rather than a pyramid. It is about equality rather than hierarchy.

A calling amounts to a conviction that God wants you to be in a certain place in life. Finding your calling helps you to make sense of things. It is your calling that gives purpose and meaning. When difficulties and doubts arise, it is to your calling that you return. Callings may also be multiple. All of us in the Lindisfarne Community are "bi-vocational." We are called to the new monasticism and its spiritual practice and called to some other place in life (in healthcare, in education, in industry, in full-time parenting and many others). Some of us are "tri-vocational." We add to the other two the calling of priesthood: a particular sacramental calling as a sign of incarnation, Christ in us and for all.

But how to find your calling?

The scriptures offer many accounts of calling by God. One delightful story is that of Samuel. As a young boy, he hears a voice calling his name. He is unsure who called and goes to Eli. Three times Eli tells the boy Samuel that he did not call him. Then the penny drops! Eli realizes that it is God who is calling Samuel. When Samuel hears the voice again, Eli instructs him to say, "Speak for your servant is listening." Little Samuel is compliant and the voice becomes clearer and God appears to him.

The story gives hints about being called. It presents us with a difficulty and a requirement. The difficulty is hearing correctly. How would I know if I am being called in a certain direction? How could I be sure it is God who is calling me and not merely my imagination? But then, perhaps my imagination is the way God calls me? Hearing the inner voice is not an easy exercise. It requires patience and practice.

It brings us to the requirement. The requirement is listening—listening to the inner voice. Being still before it. All dialogue begins with listening. There is silence before there is speech. The listening is also communal. Wisely, the boy Samuel checks out his hearing abilities with the older Eli. It is in conversation with Eli that Samuel learns how to listen to the inner voice. To discern a calling, wise counsel is required. A calling is not merely individualistic. Even then, with all the wise counsel in the world, hearing correctly and listening intently is not an exact science. There will always be ambiguity. To follow a calling is much like Kierkegaard's existential "leap into the dark" (1954).

Most callings require preparation. Over time, say, you increasingly feel that you ought to be a teacher of small children. You find your passion there. You try to forget it, yet it comes back to you again and again. You check out your sense with other folk. They agree with you: you'd make a great teacher. So you prepare. Depending on what you have already done, you will at least have to return to school to spend two years getting a masters degree in education (in the United States context), or perhaps go back to college to get a bachelors degree. It all takes time as you prepare to fulfill your calling. In the preparation time, the calling will be tested many times. When you begin to practice, the calling will not always be fulfilling and there will be arid times. There will be doubts, too, yet you return again and again to the call.

A final thought. Callings are not static. They change over a lifetime. This, too, adds complication for there is an element of provisionality about every calling. Part of the secret is to go on listening. Be often in silence. Discern the change of the season. Have wise friends. "Speak, for your servant is listening."

20. A Different Commission

When I became a Christian in the early 1970s, one of the first things I was told was that I had to become a "witness." That term was part of a strange new language that I soon became used to. What does it mean to be a witness? Go and tell people what Jesus has done for you. Why? Because it is the "Great Commission," taken from the end of Matthew's gospel (Matthew 28:6-20). We have to make as many people Christians as we possibly can.

There followed years of learning how to do it. Street witness. Frigid fingers on the frets of a guitar. Singing choruses to passers by. Embarrassing conversations. Failure. Guilt. Courses. Methods. "Evangelism Explosion"—a disconcertingly violent metaphor. As a minister, church growth was all the rage. Bigger churches. More people. More courses. More workshops. More seminars.

There is a story in the gospel of Mark where Jesus heals a leper and expressly tells him not to tell anyone. "See you say nothing to anyone," said Jesus (Mark 1:40-45). Here is a different commission. It is the great commission of silence. This different kind of commission is repeated in Mark's gospel a number of times—sufficiently so that scholars came up with the phrase "the Messianic Secret."

The difference, if taken as a priority over the other commission, would be marked. "Ah, now you are a Christian," I would have been told, "Don't tell anyone. Keep it to yourself!" At least I would have been spared the pressure to witness with its associated guilt if I had kept my mouth shut!

I am reluctant, now, to talk about my faith. I tend to keep it to myself. When people ask me directly, I tentatively give them snippets, tasters—with lots of qualifications. I listen more to their stories. I look for Christ in them. I affirm their journey.

I have tried to analyze why, for me, this is the case. There are probably unconscious reasons. A psychologist might suggest that I am in reaction to the overzealousness of youth. A friend might say, "You just got burned by it all." They both might be correct.

Consciously, I think it is that I see faith somewhat differently. Spirituality is no less important to me, but is different now than before. It is a whisper and not a shout. I am less certain about truth claims. I am more tentative about the interpretation of experience. I am less willing to make judgments about others. I am more inward.

"To be as Christ to those we meet," is an extraordinary calling. It is a life lived and not a religious view talked about. It is an aspiration and not a method. To be as Christ is to be silent, to be attentive, to welcome, to see the other as subject and not object, to build relationships of love.

"Do you follow Jesus? Shh! Don't tell anyone!"

TWO

PURPOSE IN LIFE

1. The Purpose of Life

Most of the things we do, most of the time, are teleological in nature. Teleology derives from the Greek word "telos," which means goal or purpose. The telos is that toward which something moves. If you think about most of the ordinary affairs of life, we do them for a purpose. You walk to the refrigerator to take something out. You take something out to make a drink. You make a drink to quench your thirst. Most of the things we do are of that nature. Very few things happen for no purpose. On the odd occasion when we find ourselves forgetful of the purpose for doing something, we feel foolish. "I just went into the office for something, and I can't remember what I went for. How silly!" Sadly, these increase with age and I am no stranger to them!

Among the ancients, Aristotle thought much of teleology. He suggested that everything in nature has a purpose (1962). To find out that purpose and to work with it is a good thing. It became the basis for the kind of morality that is called natural law. To say so seems quite obvious.

However, there is a common phrase that I hear a lot from students: "Everything happens for a purpose." When I hear that, I usually press the student for a meaning. The answer is usually, "Well, I don't know. I just feel that everything happens for a purpose." I ferret away at the answer because I suspect that the student is saying something more than "most everything is teleological," in the obvious and not very interesting sense. I think I am hearing "Everything happens for a *good* purpose." That is something different.

I think most people would have no trouble with the idea of the purposeful nature of most actions. Yet, I know some would have a lot of trouble with the idea that the purposeful nature of all things being toward a good end. Some things happen for quite bad reasons. Yesterday's newspaper had a story of a little boy, aged one year, who was savaged and killed by his grandparents' dog, a Rottweiller. "Everything happens for a good purpose," is quite a hollow idea in the face of such a tragedy.

There is a still deeper understanding of telos, which is contained in all the great traditions in different ways. It is that there is, indeed, an end goal, a purpose to life, but is one that we must choose. It is a purpose to which we must align ourselves. In its different guises, this goal is perfection, and perfection is a reflection of God. "Be holy as I am holy."

In the letter to Hebrews there is a phrase, "bringing many children to glory" (Hebrews 2:10). The thought is expanded, and I paraphrase it: The purpose of God (of the universe) is that all share in the perfection of God. In this world of imperfection it is not obvious what that is. We need a role model. That model for Christians is Jesus, who is a pioneer in showing us the way to God, to perfection, to the goal. Not only did Jesus know that way to God, we are told that we can share it with him. For that reason, Jesus calls us sisters and brothers. In this way of perfection there is no difference between Jesus and us.

That is an astonishing thought. Often, it is the differences between Jesus and the rest of us that people think about. Jesus is perfect; we are not. Jesus is the Child of God; we are not. Jesus is one with the Father-Mother and Spirit; we are not. Jesus is a model, yes, but an impossibly high model, a level that we cannot attain. This is reinforced in our tradition by the number of times we confess our sins! It reinforces the idea that we have failed and continue to fail. "All have sinned and fall short of the glory of God," says Paul writing to the Romans (3:23). That idea has gripped the church far more than "bring many children to glory."

There is a principle (attributed broadly to the German philosopher Immanuel Kant) that "ought implies can." If you are told, "you ought to do this," there is an implication that you can also do what you ought to do. Otherwise, it would be a cruel imperative. High jumpers in the Olympics have always fascinated me. Their achievements are amazing. Yet, if someone said to me, "OK Andy, you ought to jump over seven feet high," I would think of it as a cruel joke. Ought (obligation) can only be so if it is a possibility. "You ought to tell the truth," however, is different. Ought implies can.

So, when we come to consider the telos of life, perfection, likeness to God, modeled in Jesus, the ought to be like Christ implies the possibility to be so. This is good news.

How, then, can I become perfect? How can I reach the goal? The answer has much to do with practice and contemplation.

2. Living toward Perfection

My thoughts have increasingly been about the question, "How ought we to live?" It has become for me the most basic of questions. The answer is disarmingly simple. "We ought to love." The simplicity masks a complexity that is beyond explanation or comprehension. It is far more like art than science. I want to work away at one aspect of the answer. To love is to live toward perfection.

In Jewish and Christian traditions, the idea of perfection is very prominent. It is always important to remember that being an informal Jewish rabbi, Jesus' thought forms and expressions were Jewish too. Both the Torah and Jesus' moral teaching look to the perfect as that toward which we ought to live. The Torah clearly states, "Be holy, as I am holy" (Leviticus 11:44). God is the perfect one. That perfection is described as holiness. To live well is to live with that holiness as vision and direction. In Jesus' teaching it is: "Love . . . so you may be children of your Father-Mother . . . Be perfect, therefore, as your heavenly Father-Mother is perfect" (Matthew 5:48). The injunction is very straightforward. Perfection draws us toward itself.

Our tradition is teleological. Telos is the Greek word for the goal toward which something moves. The Greek philosopher Aristotle was the first to suggest this. Everything, for Aristotle, has a natural telos. When something lives according to its telos, its goal, its perfection, then that something lives well. In the Jewish and Christian traditions, God is the perfect and God is the telos. Humanity came from God, made in God's image, and will go back to God. People live well when they live in the light of that telos.

So simple; yet, so complex! How do we know what the perfect looks like? If we are to have it as vision and direction, what is it that must fill our vision?

In Jewish tradition, perfection is revealed through the Torah. Here, God makes practical what holiness looks like. In practice, it looks like caring for the poor, being free from acquisitiveness that leads to lying, stealing, and cheating to get what you want; it looks like caring for those who have disabilities, not hating any but loving neighbors.

The Jesus tradition is much the same but taken perhaps a little further. It looks not merely like the negative injunctions not to cheat and steal, but more positively to give to those who have need; it looks not only like loving neighbors but also loving enemies.

Yet, the direction is very much the same. How ought we to live? We live in the light of the perfect. The perfect draws us toward itself.

However, if we make those injunctions a set of rules to be kept, we will most likely miss the telos. For when those examples from Torah and Jesus become rules, we lose the perfect in the imperfect. I think that was the mistake of those the gospels call Pharisees. Jesus' critique was that they had replaced the inner quest for the perfect with an outer keeping of rules. They mistook the rules for the perfect itself.

How we ought to live has more in common with aesthetics, with art, than with fact, with science (in the popular sense).

We know the perfect through moral reflection, through contemplation. It is deeply inward, deeply personal. To love is to learn gradually and progressively what love means in experience and through trial and failure. It is to change understandings of love as love deepens. To love involves imagination; to imagine the perfect; to contemplate the beautiful.

3. Future Orientation

> Thus says God, . . . Do not remember the former things, or consider the things of old. I am about to do a new thing; now it springs forth, do you not perceive it? I will make a way in the wilderness and rivers in the desert. The wild animals will honor me, the jackals and the ostriches; for I give water in the wilderness, rivers in the desert, to give drink to my chosen people, the people whom I formed for myself so that they might declare my praise. (Deutero Isaiah 43:16-19)

Second Isaiah (Deutero Isaiah) is the unnamed prophet of the Jewish captivity in Babylon. He spoke of loss of the homeland, the place of promise. His words were addressed to exiles, far away from home. It's not that Babylon was a bad place. It was a land of good provision. Jewish exiles had done well, by and large. They had made a very positive contribution to Babylon and its culture. Yet, it was not home. The exiles longed for a return to their homeland.

This part of the biblical story has often been used as an allegory for the spiritual life. "This world is not our home." There is that deep sense in the human spirit that there is something more. The world as we know it, is a world of suffering: a world of *dukkha* (Sanskrit: suffering, stress, anxiety, dissatisfaction), the Buddha taught us. Birth, aging, death. We often miss the good things in life; too often we know the bad things in life. There is suffering in all things. In this sense, we are all in Babylon. This life is Babylon. Is there no way out, no way through?

> Beloved, this one thing I do: forgetting what lies behind and straining forward to what lies ahead, I press on toward the goal for the prize of the heavenly call of God in Christ Jesus. (Philippians 3:13)

Here a spiritual longing is more clearly expressed: a longing for what Paul calls resurrection. It is helpful to think of resurrection as more than a mere bodily resuscitation. Resurrection is the completion of humanity. It is humanity in its fullness in the presence of the Ultimately Real. All the incapacities, and failings, and frustrations and sufferings of life as we know it now left behind.

Here is the future orientation. Deutero Isaiah and Paul look to the future and tell us that in God's process all shall be well. In God there will be a way in the wilderness, rivers in the desert, mouths filled with laughter, tongues with songs of joy, restoration, shouts of joy, the prize of God in Christ.

How will it be so? Because that is the shape of the universe, shaped by God who will bring all to pass. For at the heart of the universe is not suffering but love. How did the prophets know this? They intuited it in the spirit. There can be no rational defense of God's bright future. It is a matter of faith and faith itself is a gift.

Yet, one can orientate oneself to God's future. One can side with the process. Paul did. Knowing that he had not attained the goal he made the choice of pressing toward it with his whole life. How might we do that?

Practice.

Practice.

Practice.

This is no quick fix. This is daily, reorientation of ourselves to God's future. In our practice we are saying, "Yes!" to God's process in the universe to end suffering, to bring all to resurrection.

4. A New Way of Seeing—Taking It Step-by-Step

I am intrigued by the way the early Christian church discovered an expansive vision. I think there is a key phrase in the Acts when it says that Peter began to explain it to them "step-by-step." "Step-by-step" is a *leitmotif* for the way the church began, and continues to this day, to discover the broadness of God's love for all.

It has been commented that, in the New Testament, you can see a revelation—a new seeing—and then halting attempts to put the revelation into practice. In the first century, first Peter and later Paul began to see differently. We find it encapsulated in Paul's phrase, "neither Jew nor Greek, slave nor free, male nor female" (Gallations 3:28). The love of God in Christ embraced all. There was no difference. Those who had claimed privilege (the Jewish folk, the males, the free, the rich) needed to realize that in Christ all are privileged.

Paul worked very hard in his day on the ethnicity/race question between Jews and non-Jews and the very tricky question of circumcision. Also, Paul was quite decisive at first in allowing women to work alongside men as leaders in the churches he formed. Yet, his communities did not continue with the liberated position. By the time of the deutero-Pauline letters, the Pastoral Epistles, the door had begun to close for women. By the time of the *didache* in the second century, male only leadership was reasserted and framed most of the church for the best part of 2,000 years, with a few notable exceptions. Paul and the early church worked less on the privilege of the free and the enslavement of the many. It may well be that both entrenched patriarchy and the economics of slavery were just too big to deal with. The Jewish religion was then, as now, a very small affair. The debate between Jews and non-Jews was not as widespread a social phenomenon as patriarchy and slavery.

So the early Christians moved "step-by-step," and, it has to be said, took a few steps backward as well! No blame needs be cast. Step-by-step has been quite painful at times. It was not for some 1,800 years that slavery was abolished in lands dominated by Christian sensibilities. It was even later than that when women began to receive somewhat equal treatment in society. Of course, even today neither patriarchy nor slavery has been abolished from the planet. There are estimated to be twenty-seven million slaves procured through human trafficking worldwide. Patriarchy still holds a grip in many countries overtly (Saudi Arabia, for example) and covertly (the United States, with its glass ceiling).

Still the new way of seeing remains: God's love is comprehensive. It excludes none and includes all.

Moving from the global and historical to our little faith community of Lindisfarne, we, too, have been moving Step-by-step in our own attempts to make sense of the new way of seeing. What would it mean for us to be as embracing as God's love in Christ is embracing?

We have taken baby steps in the four areas of Paul's revelation:

(1) The religious "in and out groups." In Paul's time Jewish and non-Jewish religions. In our time, openness to other faith traditions and understandings, refusing to call any "unclean." We are trying to be ecumenical in its broadest sense.

(2) The ambiguities of economics. In Paul's day it was slavery, on which Roman economics was based. In ours it is the disparities between rich and poor. In *Lindisfarne*, we are working with the marginalized in a number of different ways (with the poor and hungry, with abused children, with the elderly, with those in prison).

(3) The inequalities of gender. In Paul's day it was women and men. In our day, we are continuing to wrestle with patriarchy, but now also with the injustices of prejudice against gays, lesbians, and trans-gendered persons. This has meant, and will mean in the future, receiving all, without prejudice or judgment, as fully a part of *Lindisfarne*.

(4) The non-human world. The new way of seeing is broader than the merely human. What would it mean to include all sentient beings in the scope of God's inclusive love? What of the whole world? Step-by-step.

All of this is challenging and, to be truthful, each step has been painful in different ways, with some misunderstandings and at each step there are some who cannot follow.

Yet, like Peter, who saw the vision of the sheet containing "unclean animals" (Acts 10) and tried to work it out in practice, and then explained "Step-by-step," so must we. "What God has made clean, you must not call profane." And in Christ, God has made all clean, reconciling the whole world to Godself. A new way of seeing indeed!

5. Finding the Grain of the Universe

In the East, the essential "Way" has traditionally been called Dharma or Dao. In the West, natural law or God's law. The common idea is that there is a grain to the universe and the best way to live is to discover that grain and go with it.

When I was at grammar school, in the late sixties, most of our classes were academic: they were preparing us for university. But just in case a university education wasn't in our future, if they had made a mistake and we didn't have an aptitude for Latin and Greek and algebra, they gave us two classes to test other aptitudes: metalwork and woodwork. I was not very good at metalwork. I was marginally better at woodwork. But a few years ago, I decided to turn my hand to wood again. I started making seiza benches for meditation. A seiza bench is not a complicated affair. It is a top, roughly eighteen inches by six, and two legs. I make the portable kind and the legs are fixed to the top by hinges, so they fold for easy carrying and storage. I have made benches in oak, walnut, purpleheart, and zebrawood, amongst others. All these woods have their own characteristics. Some are hard and others soft. Some highly figured, others less so. In common for all wood is that if you are to work successfully, you work with the grain and not against it. If you work against the grain you get splinters, and if you are not careful you can split the wood. Having been successful with benches, I turned my hand to ukuleles. A different story! The pile of wood that attests to the mistakes I have made is great. Incidentally, I still don't think I have any talent for woodwork. It is simply a matter of perseverance, patience, and beginning to learn the "nature" of wood and how it is shaped, and moves and breathes.

Working with wood has helped me begin to learn that the best way to live is with the grain. Yet, finding the Way is not an easy affair. The ancients agreed that the Way is often shrouded in mystery. The Way does not reveal its secrets easily. Perseverance, practice, and daily attention are required. In time, the Way becomes clear. It often seems obvious in time, but, at first, counter-intuitive because, if you work against the grain for some time, working with the grain seems not quite right.

Here's an example. The grain of the universe, the Dao, is very humble. The Way is not about seeking honor or power or greatness. Honor, power and greatness may come to you, but are not to be sought after. In the Dao, those with humility are honored not those with hubris. Take a quick look at history. Whenever nations and empires grow and glow with pride in their achievements, watch for the inevitable decline. Say a few times, "The sun never sets on the . . ." and watch the sun sink quickly over the horizon! But humility seems counterintuitive. If you want something you ought to get it. Push yourself forward. Fight for your rights. Get what you deserve.

"Those who exalt themselves will be humbled. Those who humble themselves will be exalted" (Matthew 23:12; Luke 14:11). That is the Dharma.

6. The Argument About Perfection

British philosopher and novelist Dame Iris Murdoch makes an argument from perfection. To my knowledge, she doesn't use the phrase herself, but others have attributed the argument to her. It goes something like this:

If we can imagine the perfect, that imagined perfection can help us make a practical different in our very imperfect life now. Our imperfect lives will reflect better the life of perfection through contemplation of the perfect.

It is not an argument unique to Murdoch. She was something of a neo-Platonist, and anything with "Plato" in its descriptor will likely have something to do with an ideal, a perfection, regardless whether the ideal exists. For her part, Murdoch was agnostic about the perfect. Yet, the fact that we can imagine the perfect is very important. The perfect draws us toward itself. (It is quite possible that imagining the perfect, and knowing our own imperfection, may cause us to hate ourselves and drive us further from the perfect. But that is another story for another day.)

In Christian theology, the motif of the realm of God (Kingdom of God in non-inclusive language, or heaven in popular devotion) performs the function of the argument from perfection. Sometimes, the realm of God discussion has been termed "realized eschatology." Eschatology relates to the End, the final state, or the perfect. Realized eschatology says that it is possible to know in the present that which will be in the End. It cannot be realized in completion, but we can at least catch glimpses of the perfect, and the present can be transformed to resemble more of the perfect than the imperfect.

The realm of God is, then, an imagined perfection very different to the imperfections of the life we presently live. What is it like? An example. The imperfections of life include issues like sickness and grieving. In the realm of God, there is no sickness and those who grieve are comforted. Whenever there is a healing of sickness and wherever those who grieve are comforted, then that is a sign of the realm of God. The perfect is realized to some degree in the imperfect. There is also a spur to folk to align themselves with what looks like the perfect. Another example. In the realm of God, there is perfect knowledge and understanding. Education at its best—in the overcoming of ignorance and the many ills associated with ignorance—is a way of aligning with the realm of God. Another example. In the perfect all are accepted, regardless of gender or class or race or sexual orientation or education level or ability. Whenever there is an inclusion, there is a glimpse of the perfect. When you side with inclusion, you are aligning yourself with the realm of God.

The perfect is a happy state. Imagine away! Then look for signs of the perfect in the midst of the imperfect.

7. What We Shall Be

What we will be has not yet appeared . . . (John 3:2)

The largest ever live-streaming event on the Internet is a twenty-four-hour-a-day stream of three baby eagles and their parents. The camera is fixed on the nest and you can simply watch the day-to-day activities of an eagle family. It didn't begin with three baby eagles. It began with three eggs. The little birds hatched and have grown ever so fast. Watching the egg break open and the scrawny little fledgling make its way into the world was amazing. Seeing the parents bring food, and how they lovingly care for their young is quite an insight into nurture. Unlikely as it seems, the eagles' nest is compulsive viewing.

A large part of the fascination is to watch the changes. We knew that the eggs, should they have survived, would become little birds. We knew that the little birds would become bigger birds and develop wings. As I write the major issue of change is when and how the little birds will take to flight.

The eyrie is so high. The little eaglets are so small. We await the change. The world is watching to see what will be. It has not yet appeared.

Life is becoming what we shall be. We do not remain the same for a single moment. Our interaction with our environment is constantly changing us. Even in the stillest moment there is movement and change. The process of physical change is unremitting as we breathe and eat and drink and become. The physical processes of change reflect and interact with the spiritual processes of change. Spiritually all is flux, all is change.

Given the inexorable nature of change we have one of three choices: (1) To ignore the changes, as if the changes are unimportant; (2) to resist the changes, as if they are repugnant and must be fought; and (3) to accept the changes and to work with them.

To ignore the changes is what most people do. Life is lived without intention, without focus, without center. Life is literally wasted.

To resist the changes is the second most popular option. I have often felt a sense of tragic irony when seeing a Hollywood star looking "young" from a distance when they ought to look "old." As the camera zooms you see the stretched skin, the false "youth," the pallid visage of the almost embalmed. Change is resisted at a terrible cost.

To accept the changes and work with them is the way of the spiritual adept.

To seek to understand change was the quest of the ancient Chinese sages. The world's most ancient book (though it is hardly a book in the traditional sense) is the *Yi-Jing*, the *Book of Changes* (Wilhelm, 1997). The Yi-Jing contains ancient wisdom, added to over the centuries by commentaries and interpretations, and is the essence of all developed Chinese philosophy. At its heart is how to live in the best way with change, not yet knowing what we shall be, but working with change rather than resisting it.

The early Christians, too, had a profound sense of change. They lived with the changes of their teacher Jesus who in resurrection appears to them and is the Christ. They came to believe that the changes they had experienced in him would be changes they too would experience. There would be transformation into the likeness of the Christ. But it was not yet clear "what we shall be." For though the Christ has appeared, the Christ is yet to appear. Those who have this hope of change do not sit idly by. They work with the changes. They look toward the goal, for though "what we shall be has not yet appeared" there are glimpses. Those with this hope align themselves with the great transforming work and edge toward it.

Like the little eaglet, just now enjoying the tenderness and care of parental love in the safety of the nest, change is happening constantly. Soon the time will come to leave the nest and learn to fly. Better to prepare than not.

THREE

A VIRTUOUS LIFE

1. True Humility

In the gospel, Jesus tells a story to demonstrate that the way of humility is the better way. When you are an invited guest, never assume that you are the top guest. Always assume the lowest position. It is then up to others to invite you to the top table. It is a cute little story. The punch line of the story—what we're meant to hear, more than the cuteness of it—is that "all who exalt themselves will be humbled and all who humble themselves will be exalted" (Matthew 23:12; Luke 14:11).

We are told much the same in the Jewish wisdom literature to the effect of, "don't push yourself forward or stand with the great, take a lower position and others may invite you forward."

I think we miss the point if we see the story Jesus told and the wisdom literature as a way to get to the top—a kind of strategy, a tactic for getting where you want to get. To read it that way is to agree with the perspective that says, "the top is where we are going."

The ancients told us, "virtue is its own reward." It is a good in itself. Virtue is not a means to an end. Humility is not to be sought because it gets you to the top. Humility is good in itself: intrinsically good.

Yet, it is quite clear that this is not the way of much of life. In both secular society and in religious communities, we often face the very opposite.

In secular life, we find ourselves part of systems and bureaucracies in which it is hard to take the way of humility. For example, in the academy, to succeed, you have to demonstrate "excellence" in teaching, in scholarship, and in service. Yet, it is not others whom observe you to have these things;

you must demonstrate it yourself. You must "blow your own trumpet." It is quite distasteful and breeds all kinds of resentments, unhealthy competition, and angst.

Within and between churches there is often a very sharp competitive edge. They vie with one another to demonstrate that their version of religion is the best; that they offer the most, that their view of God is superior to others. It can be ruthless and cutthroat, particularly where money is involved.

In the Lindisfarne Community, we have tried to abandon that kind of religion.

The way of humility is something other. It is, in fact, not a tactic of the shrewd, but a way of life that reflects the nature of God. In reflecting the nature of God, it is a way that prefers the other above yourself, which honors the other, which seeks the other's very best.

In the *Way of Living* (Fitz-Gibbon and Fitz-Gibbon, 2006) of the Lindisfarne Community, in the understandings, we have:

> Such a life must be characterized by humility. We aspire to be honest, real and down-to-earth. Humility is opposed to the arrogance, isolation and deception that pride brings. We accept our spiritual poverty, our limitations and dependency and also accept responsibility for the use of our gifts and strengths for the service of God. The humble are willing to receive as well as to give. Humility respects and esteems others. It is a form of the love that does not seek its own way. We seek to be a grace-filled community as we "wash one another's feet."

In that understanding, we have tried to capture something of the flavor of the way of humility.

It is not an easy path.

Two questions occur to me: (1) Humility is counterintuitive. Why would we choose a humble life? (2) If humility reflects the nature of God, then why does God appear in so many tellings not full of humility, but rather hubris?

The great philosopher Nietzsche said that humility is a weakness, rather than a virtue (cf. 1886, 1887). If the meaning of life is the will to power, to gain, to achieve, to reach the top, then it is clear that humility is weak. You see little humility in great politicians, film stars, and sports personalities. The people our society loves and lauds are not the humble.

Yet, those who are spiritual (or seek to be) are enjoined not to emulate that kind of success, but to emulate God. "Be perfect, as God is perfect" (Matthew 5:48). So the answer to my first question (why choose the way of humility?) is, because this is the way of God.

This leads to my second question. Much God talk portrays God as lofty, infinite, demanding worship. "See how big and strong I am," says God. "I am bigger and better than anyone or anything else. I demand that you pay homage to me." If we were to find the same character traits in human beings, we would not see humility expressed!

If we are to imitate God (as the scriptures enjoin) does that mean that we are to express great pride in who we are and demand others to worship us? Definitely not.

Perhaps, our problem is that the way we human beings have often portrayed God has little to do with God in Godself and more to do with our own needs of power and importance.

In the life of Jesus, we see God portrayed in a different light. Here is one who refuses the adulation of the masses. Here is one who would rather slip away through the crowd than be made a king. Here is one who, through example and teaching, shows and tells us that the way of life is to be one of preferring others above ourselves and seeking their best as we seek to love them. For this is the way God is toward us.

This is a very different view of God than potentate, dictator in the sky! Perhaps we need to re-vision God as the humble one rather than the mighty one, the servant rather than the mistress or master, the one who lays down life, denies self, in order to serve others.

To take the way of humility is then, counter to much of religious life and much of secular life—a narrow way.

2. Mindfulness as Thankfulness

Jesus told a story about ten lepers who came to him for healing. He told them to go and show themselves to the priests. The priests were those who examined folk to make sure they were ritually clean before entering the temple.

Leprosy made you ceremonially unclean. As the ten lepers went their way, they were made clean. They were healed of their leprosy. Yet, only one came back to thank Jesus for his healing. This one was not only a leper, but an outsider too. He was a Samaritan, not one of the chosen people. Jesus commended his trust in God.

The story is rich in meaning at many levels.

I want to comment on the healed leper's thankfulness.

In our *Way of Living* (Fitz-Gibbon and Fitz-Gibbon, 2006), we commend the practice of mindfulness. This is a rich practice, which includes as a main element finding God in all things and being thankful for them.

There are two ways to think of being thankful. The first is thankfulness as spontaneous emotion. This happens when something good comes your way and you are flooded with the emotion of gratefulness. You express it more often than not with a phrase like "Thank you, so much!" or "I can't believe it. Thank you!" It is a spontaneous verbal ejaculation born of a deep feeling. The second is thankfulness as practice. A practice is a way of living born of habit. It is what we have in mind when we teach children to say "Thank you!" when they receive something. The parent repeats again and again, "What do you say?" The child responds "Thank you." In process of time, the habit builds into a practice that shapes the life and character of the child. It is not spontaneous, but habitual.

Both types of being thankful—the spontaneous, joy-filled thanks and the habitual practice of being thankful—are necessary for a balanced life. The leper who returned to Jesus probably had both kinds of thankfulness. He was truly and spontaneously thankful to be made clean. Yet, perhaps he had built a pattern of thankfulness into his life and he returned to Jesus to express his thanks. Of course, we could not know for certain.

Why be thankful?

(1) Thankfulness is a major part of well-being. It is hard to say, "Thank you!" without a smile. It creates inner well-being, inner harmony. When our inner harmony is missing we are miserable. Who wants to be miserable?

(2) Being thankful implies that you care—the healed leper cared enough to find Jesus again. Caring is the foundation of the moral life. There has been much creative scholarship (mostly feminist) on caring as a basis of morality. When we care for others (human beings, nonhuman animals, the environment), we more often act in the right way toward them. It would be difficult to kill someone you care for. If you care for Gaia, Mother Nature, you will be less likely to use and abuse her.

(3) Thankfulness implies relationship—the healed leper wants to talk to Jesus, to express his thanks, to have the beginning of relationship. Martin Buber, Jewish philosopher and theologian, spoke of relationship as

"I-Thou" and "I-It." "I-Thou" is a subject-to-subject relationship (1923, 1937). "I-It" is a subject-to-object relationship. "I-It" is when you do not respect the subjectivity of the other: you use them. "I-Thou" is when you have face-to-face relationship and respect the other as subject. Being thankful is an "I-Thou" relationship.

If we think of thankfulness as for our own well-being, as a way of caring (hence the basis of morality) and as the way of relationship, then it is clear how important the practice of being thankful is.

But how do we develop it?

In much the same way that our parents first taught us thankfulness. We need to make it a habit. We need to wake each morning and to remember to be thankful. At first, any habit needs careful remembrance. After thirty four years playing the guitar, I took to ukulele playing. My fingers had formed the practice of playing the guitar, knowing where the frets are, knowing the length of the fingerboard. Having practiced guitar for three decades, you do not need to look at the fingerboard. To change to the ukulele (a much smaller instrument) was at first quite strange. My fingers needed to learn a new practice. I made many errors. My fingers were in the wrong place. Discordant notes were many. Yet, practice has made it once again "second nature."

To train in being thankful will make thankfulness "second nature." As it becomes such, then our well-being will increase, we will find ourselves as those who care, and we will build better relationships.

3. Persistence

persistence |p□r'sist□ns| : noun

firm or obstinate continuance in a course of action in spite of difficulty or opposition: "companies must have patience and persistence, but the rewards are there."

the continued or prolonged existence of something: "the persistence of huge environmental problems." (Apple Dictionary)

I read recently that to accomplish anything worthwhile (to learn the piano, to become proficient in a sport, to learn a new discipline) requires 10,000 hours. Seems a bit excessive. But think about it. If you devote yourself to your chosen goal then at one hour a day it will take you just over twenty-seven years. At two hours a day thirteen years. At eight hours a day, about three-and-a-half years. You get the picture. Though 10,000 hours seems excessive at first glance, it's probably about right. Undergraduate students take four years to complete their degree in the United States (though it's more like five or six for many). To really excel requires a great deal of work. Daily work. Not unlike 10,000 hours. And then you are ready to go on to graduate school. PhDs take at least five more years. So, to become proficient enough to teach your subject requires at least nine years of practice. Nine years of asking the questions, searching for answers, knocking on the door of your chosen field. Persistence required!

> Ask, and it will be given you; search, and you will find; knock, and the door will be opened for you. (Matthew 7:7)

This saying of Jesus is very well known. I suspect that it is often used in a simplistic way to refer to getting what you want. Just ask for it and you will get it. In days gone by I heard sermons where earnest preachers pleaded with their congregations to just keep on praying and God would give you what you want. (Was I one of those earnest young preachers? My memory's not what it once was.) The better ones urged persistence as the key. The worst announced a quick fix way to get anything you want. The "health and wealth gospel" it was termed. (I do hope I was one of the better earnest young preachers!) Those who interpret the saying as a call to persistence in spiritual practice are closer to the spirit of the saying.

We can all accept that if you want to learn a trade, say becoming a skilled carpenter, it takes a long apprenticeship, with a lot of hard work—back to the 10,000 hours. Yet, in spiritual practice many assume an easy road, a swift attainment of spiritual accomplishment. This strikes me as odd. Meditation looks good. The benefits to body, mind and spirit seem proven. "I'll give it a go," you say. Ten minutes meditation on the first day (that was a stretch!) Ten minutes on the second day. Five minutes on the third day. On day four a useful excuse arises. By week two, meditation is more sporadic. By week four, the benefits to body, mind, and spirit are not that noticeable. Why not try something else? After a month, maybe a total practice time of three hours. Only 9,997 to go!

Clearly I am being overly simplistic and perhaps not very kind. But I think I make my point. The drop-out rate of those who begin a spiritual practice is very high. In our culture, we have tried to address it by the over-production of books, CDs, and DVDs, many proclaiming the new, sure way to the goal in the speediest possible way. Don't be taken in for a second. Listen to the saying of Jesus (and every other adept of the Way). Keep asking, searching and knocking. You'll get there. Eventually.

Enjoy the journey!

4. Contentment: An Attitude against the Stream

An anonymous ancient adept said that deep spirituality, together with contentment, is where true wealth lies.

Contentment is an attitude antithetical to life in a consumer capitalist society. It swims against the stream. I recall that, only days after the events of September 11, 2001, President Bush addressed the people of the United States (and through the media the rest of the world). He told us not to be deterred by acts of terrorism from that which really matters. What really matters is to shop. Consuming more and more stuff is what makes the world go round. Bishop Lesslie Newbigin, back in the 1980s, reminded us that consumer capitalism and Christianity were not compatible systems of thought and practice. Consumer capitalism, he said, is based on the stimulation of unremitting covetousness. And everyone knows being covetous is not a Christian virtue!

In the years before Bishop Newbigin returned from India to the United Kingdom to be appalled at British society, I studied marketing. (I have a degree in business studies and was for a time a member of the Market Research Society in London. It seems like another lifetime ago!) Marketing then, and I doubt that it has changed, was a social science devoted to: (1) stimulating unrest with what you have; and (2) provoking desire for what you don't have. In contemporary society we have become very good at this. It has been linked with industrial production we know as "built-in obsolescence." Good stuff is designed to last one season, to be replaced by equally good stuff, but slightly different good stuff next season. Seasons differ in length. Larger consumer stuff (refrigerators and washing machines) has a season of about four to five years—televisions nowadays even less. A season for a cell phone is just under the two-year contract. Clothes change with spring, summer, winter, and fall, and this year's fall colors are just sufficiently different from last year's that we all notice if you are out of style.

The stimulation of desire for stuff is psychologically shrewd. Maslow was right. We are a bundle of needs. By nature human beings consume based on needs. We consume air, water, and food. We need relationships to survive. We need a certain sense of meaning or we pine away.

Consumer capitalism taps into this human neediness and nudges it along by creating new needs. And there is no end to the new needs that have been and will be created.

It's not so bad if you can keep up with the Joneses. Needs are created and satisfied with new purchases. But none of us can keep up for very long. However much you have, and whatever your financial position, there is always the more. The system thrives on the human capacity for covetousness. The other side of the coin is that few of us are content with life, because we never have what our piqued desires tell us we need to be happy. As a culture we have more than any other in human history. I doubt that we are more content.

I don't want to be misunderstood. Nor do I want to be a hypocrite. I like my stuff. My gadgets. My clothes. My books. I don't mind shopping for things. But I suspect that, in our culture, we are out of balance. Unremitting stimulation of desire for things does not lead to contentment

Recap the ancient wisdom: "Deep spirituality, together with contentment, is where true wealth lies." If this is close to truth, how wealthy are we truly?

Contentment seems to go hand-in-glove with a deep spirituality. That's where the work needs to be done. Deep spirituality does not come easily. Like a broken record—someone explain that metaphor to the under 30s—I return to practice. Deep spirituality grows in the fertile soil of the practices: meditation, mindfulness, ritual, and the rootedness of tradition.

5. The Complexity of Simplicity

I have really enjoyed a discussion in the community on our understanding of simplicity. Between us we have demonstrated the complexity of seeking simplicity!

> We are challenged by a call to simplicity. Our deepest need is to grow in our knowledge and love of God, not the accumulation of more material things. There is a beauty in space, in openness, in solitude. We seek to enjoy beauty without owning or possessing;

to stay focused, single minded, with purity of desire (Fitz-Gibbon
and Fitz-Gibbon, *Way of Living*, 19).

A few thoughts sparked by our discussion:

(1) It is not so much what we have (though when we have to excess
while others lack, there is a moral issue) as much as our attitude about what
we have. We can have much and be utterly attached to "things" (material
and nonmaterial). We can have little to nothing, and be equally attached to
things. It is our attitude to the things, making them more than they ought
to be, that gets in the way of a deeper, truer spirituality.

(2) In the history of spirituality, folks have taken a wrong turn when
they despise the material world. The material world is good, created by
and infused with God, a world to explore, enjoy, and respect. Despising
the world, and hence the body, has had a devastating effect on nonhuman
animals at the hands of human beings. Animals are, of course, merely bodies
with no souls, and so can be as despised as much as the non-animal material
world—so we have been told. That's why the "Other"—women, people of
color, our enemies, any who differ—are compared to animals. There is a
long tradition of despising the animalistic about human beings. This is the
"lower" side of being human. This is the connection to the material world.
It is bad theology, bad philosophy. It has led to bad practice.

(3) I confess that I am a bit of a technophile. Our technology amazes
me and I keep up with it. Without technology we would not be able to
have the Lindisfarne Community in its present form. The "virtual world,"
so called, is the real world as much as any other aspect of the world. Again,
it is about attitude, attachment, and use.

Simplicity is a winsome idea. Finding the simple in the complex,
discovering the complex as simple.

6. Becoming a Certain Kind of Person

Spirituality is located in four directions: upward, outward, inward and
downward. The upward direction is to come to terms with the experience
of transcendence, the "oceanic feeling," (Freud), the divine, the Godhead.
The outward direction is toward relationship with the Other: people,
non-human animals, the environment. The inward direction is toward the
self: to become a certain kind of person. The downward direction is against
the un-Other: all that destroys relationship, injustice, hatred, the demonic,

the "dark side" of life. The spacial analogy is helpful, but flawed. The four are deeply interconnected. We separate only to analyze, but realize that there is a more profound connectedness of the all in the One.

All the great traditions have much to say about the inward direction: becoming a certain kind of person. To become a certain kind of person is character. It is not something we are born with, but something we acquire through life. We are born with personality. We acquire character. With children you see very early on the differences in personality: quiet, loud, shy, outgoing, quick, or slow. It's much the same with puppies. All of our canine companions have had very different personalities. With Molly and Lucy (our pug friends), the personality they have now as two year olds was quite clear when they were twelve weeks old.

Character is acquired depending on the way we respond to that which life brings us. We can acquire good character or bad character.

The early Christian theologian Paul makes a connection between suffering, endurance, character, hope, and love. Each produces the other.

Paul's idea, like Buddhism, begins with suffering, for in a profound way, suffering, and the way we respond to suffering, defines life. Both traditions, though beginning with suffering, bring us something hopeful. Suffering is not the last word. Try as we might, we cannot escape the world and the physical, mental, and emotional trials that being embodied brings. The way we respond to life's trials is very much about character.

Paul says suffering produces endurance and endurance character. I don't think that is true for all. For some, suffering produces nothing good at all. Suffering may produce despair. Suffering may produce hopelessness. Suffering can be meaningless.

So, what makes the difference? Why does some suffering, through endurance, produce character and some not? The difference is for Paul in two words: hope and love. I have arranged his five ideas in this way:

Love combined with hope transforms suffering through endurance into character. We can only endure when there is hope of something better. Suffering is not the last word. Love is the last word.

Where do we acquire love? Here is mystery, for love, like suffering, comes to us as gift. Christians have called it "the grace of God." It is the mystery of the *Dao*. Search for it. Long for it. Practice it. Do all you can to find it. You will not be disappointed.

7. Be the Best? Do Your Best?

Recently, after a few good games of squash, I was in the university sports center, absentmindedly glancing at a notice board. A recruiting poster for one of the teams read, "Don't be average, be the best!"

The sign echoes a much-repeated mantra of our culture that says none of us should settle for average; that we all have the ability to be better than the others—to be number one. I find it disturbing.

I am all for doing one's best—but not at the expense of others. My dad's refrain, when I was growing up, was different. He would say, "Do your best son. That's all you can do." My best might be average, or less than average. I can't remember being "the best" at anything. But that doesn't bother me. I followed dad's advice. If I fail to do my best, I am only letting myself down.

"Don't be average, be the best!" is an impossibly cruel mantra for most of us. "Do your best!" is a demanding, but realizable goal. I think that's why, in my 20s, I took up running. I wasn't trying to beat others to get into a team. I was simply doing my best.

"Don't be average, be the best!" has a worrying underlying rationale. Social theorists have pointed out a trend in our culture from a general "other-regardingness" to a "self-regardingness." The change is post World War Two and is noticeable, along a spectrum of variables, from the mid-1950s. It's not to say that before then all was rosy in the garden. It is to say that we have become more self-centered and less mindful of the needs of others than before.

The apostle said, "Don't be selfish; don't try to impress others. Be humble, thinking of others as better than yourselves. Don't look out only for your own interests, but take an interest in others, too."

The apostle came to this conclusion by meditating on the life of Jesus. Jesus is one of the world's exemplars of the "other-regarding" life. The other-regarding life is as counter-cultural now as it has ever been. It is a demanding life. It can be a quite exhausting life! But it is life to aspire to. It is a Good life.

Perhaps one day I will be looking absentmindedly at a notice board and will see a recruiting poster announcing in large letters, "Think of others as better than yourself!" I wonder what team that would be!

8. The Irrationality of Hope

By and large, we tend to believe that things are true based on evidence. We wake in the morning, the sun is already shining with not a cloud in the sky. This is the third day in a row. Every other day before the day has turned out to be warm and wonderful. There has been a trend of warm sunny days. Each has started the way this one has. We believe today will be the same, for we have some evidence. On another day, some months later, the alarm wakes us to a chill in the air. Peeking through the curtain it's clear the wind is blowing hard. The tall trees are bending. As you open the door to let the dogs out an icy chill grips you. The sky is gunmetal grey, full of snow. On this day to believe it will be warm and sunny is foolishness. It is irrational. However, based on the evidence of previous years, we can be pretty sure that there will be warm and sunny days to come, but not for a few months more. In winter to hope of spring is not irrational.

But what of hope for a better world? For the last few hundred years, in the developed world, we have grown used to things getting better. Governments have based policy on it (borrow now for the better future will pay off our debts). Individual families have based their lives on it (borrow now, and future higher income will take care of the mortgage). In recent years we have encouraged our young people to take out large education loans (the job you are bound to get will take care of the loans). This way of living seemed rational based on past trends. But as a culture we are wobbling—tottering on the brink of a steep and slippery slope. That the future will be better than the past is beginning to seem more irrational.

I am speaking of the "middle class." There has always been an "underclass"—a substratum of society we don't speak about in polite company. For them the future has never looked bright. More are joining this large group.

Data released a few weeks ago, for the United States, tells us that almost fifty million people are living in poverty. That's the highest number since the government began tracking the figures fifty-two years ago.

Still, I hope for a brighter future for the world. I am not thinking of evidence based beliefs, but rather an irrational hope, with no evidential base. I make no argument for it. Like Goodness, Hope simply is. It is a deep intuition. Hopelessness gives way to despair and despair crushes the human spirit. Hope arises deep in the human spirit and makes the unbearable bearable.

What would a better world look like? Jesus told a story in which he said:

> For I was hungry, and you fed me. I was thirsty, and you gave me
> a drink. I was a stranger, and you invited me into your home. I
> was naked, and you gave me clothing. I was sick, and you cared
> for me. I was in prison, and you visited me.

That would be a better world. The hungry and thirsty, strangers, the unclothed, the sick, and the incarcerated all cared for. That is not the world we live in. It is not the "better world" that Wall Street seeks of mere increased materiality. It is a better world of justice and fairness, and love and kindness—a world of loving relationships.

But to hope is not to daydream. To hope is to intuit the future and work toward it. To hope is to choose to act.

FOUR

THE INNER LIFE

1. Six I's and Three Me's

In Galatians 2 Paul gives us in summary form what we may term "Christ mysticism." In verses 19—21 (NRSV) we have six I's and three me's. It is not clear what Paul means. There seems to be contradiction and Paul pushes the rules of speech beyond normal usage. "I died that I might live." "I have been crucified, I no longer live, but Christ lives in me." "I now live, I live by trust." "Christ loved me, was given for me." It is not obvious who the "I" or the "me" is. What are the living and the dying? Is there a part of us that lives and a part that dies? Does Christ replace us, in some sense? Is Paul suggesting a split personality? Spiritual schizophrenia? It is, to say the least psychologically confusing!

Yet, it reaches very deep into the tradition of mystical spirituality dealing with the inner world, the life of the mind and spirit. It seems that all the great traditions of spirituality bear witness to this bifurcation of the inner life. It has been characterized in the following ways, to name a few:

- The inner and the outer.
- "I" and "Christ."
- The human nature and the divine nature.
- Human nature and Buddha nature.
- The "true self" and the "false self."
- The flesh and the spirit.
- The "old person" and the "new person."
- Self and no-self.

I am going to use the typology of Tony De Mello. He uses "I" and the "me." The "I" is the deeper self, the "me" the shallower. He suggests that most of us most of the time live in the "me," but that the "I" looks at the "me."

A few words about the "me."

The "me" is created through attachments. When asked, "Who are you?" The answers "I am a social worker, I am a mother, I am Canadian, I am a Hindu, I am a priest" are all answers concerning the "me." They do not speak of who we are in our deeper self. They are all transient attachments, contingent on some role, some function, something about life that will pass away. If identity is tied to those contingencies, when the contingency passes, what then of identity?

I think that is what Jesus was referring to in the passage about marriage: that in heaven, there is no marrying or giving in marriage (Matt 22:30). Contingent attachments have passed. It is also why, when people lose their job, they continue to speak of themselves as a "something." "I am a writer" becomes a very important statement even though I have had only one book published and that was twenty years ago. To take away that self-reference is to leave a vacuum and that is very painful if identity is built on such attachments.

It follows that the "me" is quite fragile, prone to change, easily hurt and damaged. It is why human life is so painful (inwardly painful). The "me" is the source of worry, anxiety, sleeplessness, anger, lust for things, frustration, grief, jealousy, joy of the shallower kind. Problems with the "me" are what fuel the talk therapy industry. It may also be why there is no end to talk therapy, because the me is constantly changing, in flux, demanding attention. Talk therapy is not about the deeper self. The deeper self is silent.

A few words about the "I."

It is deep, hidden, beyond words, like the wind or breath.

It comes to us not by strife, but as gift.

It is beyond theological or philosophical formulation or speculation.

We approach it through the *via negativa*—the way of negation. We can say what it is not rather than what it is.

It is the place of union with God, with the ultimately real.

It may be sought but not owned.

Theology, philosophy, liturgy, meditation, and nature can lead us in the right direction (and sometimes in the wrong direction) but they are not the "I." We often mistake the signifier for the thing signified.

Back to Paul's writing. In Galatians, Paul is grappling with these realities. Spirituality is concerned with a dying of the "me" and a discovering of the "I" and finding that the "I" is Christ. It is in the words of Jesus, to lose self (the me) in order to find self (the I).

There is universal testimony that life is happier when the true self is discovered, when attachments are viewed in their proper light. Yet, the true self is not sought for happiness sake, but for its own sake. In the words of the ancients, "virtue is its own reward." The inner is its own reward.

2. Self-Examination and Natural Consequences

Jesus told a little story to those who trusted in themselves that they were just and as a result looked with contempt on other people. The story is very simple. A religious person parades his goodness before God and compares himself over-favorably against others. A tax collector, a collaborator with the domination system, simply asks for God's mercy. The punch line of the story is that "those who exalt themselves will be humbled and those who humble themselves will be exalted" (Matthew 23:12; Luke 14:11).

I take the story to be about two things: self-examination and natural consequences.

First: self-examination. We could dodge these little stories of Jesus in this way: "Ah, Jesus told this story to the proud. Clearly not me, so I can ignore it!" But it is much better to see the story addressed to each of us. It is a story for self-examination (as all the aphorisms of Jesus are). A great part of the spiritual life is a daily self-examination. That is why the evening office allows space for recollection of the day and prayers for forgiveness. Socrates told us, "The unexamined life is not worth living" (1937).

To use this story for self-examination is simply to apply it to your self. It is a fearless look inside with the question, "Am I like that?" "Do I think too much of myself at the expense of others?" It is not about putting yourself down. It is about being realistic. When we find things not as they should be, we seek God's help to change, to be different. It is a personal spiritual exercise to help us to grow and to change. As far as I can see, all those we consider "spiritual giants" had this practice.

Yet, we must be careful. Self-examination can turn to morbidity. "Morbidity" comes from the Latin for disease. To become morbid is to focus too much on the disease. Self-examination, when out of balance, focuses on the inner disease, the disease of the self. That is not helpful at all.

It is most dangerous for those of us who have a very low self-worth to begin with. So, self-examination, yes; self-degradation, no. Care is needed.

It is also a story about natural consequences. All of our actions and attitudes have natural consequences. The story is a nod in the direction of karma, of reaping what we sow. When we are kind, kindness rebounds to us, though we are not kind for that reason alone. When we love, we are loved, though we do not love only for that reason. When we cheat, others will cheat us. If we constantly tell lies, others will no longer trust us. When we push ourselves to the top at the expense of others, we should be prepared for a fall! Yet, when we see ourselves in the proper light and do not hold contempt for others, look down on them, see ourselves as "better than," then honor comes to us as a gift, as grace.

3. Journeying by Stages

The journey has always been a fruitful picture for the spiritual life. You will know of many journey stories. In Greek lore, there is Jason and the Argonauts and the search for the Golden Fleece. In Celtic lore, there is the voyage of Brendon. He is said to be the first from Europe to "find" North America. The search for the Holy Grail is a journey, the Grail Quest. With the finding of the Grail lies immortality. The archetypal Biblical journey was that made by the Israelites leaving slavery in Egypt and journeying to the land of promise. Each journey is an allegory. It tells us of a journey we are to make with the promise of the "not yet": to find the fleece and regain the kingdom; to leave "home" to find our "new world"; to go from where we are to find the grail; to leave our "slavery" to enter our "land of promise." In Exodus it says, "they journeyed by stages" (17:1).

It is journeying by stages that I thought about today.

Movement is constant in our lives. No human life is static. At the very least we are born, we are cared for, we go to school, we work at several jobs, we die. Some of us form life partnerships. Some work, some do not. Some of us have children. Some of us have cared for over eighty! These are all stages. They may just be stages in life that pass us by unnoticed, unaccounted for. Or, we may see them as stages in the quest. If we see each successive stage as part of the quest, then there is much to learn.

Spiritually, there are very clear stages: changes of direction, important events that stand out, way-markers to trace the journey. These often coincide with the stages of life, but not necessarily. From long observation, there seem to be some more common than others. Many of us have significant spiritual events during the teen years. These often shape the next stage or two of spiritual journeying. Many people have some kind of religious awakening in those years. Middle age brings its crises, its deep questions, its regrets, and its longings. The middle period of life gives opportunity to reflect. Much has passed, more is to come. How has it been? Where is it going? What needs to be changed? Where should focus lie? Approaching death brings its own focus.

I had opportunity some years ago to chat with an elderly man about life and death. During conversation over a meal, the subject abruptly changed to the meaning of life, what happens when we die, is there purpose? I think it was a significant stage in his journey. Four months later, he died suddenly. I would like to think that I helped him a little on the journey.

Each new stage is marked by new joys, new opportunities, and new difficulties. There are new challenges to face. There are new enemies to learn to love. This does not change. I think the balance between joys and challenges changes. I think in some stages difficulties are more than other stages. Yet, the mix is always there.

For Socrates, the life well lived is the examined life; a life of mindfulness. The secret of a good life, if there is a secret, is examination. That is, not to let life simply drift by. What a miss, if life passes by with no reflection, no weighing of the journey, no learning, and no looking forward. Socrates would urge, "Be mindful!"

What is my Grail? Where is my promised land?

4. A Struggle with the Lectionary

Sometimes I find the lectionary readings disconnected (the daily or weekly readings of scriptures)—disconnected from each other, from life, from my own *Existenz*. Today the readings, for me, are like that. This perception probably says more about me than the readings, but that is the way I find them.

In Jeremiah, I found a prophet who is wrestling with his call to be a prophet. He wants to speak for God (feels compelled to do so) and yet faces derision and persecution from others. People just don't understand him and he is having a good old moan about it.

Paul in Romans presents us with a "Christ-mysticism" in order that we don't do bad things. Within thirty years of his death Jesus, the wisdom teacher and healer from Nazareth, had become the Christ of mystic experience. Death and resurrection are now a mystical motif whereby people can overcome their inner drives to do bad things. It's all a case of considering that we, too, have died and been raised. That is, our old life has died and a new life has begun. It is symbolized in baptism and experienced through a mystical identification with Christ. If you are struggling with some issue, says Paul, remember that just as Christ died so did you. Just as Christ lives to God, so do you.

In the gospel, we have a jumble of disconnected wisdom sayings. It reads to me like the early church gathered together a number of remembered sayings of Jesus and put them all together in one block. The sayings are loosely connected, but not really. I found nine sayings:

(1) Masters and disciples are equal.
(2) Everything will be revealed, even the things spoken in the dark.
(3) Don't be afraid of people, but fear God.
(4) God cares for you just like God cares for sparrows.
(5) Don't deny Jesus. If you do he will deny you.
(6) The message of Jesus doesn't bring peace but division among family members.
(7) Don't love anyone more than Jesus.
(8) Take up your cross to be worthy of Jesus.
(9) If you find your life you will lose it, if you lose it you will find it.

What to do with a jumble of sayings like that? Each saying could be used for meditation. Let the one thought be the phrase to which you bring your mind. Not all the sayings are "comfortable." You might not agree with the saying! That's OK. Life is like that.

If there is a connecting theme in these lectionary readings, it is a theme of struggle. The prophet struggled to be a prophet and didn't like it. People struggle between doing the right thing and doing the wrong thing. To follow Jesus is a struggle and you shouldn't expect anything different. Sometimes spirituality is a deep struggle and these readings reflect that.

5. Responding to Personal Hurt

Life is often rough! We get hurt and we hurt others; often unintentionally, sometimes intentionally. Much of life is responding to hurts. I am thinking not merely of physical hurts (which are easiest to respond to) but psychological hurts. Mental and emotional wounds are often quite crushing. You can live with them for days, years even. The way we respond can bring us to peace and reconciliation, or can leave us in the turmoil of bitterness and loss.

When someone hurts us, it's understandable that we have the urge to strike back—to try to cause hurt to the one who hurt us. In this response, there are the twin reactions of vengeance and justice. Behind these is the idea that this wrong should not have happened. Justice is about making it right. Vengeance is about visiting retribution and punishment on the offender. Justice with vengeance is a deep seam in our psyche and our culture.

The little child who does not get as large a piece of cake at the dinner table says, "It's not fair!" Justice requires the right to be wronged. The child may have a larger piece of cake. That seems fair. Vengeance requires that the older sister be punished for her greed in taking more than her share. She may have her cake taken away completely. She may miss the next cake. She may be spanked. So linked are these ideas that we often think that justice requires vengeance for it to be true justice.

Here are three possible responses to personal hurt. The first come to us from the prophet Jeremiah. His response is this, "O Lord, you know; remember me and visit me, and bring down retribution for me on my persecutors" (Jeremiah 15: 10-21). Jeremiah still feels the need for vengeance. He wants his persecutors to suffer. Yet, he has moved in that the vengeance to be carried out is to be God's and not his own. This is quite a shift.

Think of most of the wars between nations. The reason for war is often said to be the righting of a wrong. Retribution is taken out upon the offender. If the nations made Jeremiah's move, it is possible that there would be no war. His appeal is to God to bring about vengeance. I have read accounts of pacifism that use this same argument. They argue that it is wrong for people to use violence because God will bring about God's violence in due time. Don't kill your enemies. God will kill them on your behalf!

The second response to personal hurt is that of Paul. "Bless those who persecute you; bless and do not curse them . . . live peaceably with all" (Romans 12:14). This is a much bigger shift. It is a psychological difference. It seems that Jeremiah still holds the grudge against his persecutors. He still wants them to suffer, though he will not be personally the means of their suffering. Paul presents something new. He instructs us to begin to think differently about those who cause hurt, to bless them, to wish them well and not harm. This is remarkable and rarely practiced in politics or world affairs. But what a change such a shift would make! In personal life, it frees you from harboring grudges that lead to destructive bitterness that eats away at your spirit.

Paul does add, "Never avenge yourselves, but leave room for the wrath of God, for it is written, "Vengeance is mine, I will repay, says the Lord" (Romans 12:19). Don't you get angry accompanied by vengeance; let God get angry and bring God's vengeance! I wish he had not added that. For me, it takes away from that which he has already urged. Paul presents a new way, a different way than vengeance; one of blessing, care, love of the one who causes hurt. To add that God will repay the hurt with vengeance undermines the new way. It seems to make God less than us. Love and blessing is good for human beings, but God will exercise vengeance!

The third response to personal hurt is the gospel where Jesus refuses to walk away from suffering but to face it with courage knowing that in losing life, life is found. In the extremity of personal suffering, Jesus forgives his persecutors (Luke 23:34). He prays God's blessing on them. This theme is the one that Paul uses and is the new idea, the new response to hurt, that the early Christian community brought to the world.

In the gospel, too, is the redaction, "The Child of Humanity is to come with his angels . . . and he will repay everyone for what he has done" (Matthew 16:27). Sadly, this is much the same as in Paul. Vengeance is so deep in the human psyche that after blessing comes retribution. I wish that here too the gospel writer had remained with the mystical insight of losing life and gaining life. Vengeance rears its ugliness again! It seems strange to me that we should be urged to be kind to those who cause hurt in the knowledge that ultimately that kindness will turn to retribution. There is no retribution, no vengeance, and no repaying hurts in love. God is love, and we are to imitate God.

How do we respond to personal hurt? With love, with care, with blessing for those who hurt us and with no thought that though we bless them now they will get their comeuppance in the end!

6. Losing and Finding the Self

Those who grasp and clutch at self will lose it. Those who let go of self and follow me will find it.—Jesus

A key in spirituality is to come to an understanding of who we are. Above the doorway to Plato's academy was the inscription, "Know Yourself." In that tradition, to know yourself was the quest of a lifetime. Recently, I had a student confidently tell the rest of the class that she really knew herself. Quite a feat at nineteen!

I am fascinated by what we call the self. In contemporary society, we have a focus on the self like no other society before us. Yet, it is by no means clear what the self is, or even *if* the self is. From Plato onward, a dominant tradition in the West has held that there is a continuing entity we call the self. In its Christian version, this idea became the idea of the immortal soul—a distinct individual consciousness with a past, present and future. The idea gels with our experience and memories.

I have memories of being a little boy playing in the park behind our house in Moston, Manchester, in the 1960s. It is the same "me" who married Jane in the mid-1970s. The same "me" became a minister in the early 1980s. The same "me" is now a professor of philosophy living in a different country. Much has changed: relationships, jobs, age, ideas, the body itself. Yet, there is a sense of undeniable continuity. It is this consciousness that lies behind the idea that the self must continue after death, and that, in some traditions the self existed before birth.

In some philosophies of the East, and in a minority of those of Western tradition, the existence of the self as a unitary, continuing entity has not been held. The Buddha suggested that what we call the self is illusory and is merely a bundle of form, sensation, perception, predispositions, and consciousness. Nothing is fixed. Everything changes. Perception and consciousness combine for a while and then change. In the West, there is something of this in the mystical tradition that sees the goal of spirituality is to lose the self in God, the universal consciousness, as a drop of water would be swallowed in the ocean. David Hume—who I do not think had come across the Buddhist tradition and had no truck with the mystics—said something remarkably similar in the eighteenth century from a purely empiricist point of view. This tradition, too, gels with elements of our experience. (see Hume, 1969, *A Treatise of Human Nature*, I, IV, VI, "Of Personal Identity.")

How to choose between these ideas? Perhaps, we don't need to. Both views hold truth and speak truth to us at different times, in different contexts.

In our contemporary culture, we have a view of the self that would be owned by neither historical tradition. Its essence is captured in the phrases self-interest and self-love. To over-simplify, self-interest is the foundation of our economic system where each pursues her own interest and an "invisible hand" makes it all work out for the good. Enlightened capitalism (that is, crude self-interest balanced by moral sentiment) has given way to unbridled consumerism. We have become self-regarding at the expense of being other-regarding. Self-love (again to oversimplify) is the mantra of popular psychology, with the often repeated idea that, "You have to love yourself before you can love others." This is said so often that it is rarely challenged or analyzed as to what it might mean. Self-interest and self-love have opened wide the door to mere selfishness.

In the teaching of Jesus there is this: "Those who grasp and clutch at self will lose it. Those who let go of self and follow me will find it." This comes from the Q tradition in Matthew and Luke. It is also there in a slightly different form in the Johannine tradition. It seems so counterintuitive to the popularized focus on the self. Lose the self and you will find the self. There is a very similar notion in Eastern philosophy as non-attachment to self. Attachment to the self is the way of suffering. I think it is also clear that psychologically a preoccupation with the self is the road to neuroses.

In my work on the philosophy of love and morality, I have been developing the idea of love as "movement from the self to the other." (I have derived this in part from the work of Augustine of Hippo and Dame Iris Murdoch.) Love takes us from a preoccupation with the self to concern for the needs and well-being of the other who we love. Love is a ceasing to grasp and clutch at the self and its own needs and interests in favor of those we love. It is a losing of the self. Yet, it is in the losing of the self that the self is found, not in splendid Cartesian isolation but in loving relationship. Know yourself? You begin to know yourself in the love of the Other.

7. The Inner Journey

For it is from within, from the human heart, that evil intentions come . . . and they defile a person. (Jesus; Mark 7: 21-23)

A key to spiritual growth is the ability to look within, to take the inner journey. To examine life is profoundly important. It is also immensely challenging, for when we look within we see all kinds of things we wish were not there. With age, looking in the bathroom mirror in the morning becomes challenging. The wrinkles are obvious. There are various blotches and discolorations. The receding hairline is noticeable. The shadows under the eyes are more pronounced. It is often uncomfortable! The inner journey is more so.

In my younger days, I was taken by the idea that the older I became, the fewer imperfections I would have. I would have learned a few things. My character would improve. Now, when I look within, I see pretty much the same little boy, with the same issues, the same fears, the same wonderments, the same defects of character, the same neuroses. Of course, like a skilled makeup artist I am better now at covering them up! But they are still there.

What we see is not always pleasant. To anyone with any sensitivity, inner work is painful. What we see is a defilement of the spirit. It is a kind of death. Yet, death is not the issue. It is the fear of death that defiles, that incapacitates, that has us devising all kinds of strategies to avoid the pain that is fear.

As we grow older, most of us work out strategies for avoiding the pain of fear. These are just a few: we run away; we pretend what we see is not there; we cover it up with perfume to make it smell differently; we manipulate. Each of these is a fighting against fear. Each is a foolish strategy. Among our foster kids have been those who, for whatever reason, dislike taking a shower. Yet, also they become sensitized to how bad they smell when they do not shower. They strategize to cover up the smell. They will use more deodorant and perfume. Does it work? Not for a moment. There is nothing more unpleasant than the smell of teenage kids who try to mask the unwashed smell with perfume! Bad strategy!

Most of us do the same with what we find when we take the inner journey. Rather than face the pain of the inner imperfection, we strive for ways to avoid it.

An alternative strategy. Face it: acknowledge what you see, relax, and let it go.

Some years ago, I had a friend that looked inside and found something he didn't like. He was very happily married and loved his partner dearly. Yet, he realized that he had an infatuation with another person in his workplace. The discovery was agony for him. He wrestled and wrestled and tried all kinds of strategies to avoid the pain it was causing him. He was filled with fear. He felt like he was dying inside. In desperation, he came to talk with me. In talking with me, my friend faced what he found unpleasant inside himself. He no longer avoided it, fought against it, masked it, and pretended it wasn't there. After an hour's chat, he found that in simply facing what he had seen, it robbed it of fear and he was able to let it go. My friend grew spiritually.

8. A Divided Self?

A few thoughts about the self divided against itself. This is an important idea found in much literature. It seems to refer to the existential experience of inner conflict—a kind of inner disintegration. The aim of spiritual experience is the reintegration of the self to produce a harmony within itself, harmony with the divine, and with all things.

But what a complex idea! There is an assumption that the self exists and that we know what the self is; that there is a core "essence" of "who I am," and that this core continues throughout life (and beyond, and quite possibly before the life we now live).

Buddhism challenges the notion. There is "no self." Yet to say the self does not exist is as much an error as to say the self exists . . . hmm. It was also challenged by David Hume who suggested that the self does not exist but is merely an agglomeration of perceptions at any given time. There is nothing continuing about the self. The self is a present moment phenomenon.

The physical body reconstitutes itself every seven years or so. The body I now have is on its eighth regeneration and is different to the body I had at ages 7, 14, 21, 28, 35, 42, and 49. Molecularly different but recognizably the same. Is the self like that? Discontinuous yet continuous?

Then there is also memory. I remember things from the past. I married Jane in 1976. Was that "me" or some other self?

The narrative self also interests me. That is the way we construct our own self-identity, and the way we tell our story changes over time and undergoes constant revision. Effectively, we reinvent ourselves in the construction of our life narrative. All very interesting and no conceivable way of resolving it for sure.

It is the existential disintegration I want to think about. Whether the self is an enduring single essence or an agglomeration of perceptions changing from moment to moment, there is an all too common experience that this self is disconnected, fractured, divided. The phrase "divided self" was coined as far as I can tell by William James in his *Varieties of Religious Experience* (1982). It was used as the tile of R.D. Laing's book looking at schizophrenia. Both James and Laing see health as the self reconnected, whole and not divided.

I have toyed with the idea that in some instances this experience of disintegration happens when difference aspects of our self-consciousness are out of line with each other. Here is one way of thinking about it:

- The knowing self
- The desiring self
- The choosing self

The knowing self refers to our abilities to think things through, to come to understanding, to make distinctions. The desiring self refers to our needs and wants, desires and longings. The choosing self is that ability to act on our insights and to make meaningful decisions. Problems arise when the knowing self and the desiring self come into conflict. This is common in descriptions of sexuality, but crops up in all kinds of places. Here's an oversimplification. The knowing self has determined that to visit a friend in hospital would be a good thing; the desiring self really wants to go out to the party with other friends; the choosing self is paralyzed and a choice can't be made. The self is divided against itself. The person is miserable. The trick is to integrate thinking, feeling and choosing. In other places I have called this the formation of moral sense.

How do we move toward an integrated self? Healthy life practice. Simple, ordinary things. Healthy food, exercise, relaxation, meaningful work and activities, spiritual practices of meditation and mindfulness, rootedness in a tradition, friendship. No guarantees but this should help.

9. On Demons and Mental Illness

In the ancient world, the unexplained was given expression by a world of spirits. There were good spirits and bad spirits, and then a Great Spirit. The Great Spirit was in overall control of things. The lesser spirits were localized, bound to particular places, people, and conditions. These lesser spirits caused the various problems that we have socially constructed as mental illnesses. How to be rid of the unclean spirit? Try magic (the manipulation of nature through spell, incantation or potion) or exorcism by a holy person (and the manipulation of the gods or God).

Enlightened humanity did away with the world of spirits. The religious settled on one spirit (God) and the non-religious found no more room for the spiritual world. For them, all could be explained by what is seen.

However, the inner pain of mental and emotional upset did not go away with the social exorcism of the spirit world. A different story needed to be told. Of course, "Enlightenment" is a narrative of a particular social class. Many (the majority?) have always held on to some invisible world of cause and effect. The Enlightened called it superstition. Enlightened and unenlightened alike still suffered emotional and mental breakdown.

In modern times, mental illness—as much a mystery now as in the ancient world—have been socialized or medicalized. In other words, interactions with the social world—the self with the Other—cause the internal imbalance and inner pain. Or else it is pure biology—the physical brain malfunctions in some way and it is experienced as mental and emotional turmoil. The new shaman or priest is the talk therapist or the dispenser of brain altering drugs (psychiatrist, medical doctor or licensed psychologist). If interactions with people cause the problem, through encountering and understanding the problem in talk therapy, it will hopefully go away. If a problem in the physical brain is the trouble, do something to the brain (through chemicals or electricity), and we hope that the problem will go away. I am amazed often by the folk who place utter trust in the ability of the new shamans to fix any kind of mental and emotional issue.

The world of spirits is plausible still for many. The rational world of talk and understanding is plausible to others. The physicality of biology to still others.

Whose story? Which remedy?

Still we all have our demons. Still we all face the inner struggles. Most of the time we manage to get through it. Some of the time we feel almost overwhelmed. Very sadly, for some of us, at some points in our lives it all becomes just too much and we face a breakdown. Thankfully, these are most often only temporary. Some dear folk, very sadly, face the inner agony on a more or less permanent basis. There seems to be no help other than an empathetic "bearing-with."

The stories we tell and the remedies we seek are ways we try to make sense of the intractable problems of living a decent life of well-being. Emotional turmoil, mental agony, the affliction of unclean spirits work against our flourishing. Find help, and provide help by all useful means. At times, inner demons are best faced by spiritual means—by prayer, meditation, fasting, the authority of a deeply spiritual Other. At times, inner demons are best exorcised by talking through issues, by facing unpleasant memories, by finding new perspectives provided by a wise Other. At times, inner demons flee before the gentle rearrangement of brain chemistry provided by a skillfully trained Other. There is wisdom in not facing demons alone.

10. So You Think You're God—and Other Cool Delusions

There is a common term for those who think they are above everybody else, not subject to the ordinary rules of social intercourse: "the God complex." It is not an illness in the Diagnostic and Statistical Manual of Mental Illness (DSM-IV). Yet, we have all met this kind of person. By and large, they do not actually think they are God. It's just that to the rest of us they behave as if they have a kind of God-mandate to do as they wish. Not the kind of person you want to spend much time with.

But some people actually think they are becoming divine. Are they delusional? The DSM-IV can help us out, for here we find a reference to delusional disorder:

> **Diagnostic criteria for 297.1:** Nonbizarre delusions (i.e., involving situations that occur in real life, such as being followed, poisoned, infected, loved at a distance, or deceived by spouse or lover, or having a disease) of at least 1 month's duration.

In its sub-sections the DSM-IV includes this one:

> Grandiose Type: delusions of inflated worth, power, knowledge, identity, or special relationship to a deity or famous person.

So the person who does think they are God, or pretty close to being God, may be diagnosed as having a delusional disorder of the grandiose type. This puts most of the great mystics, adepts, saints, and religious icons as delusional. Most have been very aware of their closeness to the deity. Many have claimed that their closeness amounted to becoming divine. The best have showed the rest how to become divine too.

In the Christian tradition, the notion goes back to at least the end of the first century, when the Pauline school of theology developed a Christ mysticism. It claimed that the Jewish teacher Jesus from Nazareth was so in touch with God that he "is the image of the invisible God . . . For in him all the fullness of God was pleased to dwell"; and that just about everybody could have the same kind of experience, "Christ in you, the hope of glory" (Colossians 1:19-24). If it was possible for a human being to be divine (Jesus showed the way) then it's possible for us all to become divine.

As the tradition developed, by the fourth century or so (that's three hundred years of trying to sort out what the church should really think about Jesus) the theologians (the ones who won favor, mostly in the West) had decided that Jesus was divine in a particular and unique way. The rest of us? Miserable sinners for the most part. By then, the church largely agreed with the DSM-IV. "So, you think you're divine? You have a delusional disorder." The DSM-IV suggests treatment with antipsychotic medications. The church threatened excommunication, tried a little torture, and burned to death not a few. No more delusion.

But what if the delusional fringe is actually right? What if there is more than a "spark of the divine" in all of us? What if God is in all things, if we just had eyes to see?

Grace Jantzen wrote a helpful feminist philosophy of religion. She took the view that the masculinist corpus was beyond revision and so came up with a new philosophy of religion based on women's experience. She called her book, *Becoming Divine* (1999). Seems she too is delusional!

My own fumbling after the divine is best summed up in the word "panentheism": all is in God, God is in all. I try to see glimpses of God in all. Often I find it. In some people (and in not a few dogs and often in "nature") closeness to the divine is evident. But it's not always easy.

Becoming divine? Now that's a cool delusion.

11. Making Peace with Exile

The ancient Jewish people were exiled to Babylon from Egypt. The theme of exile and return is a prominent one in Jewish writing. The experience of exile is often close to the surface of Jewish longings for a better future. The most commonly expressed feeling of exiles is that "here" (the place of exile) is not where they want to be. They long to return home.

The ancient Celtic mystics, too, had a profound sense of exile. They often chose an exile *peregrinatio pro amore Christi*—wandering for the love of Christ. Yet, still they longed for the return home. The journey back was to the place of resurrection.

The experience of exile is existentially painful. "I don't belong here." The exile may be quite literally from one's home. For one Internet group to which I belong, my signature reads, "Andy: exile from Northumberland." It is lighthearted, but holds a deeper truth. The place of exile never feels quite right.

Yet, we need not be bound by a literal understanding of exile. Anywhere that we have the sense of "not-rightness" can become our place of exile. Listening to friends and colleagues, work often becomes a place of exile. Monday to Friday holds a certain "not-rightness." Friday evening is the homecoming. Watch people's Facebook statuses as the weekend draws near.

Perhaps the most telling place of exile is life in the world itself. "This world is not my home, I'm just a passing through" went an old song. Sometimes (for some folk most of the time) life has the quality of "not-rightness" about it. There is a shadowy memory of being from somewhere better, even when the place cannot be remembered with any assurance. Some religious traditions (and Plato among the philosophers) respond, "Of course! That's because you *have* come from somewhere else. The shadowy memory you have is a true one." Early Christian theologians expressed the longing of return, "To be at home in the body is to be away from God. To leave the body is to return to God." In exile, there is always the agony of longing.

The prophet of exile, Jeremiah, expressed a different perspective. He announced to the exiles:

> Build homes, and plan to stay. Plant gardens, and eat the food they produce. Marry and have children. Then find spouses for them so that you may have many grandchildren. Multiply! Do not dwindle away! And work for the peace and prosperity of the city where I sent you into exile. Pray to God for it, for its welfare will determine your welfare. (Jeremiah 29:5)

The prophet urged a making peace with the state of exile. Make the place of exile home. Learn to love it. Be at rest wherever you find yourself. This would be to find peace in the exile of the workplace. It would be to learn to be content in and with your body.

This may be easier said than done. As with all things, it is most likely accomplished with small steps: a daily mindfulness. Finding yourself at peace in the present moment. Could you enjoy exile? Will the longing for home ever go away? Possibly not, but the exile might be made more bearable.

12. The Three Treasures

I have been working for a while with the idea of basic ethical beliefs. These are ethical commitments so generally held (in all cultures, traditions, religions, and philosophies) that they are unquestioned. Some philosophers call them "prima facie moral axioms." That is, we hold them to be true unless we can find very good reasons for not doing so. We can't find many of them, but notions such as "not doing harm," and "doing good" are a couple of them. I came across a contender for the category as "self-improvement." The argument said that here is a basic ethical belief that we can all be better than we are, and we ought to try to be so. I am intrigued by the idea and will continue to ponder it.

A large part of self-improvement is self-reflection. In the Christian calendar we are encouraged to take two extended periods of serious reflection each year, in Lent and Advent. That's not to say that we ignore self-reflection at other times, but that at these times we make a special effort. With Christmas celebrations and indulgence around the corner, it's not a bad thing to do just now.

So, I have been wondering: what would be a good preparation? My partial answer is that preparation is an inner thing. About character. About who I am in my deepest self. It's the kind of person I am in process of becoming. Here are some characteristics to play with: Balance. Modesty. Humbleness. Quietness. Returning to the fundamental issues of life.

However, self-improvement—with its sister self-reflection—is not an end in itself. It is for the sake of the Other. I become a better person not for my sake, but for your sake. You engage in self-reflection not to boast of your achievement, but to become your best self for others. I change to love you better, more fully.

Here is wisdom from the *Daodejing*:

> I have three treasures
> That I guard and hold dear:
> The first is love;
> The second is contentment;
> The third is humbleness.
> Only the loving are courageous;
> Only the content are magnanimous;
> Only the humble are capable of commanding.

Love, contentment, humbleness—certainly elements of the inner life to treasure. Finally, wisdom from Confucius:

> The benevolent person decreases what is excessive and increases
> what is scarce. She weighs things and makes them balance.

13. Illusions, Disillusionment, Disappointment, or Reality?

These two statements seem to be true:

(1) Illusions followed by disillusionment often leads to disappointment.
(2) Illusions followed by disillusionment sometimes leads to reality.

In many endeavors it is easy to begin with grand illusions about where we are going and what the outcomes will be. In the end illusions are always shattered, for illusions are false ideas. It may take a long time, and some illusions are very enduring. Yet, finally the rigors of life have a way of dispelling illusions.

This happens in very simple ways. "I think I'll take up golf," is a fine idea. But if the notion is accompanied by illusions about your present abilities, the amount of time and practice it takes just to hit the ball straight, the number of "failures" you will face on the putting green, then the chances are you will give up after a few attempts at the game. Disappointment. Yet, this doesn't happen to everyone who has the idea "I think I'll take up golf." These folk bring with them a set of illusions, but when the illusions are shattered, they stick with the game. Reality sets in and they begin the long, difficult and enjoyable process of becoming a golfer.

Whether you take up golf is fairly inconsequential. In other areas, the disappointment has wider repercussions. Spirituality addresses us at a very deep level of our psyche. More than anything else, it shapes who we are. Spiritual illusions are, therefore, more troublesome than other kinds of illusions. To realize I will never be a decent golfer is disappointing, but I can easily live with that. I'll learn the game of chess. More within my skill range! Illusions about spiritual matters, in which I have made an investment to the depths of my being—well, that's a different matter. The world is populated with many disappointed former "seekers" who tried spirituality or religion, "got burned," and walked away with a new cynicism.

When illusions are shattered how do we make the move to reality and not to disappointment?

In the Lindisfarne Community understandings we say this:

> We know too, that our community must be for "sinners" and not "saints." We are ordinary people struggling with the realities of day-to-day life in an imperfect world. We are aware, therefore, that our way of living will always be incomplete. When people join the Lindisfarne Community, as any other intentional community, natural illusions and idealism about community will quickly be shattered. However, disillusionment leads towards reality. Discovering Christ among us is the beginning of true community.

A few reflections:

(1) It helps to begin with a more realistic view of the way people are. Just because some folk seem to have a little "enlightenment" does not then mean they are perfect. If you project perfection onto people, you will be disappointed.
(2) Give others space to make their mistakes, to grow and to change.
(3) Focus on your own growth and development, not that of others. You can't change them. You have the possibility to change yourself. You change yourself through the daily disciplines of the spiritual life.
(4) Look for Christ in all.

14. Being and Doing

In the fourth understanding of the Lindisfarne community we say, "Our spirituality is at the level of being. It is who we are in our truest selves." Being and doing are intimately connected. But we mean no hard dualism here. Being and doing, contemplation and action, are inner and outer, yin and yang. Being is contained in doing. Doing is contained in being. As contemplation ends, action begins. Action returns to contemplation. When action is at its height, contemplation is at its lowest, yet still being is contained in doing. When contemplation is strongest, action is weakest, yet is still there, at the very least in breathing as the body gently moves. You can read this in the yin yang symbol. White is action. Black is contemplation. When white if most full, there is still the small circle of black, and vice versa. Pure contemplation contains action. Complete action involves contemplation

However, when there is a general imbalance, balance needs to be restored. In our culture generally, we have lost the art of contemplation. We have forgotten how to be still. We focus on the outer. We excel at doing. We are afraid of being.

I was first introduced to stillness in the early 1980s when a new faculty member joined our college. He was a bit of a mystic. He wandered around in a black cassock. This was unusual for a Baptist college, even though he was a Methodist by tradition. One of his early ventures was to institute a day of silence and contemplation. For me, that day was complete agony! By lunchtime, I had to drive into Manchester city center simply to hear voices and noises, and to be surrounded by action. I think I was afraid of what I might find on the inside. Over time, I persevered. I have gradually learned the art of stillness, with more yet to learn.

Now at the university, before each class, I practice *zazen* breathing meditation with my students. It is good to see students learn the art of stillness. My hope is that many will make it a life practice. Yet, I know many of them struggle with it, at least at the beginning. Fidgeting, being easily distracted, legs joggling, hands nervous, eyes anxiously gazing at the cell phone hoping for a new text message. The body's unrest mirrors the restlessness inside. Students have told me that their little *zazen* at the beginning of class is the only time they are quiet during the whole week.

My early forays into contemplation in the 1980s and the experience of my students now are symptomatic of the general cultural unfamiliarity with being. Hence, in our community understandings, more is said about being than doing. In this way, we have attempted to address the imbalance. Those who are familiar with our community know that we are as active as any small group of people! Yet, in our activities we are discovering the spirituality of being.

FIVE

THE SELF AND THE OTHER
RELATIONALITY, COMMUNITY

1. Rejecting Torture

All ancient books recognized as scripture by the different religions share something in common. They are all shaped by an ancient, pre-modern worldview. This causes some difficulty in reading and interpreting as we try to bridge horizons between then and now.

It is all the more difficult when these ancient texts give us moral guidelines that are repugnant to us. In some respects, humanity has not evolved in the last 3,000 years in terms of essential capabilities of the human psyche and its associated behaviors. We are potentially just as violent and aggressive now as long ago. We are potentially just as kind and loving now.

But in that time, human thinking and expectations have evolved. There is an accumulated wisdom, much of which derives from the ancient texts and has stood the test of time. We still rely on this wisdom. I am thinking of injunctions such as, "Do not kill." Though an ancient idea, it remains very much part of that which we ought not do. Also, ancient wisdom has been supplemented and given newer explanations couched in ideas such as the dignity of the human person, the right to personal autonomy, and other human rights. We generally find it easy to reject elements of the ancient traditions that we have outgrown (and for good reasons). We have rejected the imperative to stone adulterers to death, or to cut off a hand for stealing a loaf of bread, or to consider a woman unclean for an extended time after childbirth.

Yet, religious folk still have a hard time rejecting something ostensibly from the mouth of the "founder" of a religion, be it Moses, the Buddha, Jesus, Muhammad or the Guru Nanak. For good reasons, we treat the sayings of these people with extra respect. I think that was the motivation behind the publishers who include the sayings of Jesus in a red font in some Bibles. The words in red are the extra special words among all the other special words.

Among these sayings of Jesus is a well-known passage about sorting out difficulties in a community. When a sister or brother sins against you, you are to talk to them, to sort it out. If there is no response, take a few others to try to fix it. If there is still no joy, take it to the whole community. If the offender still remains unmoved, treat them like a Gentile or tax collector (Matthew 18: 15-17). This has often been taken to mean to shun them, to have no further dealing with them. Of course, a more interesting interpretation of this directive is to treat people as Jesus treated Gentiles and tax collectors. He loved them, had food with them, and became friends with them.

Jesus then tells a story about a couple of debtors and ends with this:

> His Lord handed him over to be tortured until he would pay his
> entire debt. So my heavenly Father will also do to every one of
> you, if you do not forgive your brother or sister from your heart.
> (Matthew 18:35)

After such a wise, instructive set of teachings about forgiving offences, and a practical method of dealing with disputes, we find ourselves enmeshed again in a worldview that we find intolerable. Forgive under the threat of torture! Torture is about power over, about coercion, about inflicting pain and suffering to achieve some end. We also know now that psychologically very little good is ever produced through torture. Any confessions made or information received is often bogus. Under extreme pain, human beings will say whatever the torturer wants, to escape the suffering.

It is for good reasons that the United Nations, under the guidance of Eleanor Roosevelt, included this statement in the UN Universal Declaration of Human Rights:

> *Article 5.* No one shall be subjected to torture or to cruel,
> inhuman or degrading treatment or punishment.

Returning to the words of Jesus that tell us that God is prepared to torture people (and this is a large element in the traditional church doctrine about eternal hell fire) what are we to make of it? There are four options:

(1) This is the teaching of Jesus and we must accept it. God endorses torture.
(2) This is the teaching of Jesus, but it does not mean what it seems to say.
(3) This is a redaction of the early church. It is editorial comment and does not come from the mouth of Jesus. It is fine to reject it.
(4) Even if this is the teaching of Jesus, it reflects Jesus as a person of his own day. It is part of first century culture. We are free to reject it.

In part, the option you choose will depend on other things, such as how you treat the scriptures, and how ancient texts affect contemporary moral issues, among others. If you think every word of the Bible is inspired by God and must be accepted as true, this text will provide problems. It will leave you believing something repugnant, or else wriggling to find a more palatable interpretation of the kind, "It doesn't mean what it seems to say, it means something else entirely . . ." People have made entire careers out of explaining away what the Bible plainly seems to say.

For me, there is nothing redeeming in the idea of torture. I reject torture as demeaning to human relationships and an unworthy idea to project onto God who is love. That Jesus was a child of his day seems incontrovertible. That Jesus embraced ideas we now find repugnant—often on the basis of the other things Jesus said—also seems clear. Did the early church editors add to the words of Jesus? I'm sure they did, but sifting through the sayings and deciding which is which is, as we now say, "above my pay grade." I leave that to other specialized Biblical scholars.

2. Other Regardingness

Some years ago, I had a colleague who had spent his academic life tracing the social changes in our society since the Second World War. He noticed that many social indices began to change around 1955. (Things such as divorce rate, crimes, and child abuse.) It was an extraordinary collection of data. His interpretation of the data was that Western society had made a shift from "other-regardingness" to "self-regardingness," and that this attitudinal shift seemed to account for much of the data. Why the changes began in 1955, he had no clue. I thought then, and still think now, that he was on to something. (His idea is confirmed in works such as Bellah, 1985, 2007; and Putnam, 2001).

The way a culture is structured is very complex. Layers of social mores are added to previous layers derived from interactions between different cultures and new ideas. This is why anthropologists are fascinated by cultures that have had no contact with others. What would a culture look like that had not passed through such synthetic changes? Of course, as soon as the anthropologist enters the scene, the previously untouched culture is immediately changed by the encounter!

It is very clear that Western society, with its 2,500-year history of development, has benefited from these kinds of cultural adaptations. We are shaped by Greek and Roman ideas, by Judaism and Christianity, by Muslim culture, by the encounter of the colonialists with native peoples. It all adds to the richness and the complexity.

It is an interesting and challenging puzzle to try to isolate an idea and trace its genesis. I want to take the challenge with regard to the idea of "other-regardingness." I think we find its basis in something St. Paul said in a letter to an early Christian community, "Do nothing out of selfish ambition or conceit, but in humility regard others better than yourselves. Let each of you look not to your own interests, but to the interests of others" (Philippians 2:3).

Paul rooted this advice in his understanding of Jesus as equal with God, yet who emptied himself taking the form of a servant. Interpreting what Paul meant has had a long and difficult history. What exactly is the *kenosis* of Christ, the self-emptying? I am not going to attempt an answer, but simply note that whatever Paul meant by it, he used it as a springboard to suggest a way of living. The way was to humbly forget yourself and to think about others. In other words, here is the idea of other-regardingness rooted in what we think about Jesus.

Forgetting self and thinking about the needs of others has been a very powerful thread in the history of Western civilization. We can trace much that is good and noble (health care and social services for instance) to this principle. It has not always been received kindly. In pre-Christian times humility was considered a vice, not a virtue (at least by Aristotle). Yet, the challenge to it comes more seriously at the heart of what we now call democratic capitalism.

In 1776, Scottish philosopher Adam Smith published a book that would set the stage for the massive development of the west, *The Wealth of Nations*. Its insights were novel and powerful. Among his many ideas was the notion of "self-interest." His belief was that if everyone acted in their own self-interest, the outcome would be for the best. Self-interest fueled the industrial revolution. Self-interest fueled the growth of capitalism. Self-interest fueled the imperialism of developed Western nations. Self-interest lay behind the stupidity of the First World War, and led to the Second World War. Self-interest produced the Cold War.

To be fair to Smith, he assumed that self-interest would be moderated by moral sentiment. He called it "fellow-feeling." When self-interest is strongly moderated by concern for others it seems to work fine. Yet, the history of the West over the last 300 years has been the steady erosion of fellow-feeling with the constant strengthening of self-interest.

Self-interest and fellow-feeling are ultimately incompatible. One will be always the stronger. For all his brilliance, Smith did not foresee that. He did not realize that by introducing the novel idea of self-interest before interest for others, he would begin the steady erosion of one of the key insights of Christianity.

As I write, the United States Congress is debating whether to bail out the financial markets. The rest of the world looks on with bated breath. In the fierce debates about this economic collapse, no one seems to have an answer. Financial systems are so large, so complex, and so unpredictable. Here is food for thought. Should we have expected anything else in a culture that has left its moorings in other-regardingness for a life of self-regardingness? What would a solution be like if none looked to their own interests, but to the interests of others? In public life, the moral imagination to act so is missing. Memories of humility and other-regardingness are distant.

In 1981, Alasdair MacIntyre, another Scottish philosopher, suggested that it is in small communities of memory where virtue is kept alive. I hope we may be such in the Lindisfarne Community.

3. Relationality

Our whole being by its very nature is one vast need.—C.S. Lewis in *The Four Loves*.

Something very basic about human beings is that we are needy. I think Lewis was on the right track. Life is a bundle of needs to be fulfilled from the moment we are born. It is clear that for a life of well-being our needs must be met. Theorists from Abraham Maslow to the *Circle of Courage* have recognized this and tried to make sense of it.

Maslow placed "self-actualizing needs" at the top on his hierarchy. He placed belonging needs mid-way. I think he was wrong! He was far too influenced by Western ideas of individuality. Our greatest and highest need is that of relationship. Aristotle had said human beings are social animals. We are made for relationships with others: human beings, non-human beings, all that is, and with the divine.

4. Harmony in the Garden

We have tried to make Lindisfarne, our home and the motherhouse of the community, a safe place of openness and hospitality. Part of that is the creation of a garden where guests can wander, be still, find peace. As a place for meditation, a walking circuit takes about twelve minutes. Some years ago, we decided to abandon the use of chemicals in the garden. We wanted to have an organic garden, sensitive to the seasons and more eco-friendly. We no longer wanted to put pollutants in the earth, or destroy the little creepy-crawlies.

Yesterday, during meditation walking, realizing the Way and the permeation of God, logos, in all things, I was delightfully content. Carried, nurtured, at one with the One in all. Later, planting roses, I was pleasantly surprised, then horrified, when I unearthed brother toad, still buried in his winter refuge. He was unmoving. I feared that I had damaged him with the large spade. On examination, he was all right and I thanked God. An inch in a different direction and the little creature would have been sliced. I put the large spade away and began carefully and gently moving earth using a small trowel and my fingers. Then I thought of the chemicals that in the earth, would have damaged his sensitive skin. I was glad of our decision to go organic. Planting the roses took a lot longer than I had planned. Yet I sensed once again, oneness with the creation, with the One I perceived in brother toad, beautiful creature that he is.

5. Solitude and Community

For some time, I have been considering the bipolar ideas of solitude-community and diversity-communion.

In the Lindisfarne Community, we are seeking to live in the tension of living for ourselves before God (the idea of solitude) and with one another (the idea of community). It seems to me that the two ideas are essential for a healthy and balanced discipleship. We are to be in that place before God, which is profoundly alone (but not lonely); yet, we are not alone as we share the journey with others.

By the same token, we have sought to be diverse in welcoming those who are different—share diverse ideas, who do not replicate each other, are not clones, who do not seek to control the other—yet who are drawn together in the Communion of Jesus in the new monasticism.

Within our communion we know solitude.
Within community we rejoice in diversity.
Our community is a communion of hearts and spirits.
Solitude makes for a diversity of expression.

6. Marketing Yourself

During the medieval period, economics was a subset of ethics. In other words, economics came under the broad discipline of how we ought to live. Commerce—trade, production, and sale of goods—was not an independent activity. Trade was regulated by moral considerations. It was, for example, considered wrong to charge interest on money lent to someone. Why should you get a return for doing nothing? That didn't seem fair.

The modern period changed all that. Adam Smith's *The Wealth of Nations* in 1776 presented to the world a new way of looking at economics. The notion of a free market was born. The market was free from moral considerations, and ought to be free from interference. Free markets would produce great good. Free markets are guided by an *invisible hand*. I am not going to provide here a critique of free market economics, though Marx and Engels *The Communist Manifesto* (1967) is a very good place to start. (For interested readers I would recommend both Smith and Marx. In economics terms, everything written after them is merely a footnote.)

Even after Smith's magnum opus, economics was still a bounded discipline. The market was restrained by the moral considerations of workers (who formed trade unions) and by law, as the worst excesses of markets were moderated by fair dealings. Over the last thirty years, we have begun to see something different. More than ever, workers are now simply cogs in the machine of the market. Did anyone notice the change from "personnel" to "human resources"? We all serve the market as it works its magic.

Even more, the idea of the market has broken away from its moorings and has begun to encroach on every aspect of life. Every facet of life is now seen in terms of markets. People in hospitals are now consumers of products and not patients in need of help and care. Students have now become consumers of the product of education; teachers the deliverers of the product. The classroom is now a point of sales. It has become so pervasive that I suspect some readers of this reflection will wonder why I am making a fuss. It is self-evident that everything is marketing. That is part of the problem. Our culture has been taken over to such a degree that we hardly notice it. All is now seen in terms of money, costs, profits, and losses.

Why the fuss? In giving in to the market, we are in danger of losing (perhaps already have lost) important values. The Beatles were right—as they often were: "Money can't buy me love." Money can't buy me goodness, or truth, or beauty. Money can't measure the value of a person. Money can't measure the change of the seasons; the consciousness of well-being; the "oceanic feeling" of wonder (Freud) at the greatness of reality. If money is truly "the bottom line," then as a culture we lose.

I was chatting recently with a couple of new PhDs who are looking for jobs. It's a tough market for new professors. (See, the language is everywhere.) With a heavy heart, I advised that, in framing their CVs, "cover letters," and research agendas, they needed to "market themselves." The young scholars with whom I was talking were repulsed by the idea. Their work and learning and commitments had led them to a place where, in true Socratic fashion, they think they know less now than ever. Yet, to get a job you need to polish your image, make yourself marketable, and sell yourself.

Jesus told a parable about a self-satisfied religious man who marketed himself to God when he prayed. He displayed his achievements. Another man, a tax collector, simply looked down and asked for mercy. The punch-line was "Those who exalt themselves will be humbled, and those who humble themselves will be exalted" (Matthew 23:12; Luke 14:11).

I wonder how far my younger colleagues would get if, instead of marketing themselves, they followed the way of humility? I could not advise them to take that way. It made me sad. The ancient wisdom is a higher truth. A deeper magic.

7. Anyone Unwilling to Work Should Not Eat . . . Hmm

This week, poverty has been on my mind. In an Introduction to Ethics class, I have been discussing with students issues around poverty and a moral response to poverty. Whose responsibility are the poor? Are there any duties the rich owe to the poor? In a large and complex society, how would we begin to maximize happiness with regard to poverty? What causes poverty and how can we address those causes?

Poverty is an intractable problem. Over the eleven years that I have been teaching this class, students inevitably fall into the divisions of the "culture war." Some students express a compassionate response that whatever the causes of poverty, poor folk ought to be helped. Other students are resolute that if you are poor it is your own fault. You made bad choices. Pull yourself together and get a job. I try to help students tease out the complexities, good and bad, in both responses. I rehearse the standard conservative, liberal, and radical responses to poverty with them. I hope that those with harsh responses become softer; those with naive responses less so.

During this week I happened, in another context, to be thinking about the *Communist Manifesto* (Marx and Engels, 1967) and its prescription for a just society: "From each according to their ability, to each according to their need." Then again, in another context, the infamous words over the gates of Auschwitz: "*Arbeit Macht Frei*," work sets you free. In yet another context, the purpose of education as the cultural construction of "docile bodies" (Michel Foucault's phrase) to produce compliant workers for industrial capitalism (Foucault, 1975).

It was interesting then to read the lectionary passage and the deutero-Pauline aphorism: "Anyone unwilling to work should not eat" (2 Thessalonians 3:10). The context seemed to be an early Christian community enjoying a primitive form of communism where all was shared by all, but in which some were merely lazy, unwilling to work and thus becoming a burden to others.

It fascinates me the way in one week so many ideas converge in one's thinking. How to make sense of all this? Needless to say, I have no solution. here are a few not quite random thoughts:

> Poverty is a terrible situation to be in, and compassion for those who are poor is a much needed response. (To ponder: compassion)
>
> There are times in our lives when all of us cannot meet our own needs and must rely on the kindness of others. (To ponder: humility)
>
> We all have a contribution to make, and there are natural consequences for those who choose not to. (To ponder: diligence)
>
> Meaningful work is a part of being human. Yet, work without meaning is a drudgery and crushes the human spirit. (To ponder: purpose)

8. Pondering Social Breakdown

Jane and I returned last week from a memorable and lovely time with our families in the United Kingdom and United States. It has been for us a great summer, including a delightful Disney themed wedding. It was marred, and that only slightly, by strange weather wherever we have been. (Being British, talk of the weather is a national pastime—"if you can't think of something more suitable to say, confine your remarks to the weather," somewhere in Jane Austen's *Sense and Sensibility*.)

The summer has also given us a glimpse of social breakdown—mass murders in Norway shattering a determinedly peaceful nation; riots and looting in major British cities.

It has given us pause for thought.

Pundits of all political stripes have been quick to point fingers. Most of it has been to repeat party slogans from already entrenched political positions, sniping over the parapet at the enemy.

Suggestions as to causes have been many. Solutions have been few and unimaginative.

It caused me to think again of the great tradition of love and nonviolence shared by Jesus, the Buddha, and the Daoists. Surely, here is the solution? I think so, but not in any simplistic way.

When I teach nonviolence in philosophy classes, invariably someone raises a hypothetical case like: what about a killer attacking someone you love, or, what about the terrorist who has placed a bomb, has the information, and you have caught him? In such cases, violence is the solution. Kill the assailant. Torture the terrorist. This summer, the issue has been rather: the mass murderer in Norway, the thugs looting British cities . . . violence is the answer. Crack down hard. Arm the citizenry. The logic is compelling. Almost.

The problem with such cases is that by the time we get to thousands of youths rioting and looting, or a racist/fascist killing youngsters, as a society we have already "lost the plot." In those instances, there is no easy loving and nonviolent solution.

So in what ways can love and nonviolence help?

It helps in day-to-day simple and mundane caring and loving: living the example of Truth. In the Lindisfarne community we say, "To be as Christ to those I meet, to find Christ within them." This of course is time consuming, long-term. It is the work of youth-workers in Hackney and Manchester, of parents everywhere, of pastors and rabbis and imams. It is the work of secular-monastics buried in the world as yeast in the flour.

Of course, there are no guarantees. As the truism says, "The good die young." (Jesus was in his early thirties.) Love is often rejected.

As I have pondered the social breakdown of this summer, my question has been, "What can I do?" For sure, I can't fix it. I can't bring back the Norwegian young people whose families grieve even as I write from the safety and beauty of our garden in Ithaca. I can't repair buildings burnt in rioting, or repair the trust broken in English communities.

But I can renew my commitment to love and nonviolence. I can set my face to the daily disciplines of the new monasticism. I can seek to be a different person, to live the life of the realm of God. I can help to effect loving change in those areas where I have influence.

9. God and All Living Things

In the simplest telling of Jesus' wilderness temptations (Matthew 4:1-11) we are told that Jesus was driven into the wilderness by the Spirit, and was tempted by Satan for forty days. During that time angels waited on him and he was with the wild beasts. We are told nothing more and all else is up to our imagination. In my imagination I was drawn to the wild beasts. What did it mean to be with them?

One of our delights in coming to upstate New York was an introduction to many new wild beasts. In the United Kingdom, human development means that the native animals have all been driven away. It was rare to see non-human animals other than sheep and cows; perhaps the occasional fox. Now, in our own back yard we often have deer (a herd of nine is quite usual), opossums, woodchucks, squirrels, a whole colony of chipmunks, raccoons, and skunks. The bird life is amazing, too, with at least five kinds of woodpecker as regular visitors. I have often sat outside when the weather is warmer with a deer grazing no more than six feet away. On one occasion, I was in kneeling mediation on a *seiza* bench and a chipmunk scampered over my toes and began washing herself not two feet away.

In the mystical tradition, many stories are told of monastics (often in the wilderness or the forest) with companion animals—not merely dogs and cats but all manner of wild beasts. My thoughts below are excerpts from a book chapter in a collection on religion and animals.

Whilst seeking ultimate reality led many mystics to shun the company of other human beings, their search led them toward the friendship of nonhuman animals. Myths surrounding mystics often seem unlikely as history. It is not necessary to claim them as such. Their many animal narratives provide a strong tradition of care for nonhuman animals. Whether Saint Cuthbert's feet were literally dried by his friends, the sea otters, on return from a night of prayer in the ice-cold sea, is beside the point. What matters is the conglomeration of stories about animals associated with mystics.

Helen Waddell translated many of these animal narratives from Latin into English (Waddell and Gibbings, 1934). She focused on legends from the desert fathers and mothers from the fourth century, and Celtic traditions from the sixth and seventh centuries. Both traditions sit broadly within the mystical corpus. Edward Sellner (1993) also compiled stories of Celtic mystics. In these stories, hermits, having chosen a life of solitude, encounter animals in delightful ways. Universally, the relationship between mystic and animal is positive. Though there is some sentimentalization, animals continue to exhibit animal-like behavior. A few instances suffice to make the point.

From Waddell (Waddell and Gibbings 1995):

A desert monk whose sole friend is an ox and who feeds a lion dates by hand. (3)

A horse that mourns before Columba's death. Columba calls the horse "this lover of mine." (42)

A lion that is helped by abbot Gerasimus and then becomes the abbot's disciple. On the abbot's death the lion is distraught and lies on the old man's grave, where he dies. (23)

A wolf shares a monk's bread and then becomes penitent after stealing bread in the monk's absence. (6)

Macarius who heals the eyes of a hyena's whelp. The hyena brings a sheepskin to the saint, who refuses it: "As that which thou has brought to me comes of violence, I will not take it." (13)

The saint rebukes the hyena and makes her promise that "I will not kill a creature alive" but from that day will only eat what is already dead. If the hyena can find no dead animals, then the monk promises to feed her on his own bread. (12)

From Sellner (1993):

Ciaran befriends a fox, who carries Ciaran's psalter. The mystic hides the fox under his cowl when hounds come hunting the fox. (80)

A stag visits Ciaran and allows the monk to use his horns as a reading stand. (82)

In the story of Kevin, "one Lent a blackbird came from the woods to his hut and hopped on the palm as he lay on the flagstone with his hand stretched out. Kevin kept his hand so the blackbird would have a place to build her nest. He remained there until she had hatched her brood." (161)

Animals work alongside monks but are not called upon to do anything overly burdensome. Mystics, more often than not, show sympathy, kindness, and protection toward their animal friends.

Perhaps the mystic most well known for relationship with non-human animals is Francis of Assisi. Again, we are dealing with hagiography, and many of the stories are historically suspect. Nonetheless, the Franciscan tradition of kindness toward animals is important. Thomas of Celano (c. 1200-1260) wrote three volumes about Francis shortly after his death. Thomas says of Francis, "he was a man of great fervor, feeling much sweetness and piety even toward lesser, irrational creatures" (Armstrong and Brady, 74). Francis talked regularly to animals and exhorted them to love God. The "irrational creatures" in their turn "sensed the sweetness of his love" (75). Francis's concern included all creatures: "He had the same tender feeling toward fish. When he had the chance he threw back live fish that had been caught, and warned them not to be caught again (75). And further on:

> Even for worms he had a warm love, since he had read this text
> about the Savior: I am a worm and not a man. That is why
> Francis used to pick worms up from the road, and put them in a
> safe place, so that they would not be crushed. (90)

Stories of Francis are stories of tenderness toward waterbirds, bees, pheasants, and a singing cricket whom Francis calls "my sister cricket!" (275).

Besides animal narratives, the prayers and poems of mystics offer a glimpse of their relationship toward animals. Alexander Carmichael, in the late nineteenth century, traveled the highlands and islands of Scotland, listened to the old Gaelic prayers, poems, incantations, and charms, and translated them into English. Though it is unlikely that these delightful runes go back to the early Celtic church, it is clear that they are part of a long and unbroken tradition rooted in the premodern world. These poems reveal a world in which animals are greatly respected and loved, used by human beings to be sure, but given a more intrinsic than instrumental value:

> The charm placed of Brigit
> About her neat, about her kine,
> About her horses, about her goats,
> About her sheep, about her lambs;

Each day and each night,
In heat and in cold,
Each early and late,
In darkness and light;

To keep them from marsh,
To keep them from rock,
To keep them from pit,
To keep them from bank. (Carmichael 1992, 339-40)

And further on:

Give the milk, my treasure,
Give quietly, with steady flow,
Give the milk, my treasure,
With steady flow and calmly. (346)

It would be overly optimistic to expect to find, in the Western mystical tradition, a full-blown understanding of animal rights. Nonetheless, taken together, the theoria of the mystics (that all is/are One, that the divine is in all, an ethic of compassionate love for all) and their praxis (shown in tender stories about animals and in prayers, poems, and incantations) suggest a way of life deeply sympathetic to animal advocacy.

This is a delightful tradition that encompasses all as cared for by God and in unity in God's wonderful world.

10. The Problem with People Is . . .

I was reading the Daily Office this morning: Genesis 9, the myth of Noah and his sons:

The fear and dread of you shall rest on every animal of the earth, and on every bird of the air, on everything that creeps on the ground, and on all the fish of the sea; into your hand they are delivered. Every moving thing that lives shall be food for you; and just as I gave you the green plants, I give you everything.

I had a flash of insight. Here's the first problem with people: Domination. Human beings spread fear and dread. Every animal. Every bird. Everything creepy crawly. Every fish. We dominate, kill, and eat.

Here's the second problem: Be fruitful and multiply, abound on the earth and multiply in it. There are too many of us. The planet cannot long sustain life as we know it, if we keep growing.

11. The Trouble with Bodies

I punish my body and enslave it . . . (Paul, 1 Corinthians 9:27)

Jesus stretched out his hand and touched him. "I do choose. Be clean." Immediately the leprosy left him and he was made clean. (Mark 1:42)

Bodies have always been troublesome for the spiritually aware. In truth, bodies have been troublesome for everyone.

Burping, farting, dumping . . . bodily functions are the source of acute embarrassment and much merriment. The earliest humor I remember was the sing-song rhyme that began, "In days of old, when knights were bold, and toilets weren't invented . . ." Little boys humor! But it doesn't stop with little boys. We have never been quite sure what to make of bodies and what bodies do.

And then there's sex. Most enjoy it. Some loath it. Most talk about it abstractly. Most keep their deepest thoughts, desires, and fantasies to themselves. The sexual body seems to have a mind of it own, and causes trouble for the "other" mind. The body's sexuality pops up at the most inconvenient time (pun intended, at least for male readers!)

Still, we love our bodies and when they get sick we try all we can to get them well again. We keep them clean (most of us). We beautify them as far as we can (hair styles, makeup, body sculpting, dieting, and clothes). Yet, we are conflicted about the body. Many of us have a love-hate relationship with our embodiedness.

Spiritual traditions share the conflictedness. All the great traditions lean toward the ascetic (with disciplines such as fasting). Some go to extremes of self-denial and physical punishment (helped along by St. Paul's view of the body quoted above). All the traditions urge moderation of the body's sexual appetites. Some go to the extreme of decrying sexuality as impure and any sexual activity as getting in the way of true spirituality.

At their best, the spiritual traditions give us a balance—a true appreciation of the body's innate goodness, together with an awareness that the body, at times, does need to be controlled, its excesses reined in. The Buddha rejected the more severe forms of asceticism to take the middle way. St. Benedict designed a Rule for his communities that was not arduous—disciplined and demanding to be sure, but not extreme. The Laozi gives us the balance of yin and yang, which laid the foundation for the complex and beneficial body practices of *qigong*. Jesus healed the sick bodies of those who came to him. And Jesus (God in a human body) rose bodily from death. I'm a fan of the middle way.

(I have an article in *Social Philosophy Today*, 2012, "Somaesthetics and Nonviolence," where I look at some of these issues in more detail.)

12. An Inclusive Trinity

Recently, I was in a conversation about liturgy—formal prayers and such. I told my conversation partner that many years ago, we determined to remove masculinist language from our prayers in the Lindisfarne Community.

"So, as often as not, we tend to call God 'Father-Mother'," I said. "And we say 'child' instead of 'son'."

"Well, I'm a Trinitarian," came the reply. "I have no problem with Father and Son language."

I have always thought of myself as a Trinitarian too, and intrigued by where the conversation was heading, I continued.

"But wouldn't a person off the street, who had never heard Christian liturgy before, assume that 'Father-Son' language is masculinist?" I suggested. "Doesn't that language privilege males?"

My conversation partner disagreed. "It's not meant to privilege males. 'Father-Son' language is not about gender.

"Sounds like it to me!" I said, perhaps not very helpfully.

"By calling God 'Father-Mother' and calling the son 'child,' *you* are bringing gender into the discussion," my conversation partner accused me.

I was a little taken aback, but left it at that.

It has caused me to think about God language again. To speak of the Trinity is rather strange language—quite difficult to get your head around.

Of the many things we could say about Trinity, I mention two interesting points of significance.

First, all language about God is, in the end, impossible. If God is the infinitely Real—"in light inaccessible, hid from our eyes" as the hymn says—then all descriptions about God, if taken to have literal rather than metaphorical meaning, become idols. For God is not that which we say God is. That God is One and Three reminds us that language is always inadequate.

Second, the most meaningful understanding of Trinity (for me) is that its speaks of relationality. If God is at the heart of the universe, then at the heart of the universe is a relationship, and by all accounts a relationship of love.

To put the two together: to talk about God is ultimately impossible, but when we do our best attempt is to talk about a relationship of love.

In our human terms (though I want also to include non-human animals in relationality) any picture language (or artistic depiction) of Trinity would need to be inclusive. If the picture is only of two males (an older one and a younger one) then it is too exclusive.

Is there anything to privilege the father-son relationship over the father-daughter, or mother-son, or mother-daughter relationships? In other words, is there something about fathers and sons that makes them a better picture of God than a picture with a female in it? I can't think of any.

It is why I like those icons of the Holy Trinity that depict the humanity of the Three in gender ambiguous ways. Are we looking at males or females? Or, rather, are we looking at three persons, gender unknown, who are in loving relationship?

Of course, the advantage of traditional depictions of the Holy Trinity (older male with a grey beard, younger male with a brown beard) is that the third is none human—a dove. The female is excluded, but the non-human is included. Oh for an inclusive vision of loving relationship!

SIX

LOVE AND NONVIOLENCE

1. Choose Love

If we ask the question, "How then shall we live?" one answer is to say, "We live by our obligations." The best kind of life is one where we follow our duties.

This general answer has a long and noble tradition. It is, of course, very much a part of Judaism with its emphasis on following the commandments of God. That typically Hebraic answer is not the only one. Immanuel Kant, trying as hard as he could to divorce morality from tradition (including religious tradition) said that reason alone would tell us what our obligations are. He called the moral result of the reasoning process the "categorical imperative" (1964). Kant tells us that to be a good person is an obligation, a duty we are bound to perform. It is an obligation regardless of the outcome. When we add an "if," a condition to the imperative, such as "If you want to succeed, then do this," it is a hypothetical imperative. Categoricals are always true and have no conditions attached to them. In that way, his categorical imperative is very much like the command of God.

There are other answers to the question about how we should live—such as by becoming a certain type of person, or by considering the consequences of our actions—but I want to consider this idea of obligations.

Jesus, as a first century Jewish teacher, when asked which commandment was the greatest answered, "You shall love the Lord your God with all your heart, with all your soul, and with all your mind. You shall love your neighbor as yourself" (Luke 10:27). This is, perhaps, the core ethical teaching of the

New Testament. If you were to ask Jesus "How then shall we live?" this would be his answer. You are to love God and love your neighbor.

It is such a simple thought, yet its depths have challenged the greatest minds and spirits of Western history. I want to consider just one facet of this imperative: can we command love?

Kant suggested that any imperative contained the implicit idea that, of course, carrying it out is possible. If you have an obligation, then you have the ability to fulfill it. That seems reasonable.

If you apply that to what Jesus said, then the answer to my question is, "Yes, love can be commanded."

Yet, what is it that is commanded? Love arises from the passions. Love begins as feeling. Love is that feeling that moves the self from preoccupation with itself to the Other. Love is movement toward the Other. Can a feeling be commanded? A mother could rightly say to her daughter, "Eat your broccoli, it is good for you." It would be impossible to say, "You should love your broccoli as you love your ice cream." A young man looking for a partner could hardly be told, "Love this particular one." Love is something into which you fall. It comes to you as gift. Compassion for the poor arises as a deep passion. To be sure, it often turns to action, to the choice to do something, but its genesis is passion, deep feeling for.

For these kinds of reasons, scholars have separated out different kinds of love. Romantic love, affection, or compassion, as feeling is one kind of love. There is another kind of love that is detached from feeling. It is a love based in reason and directed by will. It is love as seeking the best for the Other. It is love regardless whether you feel love. It is pure obligation to do the best for the Other. As such, this kind of love has been proclaimed as the better kind of love, as moral love rather than sentimental love. Kant called love based on natural feeling "pathological love."

In his 1966 *Situation Ethics*, Joseph Fletcher took this approach. Love for him for purely a choice based on reason. Feeling was removed. It became a utility calculation.

Yet, if we remove feeling from love, do we have love left to speak of? I leave that for another day.

2. Knowledge and Love

Early Christianity was inextricably influenced by then current Greek and Roman ideas. What we have in the New Testament is a complex synthesis of ancient and contemporary Jewish ideas, Greek and Roman philosophy, and some genuine creativity—most clearly in the life of Jesus, but also in the first Christian teachers. The early Christians were particularly fond of Plato and of the Roman stoics. Scholars tell us, for instance, that the *haustafeln*, the household codes of Pauline communities, are replicated in Stoic writings. There are many similar allusions, borrowings, and modifications of then current ideas.

When contemporary fundamentalists insist that we "get back to the Bible" and to the "pure word of God" it is not clear what they desire. I think such comments follow from an idea that the Bible, as inspired by God, was dictated to the writers by God, or that in some way the Spirit of God oversaw the writing in such a way that the writer's personality and errors were extinguished. It is not only a strange view, but relatively recent.

This was not the view of the writers of the scriptures, nor of the early Christians. Its provenance is the turn to modernity and scientism when knowledge, to be true, had to be empirically based in provable facts. The Bible, as inerrant word of God—for fundamentalists—became the deposit of such facts. Story, legend, myth, allegory, and poetry were reduced to literal truths. Fundamentalists, like scientific positivists, can only see truth in literalism. Both worlds are all the poorer for it.

The early Christian movement saw no problems in a synthetic approach to truth seeking. All truth was God's truth, whether spoken by Moses, Jesus, Socrates, or Marcus Aurelius, who was no friend to the Christian movement, yet whose meditations Christians have used for centuries. Second century theologian, Justin Martyr, believed Plato and Socrates were "Christians before Christ" (Apology 1.46). Like many, then and now, he saw that the similarities and connections were remarkable.

I detect a borrowing from Plato in Paul's words to the Corinthian Christians when he speaks to them about knowledge and love, "Knowledge puffs up, love builds up. Anyone who claims to know something does not yet have the necessary knowledge; but anyone who loves God is known by God" (1 Corinthians 8:1).

The Socratic dialogues, where Plato writes in the persona of Socrates, usually focus on one issue—virtue, justice, friendship, love in different dialogues. Socrates and his conversation partners tease out possible meanings of the idea. They test it against lived experience, modify their understanding, and test it again. In the early dialogues, the closest to the "real" Socrates, the conversations end with no solution to the problem. For Socrates, to have knowledge is to know that you do not know. Paul echoes that idea, "Anyone who claims to know something does not yet have the necessary knowledge" (1 Corinthians 8:2).

Knowledge as wisdom does not come easily and rarely to the young. When I was a young, fresh, and arrogant minister of twenty-four years of age, I knew everything. I was a voracious consumer of theology and doctrine. I had aligned myself with the Puritan/Calvinist School of theology—a vigorous and carefully worked-out system. In any argument and there were many, I had an answer for everything. I knew my stuff! Oh dear! Thirty years later, I am prepared to confess my ignorance. Yes, I still "know" a lot of stuff, probably more stuff than is good for anyone—but what do I "know"? Knowledge puffs up.

The second idea in which I hear Plato is Paul's contrast of knowledge with love. Love is that which builds human society. Love values the Other as a person in her own right. Love affirms freedom to be. "*Amo: Volo ut sis.*" I love you, I want you to be. The love of God, the love of the ultimate Good is the way of true knowledge, true wisdom.

In Plato, the love of the good is the ultimate goal of human life, though in the Socratic dialogues Plato uses the Greek word *eros* and not the *agape* or *philia* of the New Testament. Love is the desire for what we do not yet possess. In its lowest forms, love takes on the guise of sexual desire, the desire for the Other who we do not possess—the Other who completes who we are. Yet, love does not remain there, for when the other is possessed, there is the realization that we are not yet complete.

Sexual desire is not bad in itself (as, sadly, Christians later came to believe); it is merely incomplete, a step on the ladder to perfection. Sexual desire is desire for the divine Other, though at an early stage of its development. In Plato, desire moves beyond the physicality of sexual needs to the desire for eternity. "Our hearts are restless, till they find their rest in you," said Augustine echoing again the Platonic thought (1952).

I hear the same echoes in Paul's words. If you think you have knowledge, you do not. Love the divine, love the eternal, and then you will know truly and be truly known.

3. Everyone Who Loves Is Born of God . . .

I teach a course called "The Ethics of Love." It is a course based around my book, *Love as a Guide to Morals* (2012). According to the students, and my perception too, it turned out to be a very interesting course. One of the

assignments is to write a critical philosophical book review of C.S. Lewis'
The Four Loves (1960). One student, admitting that she is not religious,
wrote that she has a greater appreciation for Christianity now because,
according to Lewis, the Christian God is all the love in the world. I thought
her understanding profound.

Love is an extraordinary expansive and non-exclusive idea. Religions
often tend toward exclusion: who is in and who is out, and what you
have to do to be in, and what things keep you out. Of course, we cannot
live without making distinctions. It is important to know the distinctive
features of apples and oranges; of water, vodka and bleach. If we don't
make such distinctions, we could get ourselves into all kinds of trouble!
Knowledge and understanding (in fact the whole of philosophy) is built on
making distinctions. The education of little children is all about helping
them understand the distinctions between what is good for them and what
is bad for them.

However, in relational terms, when we use arbitrary distinctions
to exclude, great human problems arise. Racism, sexism, heterosexism,
classism, speciesism, ableism—all of the "isms" really—are based on the
exclusion of the Other based on some distinguishing feature that makes us
"in" and the Other "out."

One such distinction made popular in the twentieth century was the idea
of being "born again." The idea originated in the writings of the Johannine
community in the scriptures. It was variously called "born again," "born
from above," "new birth," and "born of God." In usage it is very close to
the idea of becoming enlightened. As an idea, it has been present as one
of the ways of talking about the human experience and knowledge of God
since ancient times. Yet, in recent days, it has become a catch phrase for
exclusion. The "born-agains" and the "non-born-agains." The meaning of
"born again" has also narrowed to a particular form of Evangelical religion.
For some it is, "Have you signed the response card?" For some, "Have you
said the "sinner's prayer"? For some, an intense religious experience, filtered
through a particular interpretative framework. For others, the assent to a
particular set of religious doctrines. Whichever way, it becomes a badge to
indicate who is in and who is out.

However, for the Johannine community, everyone who loves is born
of God. Love is expansive and non-exclusive. "God is love, and those who
abide in love abide in God, and God abides in them." Simply, yet ever so
profoundly, to be born again is to love. To know God is to love. To live in
God is to live in love. The implications of this are far-reaching, imaginative,

and controversial. Love cuts across religious lines of demarcation. Love cuts across dogmatic differences. The Muslim who loves is as born of God as the Christian who loves as the atheist who loves—for God is love.

I think my student had seen the great possibilities of love. I am grateful to her.

4. Love and Nonviolence

I want to say a few words about love and nonviolence. But first, a few words about faith, for I want to situate love and nonviolence in faith. There is a popular idea that faith is believing in something that is very hard to believe in, because the thing believed is most unlikely. If it is likely, you do not need faith. The tooth fairy comes to mind. That such a fairy exists is most unlikely. We might even say it is unbelievable. So to believe in the tooth fairy, you throw away any credibility or plausibility test, and believe the impossible anyway. For many people, faith in God is like that.

Paul Tillich said something different about faith. He said, "Faith is the state of being grasped by an ultimate concern" (*Dynamics of Faith*, 2011). Notice that faith is not something that you do. It is something that happens to you. Something grasps you. An ultimate concern gets a hold of you. You can't shake it off. It becomes the most important thing for you. It defines you. It shapes you. It changes you. That is a very different view of faith to the popular "believing in the incredible and unlikely." I like Tillich's way of thinking about faith.

That brings me to love and nonviolence, for I have to say that I have been grasped by an ultimate concern, and that ultimate concern is love. Love is closely connected to nonviolence. Let me explain what I mean.

Aristotle said that human beings are social animals. In 1624, the English mystical poet John Donne said:

> All mankind is of one author, and is one volume; when one man dies, one chapter is not torn out of the book, but translated into a better language; and every chapter must be so translated . . . As therefore the bell that rings to a sermon, calls not upon the preacher only, but upon the congregation to come: so this bell calls us all: but how much more me, who am brought so near the door by this sickness . . . . No man is an island, entire of

itself . . . any man's death diminishes me, because I am involved
in mankind; and therefore never send to know for whom the bell
tolls; it tolls for thee. (1959)

Philosopher and mystic alike tell us something important about human
life: we are made for relationships. Where Aristotle says we are social, I
prefer to say we are relational. Social is too humanistic for me. We are made
for relationship not just with other human beings (the social aspect of life)
but with non-human animals too, and with the environment we live in,
and with the divine herself. We are relational animals. We are part of a great
web of interconnectedness.

We relate to the Other. I have capitalized the word Other. When you
capitalize a word where it would not normally be so, you indicate that
you are speaking of a particularly rich concept. Other (with a capital "O")
stands for all those with who we are in relationship. So, from now on, when
I say Other, I mean all those others (people, animals, fishes, bugs, rivers,
trees, all that is, the divine). We are made for relationship with the Other.

The tragedy of human life is that we have so often made a mess of
that relationality. We have used and abused the Other. We have hurt and
ignored the Other. We have focused on ourselves and our own needs at the
expense of the Other.

How it might be otherwise is the thought that has grasped me. That
is my ultimate concern. That is my state of faith. That which has grasped
me is love and nonviolence. You might find it strange that I join those
two words. But love and nonviolence have been used interchangeably by
adepts of spirituality, including Mahatma Gandhi and Martin Luther King
Jr. If you read their writings, you will often find the two words used to
mean the same thing. To love someone is to be nonviolent toward them.
To be nonviolent is to love. Both words are very full words, like *shalom* in
Hebrew.

Shalom means peace, but more than the mere absence of war. *Shalom* is
the fullness of well-being; life lived in all its goodness and glory. *Shalom* is
life thriving in goodness, peace and well-being. Love and nonviolence are
words like that. More than the mere absence of hatred or violence. Love
and nonviolence are very positive concepts that speak of life as it could be
if only we achieved our potential as divine image bearers.

Love and nonviolence are relational words. They speak to us of the
Other. The Other is everyone with whom we have a relationship, and we
have a relationship with everyone and everything. I grant it is not the same

relationship with all that is, but, still, we do have a relationship. It is a universal requirement to love.

In my writing, I have been working a lot with the ideas of love and nonviolence and I can't say much in this reflection. I will share just one aspect of love and make some practical application of it.

The aspect I call the fourfold effect of love and nonviolence. The effect is how nonviolence looks in practice; how love looks in practice.

> To do good for the Other (beneficence).
> To do no harm to the Other (non-maleficence).
> To respect the personhood and integrity of the Other (autonomy).
> To work for the justice of the Other (justice).

How does this work out in our lives? Nonviolence—love—becomes our guide. We relate to the Other in loving, nonviolent ways. We seek good and no harm, we respect the Other and where justice is lacking, we seek justice for the Other. So far, so good! But that is very general. It is important for each of us to find a sphere of influence where we can practice nonviolence.

For me, I have found my sphere in leading, with Jane, a small ecumenical religious order where we try to practice these things. It is in teaching at the university where I seek to be a loving nonviolent mentor to students. It is in writing about these things in books and journals. It is also, for us, in the area of foster care. We have three grown children and we have cared, over the years, for more than eighty other children. These children have been mostly victims of physical, psychological, and sexual abuse. Most have known little love. Most have been socialized in violence. We have made it our task to create a nonviolent home where we demonstrate to these children a different way: a way of nonviolence and love.

Love is the work of a lifetime. Nonviolence is a life-long practice. I hope that you have been grasped by such an ultimate concern. I hope that you have found or are finding a sphere of influence where you can be a nonviolent, loving presence to the Other.

5. A Realm of Love?

For quite a while, I have found "kingdom of God" language difficult, if not alien. It may be that living in a republic makes talk of "kingdoms" awkward. It was easier living in the United Kingdom. At least in the name was reference to kingdom—though with a queen in charge since 1952 kingdom language is still a stretch! Perhaps it should become the United Realm.

Yet it would still have the idea of being united under a single sovereign. Most democracies have long since abandoned the idea. That Britain did not become a democratic republic in the seventeenth century has always been a mystery to me. Historian Christopher Hill called it a "stop in the mind" (1980, 53). The slow development of a constitutional monarchy was an accident of history and was something of a compromise—a monarch as figurehead without any real power. Power to the people, then?

People power, too, is problematic. I have sympathized with Plato that the people on too many occasions make bad decisions. Give the people a chance and they will kill Socrates. The crowd bayed for Jesus to be crucified. Monarchs or people—not much to chose between them. Plato favored an aristocracy with philosophers in charge. But then he probably hadn't attended a conference of philosophers who never agree about anything! (Philosophers, they say, are like manure: quite good if you spread them around the countryside. But put them together in one place and they become a public nuisance! Of course this is not true of my favorite group of philosophers, *Concerned Philosophers for Peace*. We would make a decent job of running the world!)

I write these thoughts on the Sunday in the ecclesiatical year called the Reign of Christ. In the liturgy of the Lindisfarne Community, we changed all references to "kingdom" to "realm." In the prayer of Jesus we petition, "Your realm come . . ." What would a realm without the domination, power and control look like? It would look like a realm of voluntarism where none are coerced and all are free to choose. It would look like a realm of kindness and compassion where all are cared for. It would look like a realm where wrongs are forgiven and punishment is abandoned, where all can reach their full potential. It would look like a realm of love.

6. Love at the Heart of the Universe

During our community online chat this week, one of the issues we discussed was "plausibility structures." This idea comes from the sociology of knowledge and is a concept from the 1960s. A plausibility structure is a foundation level belief (or set of beliefs) that we hold and which is largely unquestioned. We hold these base level beliefs about life in lots of different ways, about lots of different things. Often a plausibility structure is held at an unconscious level. We often only become aware of it when it is challenged or when something triggers it to the fore. Conscious self-awareness will do that. Talk therapy, in an attitude of open and honest dialogue, will also do it.

Someone in the chat asked me, "So, Andy, what is your plausibility structure?" I answered without much thought, "Love is at the heart of the universe."

Someone else asked, "Andy, how can you say that when there is so much un-love?" which led to a fruitful discussion. Here is a more thoughtful answer (without the typos of online chat!)

I can make a case (as others have done) that says all the world's great traditions have a central ethical concept of compassion. Though it is a theme in all the great religious and philosophical streams, it often becomes overshadowed by dogma and the sheer weight of debate. Nonetheless, if you look for it you will find it. It is an optimistic foundation level belief about the universe. You see it, for instance, very prominently in the writings of both Mahatma Gandhi and Martin Luther King Jr. Love is at the heart of things.

Profound ideas are often best expressed in the context of stories. In the telling, stories have depths and nuances that engage hearers at multiple levels. Story-telling has been a primary human way of transmitting the most important and foundational ideas that make sense of life from one generation to the next. Our plausibility structures are expressed in narratives, even when we can't give adequate conceptual voice to them.

In the Christian telling, two important stories point to love at the heart of the universe. The first is the story of God as Holy Trinity. The second is the story of Christ crucified.

Let me tell the story of God as Holy Trinity in vaguely Augustinian ways. There is a lover, there is a beloved, and there is the energy of love between them. At the heart of all that is there is a relationship of love. The mystics have long told us (Jesus of Nazareth chief among them) that conceptions of God as "out there somewhere," "detached and distant," "unmoved mover" are inadequate. God is here, now, everywhere. "The realm of God is within you." God is in all things. All things are in God. If this insight is true, then in all things—at the heart of all—is relationality. In the neo-Platonic tradition, that was very important to early Christianity, all is One. It happens that this One is a relationship of love. Love is the movement of one to the other for the other's good.

The second Christian telling more directly answers my friend's question, "How can you say that love is at the heart of the universe when there is so much un-love?" The Christian story tells of the unjust killing of one who spoke of love. In the telling, this one (who was so in tune with God that he was called the Child of God) shows us that God suffers with all those who suffer.

In situations where there is un-love, where is love? Love is suffering with. Love is present as suffering. In fact, that is the Latin root of what compassion is: to suffer with.

Love at the heart of the universe is a trustworthy guide. It leads us to seek, to build, and to cherish loving relationships with all. Where there is suffering, love leads us as compassion to suffer with and to work toward loving resolutions to complex and hurtful situations.

What's your plausibility structure?

7. Nonviolence? Nonresistance?

When Dietrich Bonhoeffer tantalizingly called for a new monasticism, he said it would have nothing in common with the old, save for a commitment to the teachings of Jesus we call the Sermon on the Mount. I am always impacted by these sayings of Jesus. Here is a part that has always been important to me.

> You have heard the law that says the punishment must match the injury: 'An eye for an eye, and a tooth for a tooth.' But I say, do not resist an evil person! If someone slaps you on the right cheek, offer the other cheek also. If you are sued in court and your shirt is taken from you, give your coat, too. If a soldier demands that you carry his gear for a mile, carry it two miles. Give to those who ask, and don't turn away from those who want to borrow. (Matthew 5:38-42)

Few have taken these sayings seriously. It is easy to "spiritualize" them—something like, "Of course Jesus didn't mean this literally. How could he? Things just wouldn't work if everyone took a nonresistant stance."

Clearly things wouldn't work the way they do now. We would live in a far less violent world! It was through trying to live out these ideas that

I became a nonviolentist over a quarter of a century ago. It is not an easy road, and I have not always lived up to my highest aspirations. Working out the practicalities is a challenge. The inner violence of the psyche is a major stumbling block.

One of the questions I have been asked often is, "Doesn't this mean you will allow the aggressor to walk all over you?" I have found this difficult to answer, and have usually resorted to the answer that, regardless of the consequences, nonviolent is the right way to be.

Historically, in some understandings of nonresistance this has been the case. It was true, for instance, for the early nonresistant Anabaptists in the sixteenth century. It continues in the Amish and Mennonite traditions. It is a thoroughly deontological position. It is a simple duty to be nonviolent. None of us can foresee the consequences of our actions. Our responsibility begins and ends with our intentions to comply with duty.

Yet, it is difficult to ignore consequences, for consequences matter. To allow the aggressor to use violence is to collude with violence. It is not a nonviolent action.

How to resolve the dilemma?

It is often set up as: aggressor threatens violence, either (1) be nonresistant and allow the aggressor to use violence; or (2) resist the aggressor with force. Violence against violence. Perhaps, there is a third way.

I have received new insights from my practice of *taijiquan*. In *taiji* when the aggressor threatens violence, you neither resist violently nor simply give in to violence. In *taiji*, nonresistance means to deflect the violence of the aggressor away from yourself in a way that causes no harm. In Chinese, it is *lu*. In English "roll back." In this way you are not "walked all over," nor do you use violence. It is a nonviolent way of disarming the violent. The goal is to reduce the violence of the total situation, rather than merely not to use violence yourself.

8. Owe No One Anything, Except to Love One Another

"Owe no one anything except to love one another," so said St. Paul (Romans 13:8).

Yesterday was my birthday. It was not an auspicious one (18, 21, 30, 40, 50, 60, 65, 70, 75, or 80). Just a regular, common or garden birthday. I had a wonderful day from waking to sleeping. I felt very glad, warm and fuzzy, rambling through the day in a gentle cloud of well-being.

I was taken by surprise by the sheer amount of affection sent my way by so many people—old friends, new friends, former students, former foster kids, and family, of course.

Affection is an important way of loving, and perhaps the least noticed or appreciated. Books are legion on romantic love. Altruism, compassion, and charity have their champions. But affection? C.S. Lewis said of affection that is like a favorite pair of old slippers! Comfortable. Hardly noticed. Yet, oh so welcome at the end of a hard day on your feet, or a cold morning when the floor feels a little icy.

Affection is not the love of grand gestures. It is not the over-heated love of new romance. We may "fall in" to that kind of love, but we do not "fall into" affection. Also, affection does not have the intensity of compassionate acts when your heart feels like it is breaking because of the plight of some needy Other.

Affection, rather, creeps up on you when you are unaware. As I write, I am looking at Jack the little pug we rescued a few months ago. My feelings? A warmth somewhere deep inside. A kindness toward. I can't help a little smile. When we rescued him we were motivated by compassion. He had been ill-treated. He had a few bad manners. As a pug, he's not up to "show standard." He's misshaped. We call him affectionately our little belly-flop (the name given to misshapen Jelly Bellies). We didn't know how he would fit in with the household, or whether we could manage his behavior. He was in bad shape and needed help. That was it, as far as we were concerned. At the beginning we felt compassion, with no real relationship with this waif and stray. Of course, compassion too is a way of loving, but that's not my point at the moment. As time passed affection crept up on us, as is its way. Jack grew on us as we got to know him.

Affection is the love that oils life. Things go more smoothly. A life without affection must be a poor life indeed.

When the Apostle said, "Owe no one anything except to love one another," I don't know whether he had affection in mind. If he hadn't, I wish he had. And whether he had nor not, I shall read it that way!

Today (54 years-old and one day) I feel immensely grateful to know so much affection. I'm glad I noticed it. Notice the little things. All shall be well.

9. Un-Selfing for Love's Sake

Western culture is characterized by the cult of the self. Since the 1970s, popular psychologists have told us that before we can love anyone else, we must love ourselves. Read just about any popular book on love or relationships and it will begin with the mantra, "learn to love yourself and all will be well."

This emphasis is not new and has its roots at the very beginning of modernity when Adam Smith in the eighteenth century told the world that "enlightened self-interest is what makes the world go round" (my very rough paraphrase of *The Wealth of Nations*). It takes a while for the ideas of the great and the good to filter down to the rest of us. Some of their ideas get stuck in books. This one—the cult of the self—has become so pervasive that it is now common sense. Question self-love and people will look at you as if you belong to another realm.

Jesus did belong to another realm—the realm of God. Like all the great wisdom teachers, Jesus told a different story. Lose yourself to find yourself. Be non-attached to your self and your self-interests.

> That mortification is best which results in the elimination of self-will, self-interest, self-centered thinking, wishing and imagining. (Huxley, 2009, 101)

How uncomfortable does that make us feel! Mortification is the old term for self-denial, and self-denial has been taken to extremes in all religious traditions. If self-denial is seen as an end in itself, then it is simply one more religious error leading us down one more rabbit trail.

To lose the self is a means to another end. That end is Love. The most wise speak of non-attachment to self in the context of love.

Iris Murdoch called it "un-selfing." Aldous Huxley called it "self-naughting." To lose the self is for the sake of the Other. Jesus said it, "Those who lose their life *for my sake* . . . Those who lose their life *for the gospel's sake*." What is the gospel? The way of love.

Loss of self and loving the Other may sound counterintuitive, but there is a deep connection. Love is a movement from the self toward the Other. We have been fooled into thinking that love is merely about what I get from the Other, how the Other meets my needs, how my desires are satisfied. If that is the case, then love is preoccupation with the self *par excellence*. St. Augustine told us that love is always motion. Love is movement away from the self toward the object of love. The lover loses herself in the preoccupation with the Other. Love and beauty are closely associated. Gaze on the beauty of a sunset, find yourself lost in the sight of the first heavy snowfall when all is a white winter wonderland, look into the eyes of a newborn baby—the last thing on your mind is your self. In the encapturing of beauty you lose your self. It is why animal companions are such a gift. Your little kitten draws you out of your self toward her. In love is the loss of individuality, the melding of individuation into the One, into Love-itself.

Pre-modern cultures had a clearer sense that loss of the self was a good. Yet, the zeal to lose the self through mortification took many wrong turns. In order to lose the self, to find non-attachment to self-interests, ascetics dreamt up all kinds of self-tortures. But self-flagellation misses the point. You learn to lose yourself in everyday relationships when you make the Other first and not yourself. You practice non-attachment not in a lonely mountain shack, nor in a desert cave, but in the office where you work, in the check-out line at the store, as you sit in the doctor's surgery, as you wait the results of a test.

> Self-denial should take the form, not of showy acts of would-be humility, but of control of the tongue and the moods—in refraining from saying anything uncharitable or merely frivolous (which means, in practice, refraining from about fifty percent of ordinary conversation), and in behaving calmly and with quiet cheerfulness when external circumstances or the state of our bodies predisposes us to anxiety, gloom or an excessive elation. (Ibid, 102)

I give the final word to the fifteenth-century Indian mystic Kabir:

> The devout seeker is he who mingles in his heart the double currents of love and detachment, like the mingling of the streams of Ganges and Jumna. (Quoted in ibid., 105)

10. No Greater Love

Twice in my life I have had to make a serious decision about military service. Neither was in case of national emergency, or a draft of young men into the military. Both times were matters of conscience. The first was in 1983, when I seriously considered becoming a British Army Chaplain. I attended a weeklong recruitment session at the Royal Army Chaplain's Department at Bagshot Park in Surrey. Military service was then a very tempting proposition. I decided not to, on a point of conscience.

The second time, I faced a similar conscientious choice was with regard to the oath for United States citizenship. It is a mere happenstance, an accident, where you are born. You do not choose it, nor think about what it means to be a citizen of your place of birth. When you live in a country not of your birth, and want to take participation in that country seriously, then usually you have to make some kind of statement about it. In the United States, the citizenship oath says that you will participate in the military if called upon to do so. This too became a point of conscience, and for the same reasons that in 1983 I chose not to become a military chaplain, in 2012, I chose not to agree to serve in the military if called upon to do so. At my age, it is most unlikely that I would ever be called into military service. Still, it's a matter of principle.

The issue of conscience is quite simple. Jesus of Nazareth, and the first Christians (for at least a couple of hundred years) were pacifists. They eschewed participation in violence. I have tried to follow that Way.

It is a simple matter, yet entered into after much deliberation, for the truth is I have a great deal of sympathy for soldiers. I don't have sympathy for governments who declare war because "We have no other choice." There are always other choices. It is not government officials who die, but young men, and now young women. Nor do I have sympathy for generals, who by and large orchestrate the killing. My sympathy is with the young boys (and now girls) who "join up" and don't in truth know what they are doing. Jingoism, peer pressure, money, the promise of travel and adventure, "glory," these are the reasons. They mask the awful reality of "kill or be killed" for a cause that is not understood, or for a lie, or for something ignoble, such as land, or gold, or oil, or power.

I read recently Adam Hochschild's *To End All Wars* (2011). (I wrote a review for *The Journal for Peace and Justice Studies*, 2012). About the First World War, the book looks mostly at those who resisted the war for conscientious reasons. It reads like a good novel, but is great history. It is profoundly moving. I was struck again by the insanity of total war and the great toll it takes on people—especially the young.

In the aftermath of the War to End Wars, all over Britain monuments were raised to the dead. Every village, every town has its war memorial with lists of the young men who were killed. Usually, as part of the memorial is a verse from the Bible: "No man hath greater love than this, that a man lay down his life for his friends" (John 15:13). In the First World War, this was profoundly true as many of the young men who died were best friends, neighbors, and class mates who all joined the same regiment, in the same battalion, on the same day. In France, they shared intimately every aspect of life: eating together, sleeping next to, enduring all the same discomforts. The bonds of friendship were strengthened in ways almost inconceivable in peacetime. Often they died within minutes, seconds even, of "going over the top" of the trenches.

By all accounts, from the letters of soldiers who died, and stories of those who survived, soldiers fight and die not for some grand purpose, but for the soldier next to them in the line. They fight and die for each other. So, there is a profound sense in which the saying is true, "No man hath greater love than this, that a man lay down his life for his friends."

There are philosophical and moral issues to face with regard to love and killing for love's sake. For myself, I determined that it is not acceptable to kill another for love's sake, for love is due to all. But to die for love of the Other is something different. Many young people have faced that with courage and fortitude. I have great sympathy for young soldiers who face that in a way that I have never faced it. In the Iraq war, nearly 5,000 United States soldiers were killed. Over 32,000 were seriously injured. In previous wars, many of those would have died. Today, they live with the terrible legacy of their injuries. This does not take account of the countless numbers who suffer today from Post Traumatic Stress Disorder.

Today, I spare a thought for those young men and women, and for those who still face the choice to lay down their lives for their friends.

11. A Question of Conscience

Being a good citizen. Paying taxes. Serving the community. Being political. The *Social Contract*. Patriotism. Nationalism. When the state asks for something do we give it? How much do we give?

In the year 2000, my book, *In the World But Not of the World: Christian Social Thinking at the End of the Twentieth Century*, was published. It was the culmination of fifteen years thinking that produced three advanced degrees along the way.

If you boil it down, what I was thinking about then was loyalty to a way of living—a life committed to loving nonviolent relationships (following the Christ, and other witnesses to the realm of God)—in the midst of a culture that all too often pulls in a different direction. I am still thinking about it now.

You see, life is dandy when the culture and the Realm of God get along fine. Problems arise when they conflict. Then it becomes a matter of conscience.

H. Richard Niebuhr wrestled with this in his classic *Christ and Culture* (1951). If you haven't read it, it will be worth your while. Niebuhr gives us five typical positions. When you read the book you will probably switch between the positions. Is there opposition between the Realm and culture, or perhaps similarity, is one above the other, is there an unsolvable paradox between them, should we seek to change culture to make it more closely resemble the Realm?

The issues are real. After September 11, 2001, my thinking about war and violence did not change. It brought me into conflict with good friends who thought the only response should be a violent one. I lost quite a few friends who just couldn't understand a loving nonviolent response to terrorism. For me, it was a matter of conscience.

How far do you take these matters of conscience? Well, that's a matter of conscience! I know folk who would be conscientious objectors to a draft into the military. This has not been tested for a long time. It is unlikely to be tested again anytime soon. I know others who are "tax resisters" and refuse to pay the percentage of taxes that is used for military purposes. I have never felt drawn to this step, but respect those who have. It seems to me to be a symbolic stance, as once the money is in government hands, it's all in the same pot.

I am watching the "Occupy Wall Street" movement with great interest. Here are citizens who have had enough of the status quo and are taking a step of conscience to resist. I am unclear what they are resisting or what change is to be effected. But the social movement is fascinating.

In my book, I drew the tentative conclusion that small groups of loving support were the most hopeful structures to help us make sense of "being in, but not of the world." I have not changed that viewpoint, though I hold even that more tentatively than before.

British philosopher and ethicist G.E. Moore came to the conclusion that a good life was one that enjoyed friendship and experienced beauty. I like the simplicity of it. When you read his work you realize that "friendship" is code for the ethical life as relationships characterized by love and goodness. If we can achieve that, that would be a happy achievement. It's all a matter of conscience.

SEVEN

METAPHYSICS—THE ULTIMATELY REAL, GOD, JESUS CHRIST

1. The Big Picture

A spiritual view of life ought to be expansive. It should help us with the big picture, the sense of meaning. Of course, it is not to say that we will have all our questions answered. Rather, that we will have something like a map. Not the small scale, detailed map that shows street by street, but the continents, the oceans, the vastness of it all—a making sense for us. I have just finished reading John's Hick's *The Fifth Dimension: An Exploration of the Spiritual Realm* (2004). Hick skillfully presents just this sort of big picture.

I first encountered Hick's work as a rather Calvinistic student at Northern Baptist College, Manchester. Then, I hated his writing! His vision of God and goodness, and the inevitability of love winning all, was far too large for my limited thinking. One of the darker sides of religion is that it restricts and narrows. It separates the sheep from the goats. Too many of us are confident that we are the sheep!

Like bellybuttons, religion too often divides humanity into the "innies" and the "outies." A big picture of the love of God—God who is in all things and above all things—will not be content with the dismembering of humanity.

Could it be that all are included in the love of God? That God seeks all and that all seekers find God? That in "worlds to come" all will be seekers? If you have a mind to be stretched, check out John Hick.

2. Something or Nothing

From time to time, we all think of the fundamental question, "What happens when we die?"

A simple answer might be, "Something or nothing." Either something happens or nothing happens. The human person continues in some way or other or the human person ceases to be.

Let's survey the options, all that occur in scriptures in different places:

(1) Nothing. The human person is so intimately tied to the material body that when the body dies, the person dies with the body. Human life is merely material, a product of brain function. When the brain ceases to function, consciousness ends. In its way, that is a quite comforting thought. However painful the process of death might be, when death comes suffering ends.

(2) Something. Human consciousness continues with no break. The person enters a new realm. This may be good or bad. It may be like summoned into a court to face a judge. If you have done well (according to certain criteria, the content of which need not trouble us at the moment), consciousness continues as pure joy. If you have not done well, then you suffer, either for a short time to make you better (and then you will know pure joy), or for a long time, perhaps forever (your suffering is infinite).

(3) Something alternative. The human person falls asleep, to awake at some future time. When the person awakes, it is much the same as the first "something."

(4) Alternative something. There is no reckoning, no judge's court. The life after life is not like this life in any recognizable way. There is no pain, suffering, tears, or anything recognizably bad. It is all good. Everyone enters this life, irrespective of what happens in the life we know.

(5) Something alternative redux. The human person finds another body, maybe human or maybe not depending on how well life was lived.

I think I have covered all the something and the nothing. How could we know? Put simply, we cannot know. We cannot know in the sense of knowing something that is empirically verifiable. There is no test we can carry out to look at the results. We cannot know either in the other sense of knowing, "I know beauty, or love or goodness." That kind of knowing is part experience, part intuition.

In another way, however, we can know. We can know in the way a child knows some things. We tell a child, "the grass is green, water is wet, two plus two equals four." The child knows things (and we know them now) because we have been told that they are true. Everyone knows that water is wet. It is part of the structure of language itself. (Perhaps, there is nothing other than language.) The answers to the question I considered above are of this latter type. They are claims to knowledge within a particular way of thinking about life, a particular language game. We know the answer because someone told us, and there is no way to verify the answer.

What happens, then, when we die? Do you believe what you have been told?

The second letter to the Thessalonians in the New Testament gives one perspective. In this letter, the folks seem particularly troubled that Jesus has not returned to the world. This was troubling because they had been led to believe (they had been told) that Jesus would return soon and that when he did, there would be a general resurrection. "The dead would rise to meet the Lord" (1 Thessalonians 4:16). This implies something like the option that when you die you fall asleep and you wait. They had been waiting now for over twenty years (if you date the letter early) or perhaps fifty years (if you date it late). Some of their number had already died. They were beginning to get worried. So, the letter is written to encourage them to wait with patience. A tale is told that some other things would have to happen before Christ comes to the world again.

A gospel, tells of a group of folks who believed something like the first option: when you die there is simply nothing. When the Psalmist asked, "Can the dead praise God?" these folk answered "No, because the dead are dead." There is nothing (Psalm 155:17).

In response to this, Jesus said that as God is the God of Abraham, Isaac, and Jacob, and as God is the God of the living; they must be alive after they have died. This implies something like one of the other options.

But it says nothing about any kind of reckoning. We must assume that either there is not a reckoning or else that Abraham, Isaac and Jacob passed with flying colors.

So, can we answer the perennial question: what happens when we die? I think not with any certainty, not with any knowledge claim that means much.

The final thing Jesus says is "To God all of them are alive?" (Luke 20:39). This is very hopeful. As a follower of Jesus, this is enough. What happens when we die? We are alive to God. How do I know? Jesus told me.

3. Making Sense of Transcendence

This week, I had opportunity to talk with students about the causes of war. A number of students came up with the answer: "Religion is the number one cause of war." One said, "Religion has caused more wars and deaths than any other human phenomenon." His view is a fairly common view. It is easy to create a long list of religious wars and wars that began or continued with a religious legitimation. Though that is true, I think it is an exaggeration that through repetition has gained the power of truth. Recently, I reviewed a book for *The Journal for Peace and Justice Studies*, Tina Beattie's *The New Atheists* (2008). The book is well worth a read. Among other things, Beattie challenges the assertion that religion has caused the most wars.

Nonetheless, I have great sympathy with my students. Religion may not have caused more wars than non-religious ideologies, but it has caused sufficient numbers for us all to be appalled at its track record. And not merely wars; religion has a bad record in human rights abuses, in intolerance, in bigotry, in ethnic cleansing, and racism.

For these reasons, many thinking people want to distance themselves from religion. At the same time, we human beings cannot get away from the essential spiritual nature we carry with us. We grapple with the sense of transcendence (Freud called it the "oceanic feeling") and experience wonder, awe, and sometimes fear. "The idea of the holy" will not go away. On more than one occasion, colleagues have said to me, "I am not religious, but I am spiritual." I have taken it to mean that they want to distance themselves from the dark side of religion and yet hold on to the essential spirituality of being human and our connection with transcendent reality.

I have great sympathy with those colleagues. At times, I have been ashamed to admit that I am a deeply religious person—or is that deeply spiritual? The problem is that though the desire to separate religion from spirituality is a strong one, sociologically, psychologically and philosophically it is impossible to do so. Unless we make a stipulative definition of the kind, "By spirituality I mean something like religion, but without all the garbage that religion often has!" Of course, if folk want to make that move, that is fine too. But it does seem the components of spirituality are clearly religious, and religion is rooted in spirituality.

When I try to help future high school teachers think through what religion means (for future social studies classes) I suggest, "Religion is the human attempt to make sense of the experience of transcendence." As we try to make sense we create the structures of religion. These structures can be for good or ill. Besides being the cause of much strife, religion is also the cause of much good. Daily, countless millions of folk do good and kind things rooted in their religious/spiritual understanding and practice.

At times, I find is psychologically painful to live with the tension of the good and the bad in our spiritual practice. My way forward is to try, with integrity, to live deeply in my spiritual practice, with kindness to all.

4. Appearance and Reality

This week, Jane and I attended a presentation on what we might or might not know about the brain, how experimenting on non-human animals might or might not tell us something, and how what we might or might not know might possibly give us insight into child behavior; finally, such knowledge might or might not help us find new interventions to help troubled children. The conclusion seemed to be that all is guesswork, but at least it is worth subjecting other sentient beings to pain in order to keep guessing. We came away frustrated on a number of levels.

Here is one of my frustrations with the talk. The presenter had a particular view of knowledge: what it means to know something and how we get that knowledge. She was an unacknowledged positivist. A positivist is someone who thinks that we can only know something if we can perform an experiment and empirically verify the result by repeating the experiment a number of times and reaching the same conclusions. Only then do we have knowledge. (It is called the verification principle.)

I have no problems with that kind of knowledge. It is the basis of our technological and scientific breakthroughs of the last few hundred years. (Though I do dissent from seeking that kind of knowledge by subjecting other sentient beings to great pain.) My frustration comes when empirical knowledge is announced as the only knowledge; that all else is truly meaningless as a truth claim. The empirical, by its nature, deals only with appearance: how things are perceived by us and not with the "thing-in-itself."

Philosophers have wrestled with the issue of appearance and reality since they began pondering about life. They have reached no firms conclusions. Immanuel Kant, an eighteenth century German philosopher—and very important as philosophers go—said that it is impossible to know a "thing-in-itself" (which he called the *noumenon*). We can only know how something appears to us, filtered through our own experience and limited thinking (which he called the *phenomenon*). The presenter of our talk this week seemed to think that appearance is reality; that *noumenon* collapses into *phenomenon*. At least Kant left room for the *noumenon*, even if he thought we could never know it.

The spiritual impulse is different. It is the search for the *noumenon*. It is to move beyond appearance to find reality. W. R. Inge said, "the only true mystic is one who sees realities and knows how to distinguish them from phantasies" (1947, p. 142). God said to the Jewish prophet Samuel: "God does not see as mortals see; they look on the outward appearance, but God looks on the heart."

In John Hick's phrase, God is the Ultimately Real. The Ultimately Real sees the "thing-in-itself." The goal of spirituality is to become one with the Ultimately Real. To become one with the Ultimately Real is to be enlightened—to see truly. Things aren't what they appear to be. Do you want to be a *bodhisattva*? Keep seeking! The mystics have told us that the fully real is fully knowable.

In the Christian context, monasticism (or something like monasticism) has usually been rooted in a desire for a deeper spirituality that goes beyond mere formality or theory—a deep connectedness with the Ultimately Real. Central to the monastic spirit is the formation and living of a spiritual practice.

As we developed the "Rule" of the community in the late 1990s, we arrived at six habits that help form the practice of spirituality for our members:

> Eucharist (the central rite of historical Christianity that roots us in the great tradition)
> Daily Office (prayers and reading of sacred writings, scriptures)
> Meditation (quietness, stillness, contemplation, sitting, standing, walking meditation connecting body, mind and spirit)
> Mindfulness (developing awareness with thankfulness in the whole of life)
> Study (reflective and meditative development of understanding)
> Service (the outworking of spirituality in loving concern for the Other—people, non-human sentient beings, the environment—focused often on the marginalized)

To build a spiritual practice is to find balance in these daily habits. If you are from a different tradition, these habits are easily modified. For Eucharist, substitute the rites and rituals of your own tradition. For the Daily Office, substitute the prayers and sacred texts that are meaningful to you. The other habits easily translate across traditions.

But how to build a practice? In traditional monasticism, you either became a cenobite (joined with others in full-time monastic life, separated from the world) or an anchorite/eremite (a solitary, living alone, given to full-time pursuit of prayer and contemplation). In the new monasticism, we are trying to develop the spirit and habits of monasticism in daily lives lived in, and not apart from, the world (neither cenobitic or eremitic). This presents great challenges! It is why I like the term "secular monasticism" (a phrase coined by our good friend Fr. John Skinner in the 1980s). The term fuses two ideas that have been traditionally mutually exclusive (not unlike Bonhoeffer's "religionless Christianity.") In the Lindisfarne Community, we are monastics in the world. Hidden. Buried. Anonymous.

Building a spiritual practice is challenging.

Here's a few reflections:

- Be realistic. To set impossible goals will only end in defeat, frustration and guilt! The goal of "two hours in prayer a day" combined with a family, a full-time job and the sundry other commitments of everyday life is a stretch.
- Be creative. Meditation does not have to happen always sitting on a cushion, with incense and soft music. Do you drive to work? Turn off the radio. Meditate. Do you walk? Meditate. Use every opportunity to become mindful.
- Use technology. Smart phones, tablets, laptops, podcasts. Don't be enslaved by technology, but simply use it. There are versions of the Daily Office you can listen to. For example, you can have the Lindisfarne Way of Living (Fitz-Gibbon and Fitz-Gibbbon, 2006) on your phone, Kindle, Nook or tablet, and in snatched moments during the day read the office.
- Start small. Baby steps. Little habits soon become bigger habits. You are less liable to fail in a meditation habit if you begin with just five minutes in the morning before work than an hour.
- Build habits that you enjoy and find beneficial. It's much easier to do things you like doing.

- Think long-term. A spiritual practice is a marathon not a sprint. You are building a life-practice. You don't need to do it all at once.
- Recognize that over time your needs and interests will change. You may spend a year or two focused mostly on meditation, with the other habits in the background. That's fine. Prayer and reading will have more relevance for some periods and less for others. That's fine too.
- Despite all the above, a spiritual practice requires discipline. It does not "just happen." It is conscious, intentional—living against the grain.
- Be kind to yourself. When a well-intentioned plan doesn't work, don't beat yourself up. A spiritual practice is there to help you. It's a way to lead you toward flourishing in loving relationship with God, yourself, your family and friends, and all that is.

5. Retreat Thoughts

The meditation exercises in which we have engaged on this retreat (and I hope that you will continue to practice) have been related to an awareness of the body. The mystics have this in common: they try to move us beyond words and then beyond images because God is beyond words and beyond images. It was the great insight of the ancient Jewish people that to create an image of God is idolatrous.

Of course, words are themselves symbols and, when we substitute the symbol for the thing symbolized, we have mistaken the use of language. The word "tree" is not the tree itself. The word "lake" is not the lake itself. Words are shorthand symbols for a far greater reality. How can all that you see out there be captured in the word "lake"? The word has meaning for us only when we have truly experienced what it is like to be here, to sit outside, to see, to feel, to hear, to experience, to put you toes in the water, to kayak the lake.

So, God beyond words.

Today is Trinity Sunday, the day when the church worships God for the wonderful revelation of Trinity in Unity, the One and the Many, the Three and the One. If the idea of Trinity teaches us anything, it is that God is beyond words and beyond images. That three are one makes no linguistic sense. (Or should we say that three is one? We do not even have adequate syntax to express the idea). When well-meaning theologians have tried to popularize the idea of Trinity—St. Patrick's three-leaf clover, or water, ice and vapor, for example—they have distorted the idea. By trying to make the concept accessible, they lose the mystery. They turn reality into error.

When great artists represent Trinity, the image is invariably of the Three and we lose the One.

The idea of the Holy Trinity is to confuse us, to make our brains ache, to have us throw our hands up in exasperation and say, "It makes no sense!"

Our friends the Unitarians have missed the point. "The Trinity makes no sense," they say, "so let's lose the idea of Trinity."

Yet, that is the point. The Trinity makes no sense. The Trinity is, in fact, none-sense. Trinity is mystery. God is mystery. God is beyond words to formulate. God is beyond images to depict. If I can make sense of God, then I have reduced God to my understanding.

The ancients insisted, "God is that than which nothing greater can be imagined." If I can imagine God, then I have failed in my task. I have something less than God. God is beyond my ability to imagine. God is beyond my ability to describe in words.

Let's not think about God for a moment. Let's think about a lime. You can create an image of a lime, a painting, a digital photo. Yet, none of those representations is the lime itself. The imagery may help convey the concept of the lime. But if you say the image is the lime, you have missed it.

It is like a finger pointing to the moon. If you remain with the finger pointing, you will miss the moon.

You have a friend. Your friend is particularly partial to limes. She has never seen, touched, smelled, or tasted a lime. She has only seen a picture of a lime. She might be able to recognize a lime were she to come across a real one. But she has not experienced one. You, who happen to be erudite in the extreme, a true wordsmith, a philosopher of all things citrus, try to help her. You describe the texture of the skin, the feel of a newly ripe lime. "It is like a lemon, similar in shape but not quite, a little harder usually, the smell is tangy, but not as sharp, a somehow softer smell. Bite into the lime and it is tart, more so than the lemon, but not as much as vinegar. You will never mistake a lime for a lemon . . ." And on it goes—a PhD in describing limes! All very good in its own way, but until she experiences the lime for herself, she has missed it.

Now back to God. If we cannot through words and images do justice to a simple fruit, how could we expect to do justice to the Ultimate Reality of the universe?

I do not want to belittle religious art, iconography, theology, or philosophy. I think they are all very important and I am happy to give my life to reading, thinking, and writing. But at best, these are all but signposts—they point the way. Religion is not the truth. Religion points in the direction of truth (at its best) and is a hindrance to truth (at its worst, and sadly we see so much of the worst).

Therefore, we cannot remain with the words, with the image. We must move beyond to the experience of God directly. And in the words of the old Gloria Estefan song. "I'm trying to say I love you, but the words get in the way!"

Alongside the daily office, Bible reading, speaking or thinking prayers, and study, build in the practice of silence, awareness, going beyond. That is why we have had a focus during these few days on meditation exercises that do not feature words or images, but sensations, awareness of breathing, of our bodies. Christ in you. Without concepts. Without words.

I was sitting outside this morning looking over the lake. There is a deep silence in creation. But it is not an auditory silence. It is very noisy! The water lapping the shore. A thousand birds all singing at the same time. Flies buzzing. Fish jumping out of the water. The wind in the trees. A million leaves crashing into each other. A woodpecker banging the tree trunk. Yet, in it all, is a deep silence. Awareness brings us to that. Beyond words, beyond images we find God.

6. God a Judge?

All we can say about God is metaphorical. It is always, "God is a bit like this . . ." There can be no literal language for anything that can be said about God for God is always other. Language is our way of trying to make sense of the inexpressible, the ineffable. In 1 Timothy and Luke, there are three metaphors: two obvious and one not so. In Luke, the metaphors are embedded in stories Jesus told, a shepherd who loses sheep and a woman who loses some coins, and there it's obvious that coins and sheep represent something other. In Timothy, the writer speaks of Christ as making a judgment; that he is like a judge. For most Christians, Christ is God. Yet, the message is not that Christ/God *is literally* a judge, but that God is *like* a judge. It is as clearly a metaphor just as in the case of the shepherd and the woman.

The writer of the letter to Timothy is very grateful. (Most scholars think that it is not Paul, as traditionally thought, but someone from the Pauline community writing in Paul's name, probably sometime after Paul's death.) He is thankful for the mercy of God shown to him as a sinner who acted in ignorance. At one time, he was a persecutor, a violent man. Yet, he carried out his actions in ignorance, and the judge, because of his ignorance, was merciful.

Now that is interesting as a moral argument. Picture the judge sitting in formal robes, raised above the courtroom on a dais listening to the defendant. "Your Honor, I admit to persecuting people, I admit to blaspheming the name of Christ, I admit to violent acts, even to the point of killing people. But I acted in ignorance. I did not really know. I did not understand. I am truly sorry."

How would the judge make her determination? The judge would probably take into account true contrition and ignorance. Yet, in capital offenses, ignorance is finally no excuse. The defendant in this case has committed murder. If the defendant had filled in his tax forms and made a huge mistake in his own favor, not truly knowing the rules (that is, in ignorance) the tax authorities may be lenient with a fine. But I suspect not in the case of murder. The sentence might be commuted to manslaughter, but some judgment would be made against the defendant.

In Timothy, the judgment is made in the defendant's favor. Why? Because the judge is a merciful judge and overlooks ignorance.

That is the picture of God given to us. That is why the letter's author is grateful. God is like the kind of judge who takes ignorance into account. If we are ignorant when sinning, then God will have mercy on us. Good news? Partially so.

As I pondered this, I became unsettled. I am unsettled because I know myself. I sometimes do things that I ought not do in the full knowledge of what I am doing. I cannot plead ignorance. I willfully do things in my own interest and against the interests of others that I know to be wrong. Will the judge be merciful?

The inner struggle between "want to" and "ought to" has been noticed throughout all the centuries of philosophy and theology. Many times the two are in conflict. This epitomizes the existential moral dilemma. Progress in character means that the "want to" and the "ought to" become much closer together. In the saint or sage, the "want to" and the "ought to" are identical. The saint wants to do what she ought to do. I know myself to be some distance away from sainthood!

So, given my reality, on the basis of 1 Timothy, will the judge be merciful? I see no hope of that, for I cannot plead ignorance. I know what is right. I just do not always want to do it.

The question is, is God like that judge? Merciful when ignorance can be claimed, but not when there is willfulness?

The stories of Jesus are ultimately more hopeful. The shepherd looks for the lost sheep, the woman looks for the lost coin, without consideration of the motives of the errant sheep or the missing coins. There is no thought of whether the sheep or the coins deserve to be found. In Timothy, there is at least a hint of just deserts. The defendant relies on the mercy of the judge, yet his ignorance deserves at least some attention. It is a mitigating factor. As I cannot plead ignorance, I would much rather be that lost sheep or lost coin! In those stories the emphasis is solely on the good nature of the shepherd and the woman. There is no consideration of whose fault it is that the sheep and coin are lost. Our attention is directed to God, who is like a kind shepherd who goes out of his way to find the lost one. God is like a woman who turns the house upside down to find the one lost coin.

Today then, I find comfort in the stories of Jesus. My hope is that God will find me despite myself. Jesus tells me that he would leave ninety-nine just to look for me. Jesus tells me that he would turn the house upside down just to find me. I do not plead ignorance, for I know that I am lost because of my own foolishness and weakness of will.

7. The Will of the Father-Mother in Heaven

How should we live? We live toward perfection, toward holiness. "Be perfect, as I am perfect," says God. "Be holy, as I am holy" (Matthew 5:48). If we locate perfection not as a state of being, but as a place, a realm, then we would call it something like "the kingdom of heaven," or better, "the realm of heaven." The realm of heaven is that place where all will be perfect. There will be no more sadness, or sickness, or violence, or suffering, or anything bad at all. The lion will lie down with the lamb. Children will play with once poisonous snakes.

The images are many and varied, but universally they all look toward a place of perfection. It is the longing of the human spirit. We cross the Jordan to get there. It is the good land, the land of promise. Most poignantly, Africans enslaved by white imperialists sang of it. Their songs became the basis for all forms of modern music—blues, jazz, rock 'n roll. The music was born of longing for that perfect place.

When Jesus spoke of this perfect place, he most often spoke in parables—little stories that give us hints and glimpses. "It's a bit like this." Or, "It's not at all like this."

He told of the wise person who built a house on the rock. When the wind and rains came, the house stood firm. He spoke of a foolish person who built a house on sand. When the winds and rain came, the house fell flat, with great loss to that foolish person.

The moral of the story was how to be a wise person. The wise person is the one who does the will of the Father-Mother in heaven. The foolish person is the one who does not do the will of the Father-Mother. To do the will of God is to prepare to enter the realm of heaven.

Jesus made it very vivid by emphasizing what is not the will of God.

It is not prophesying. It is not casting out demons. It is not doing deeds of power. This is quite surprising.

It is often these kinds of activities that draw great attention, great adulation. It is often these kinds of activities that are said to prove there is a God. "There must be a God. Look at the miracles."

In the early 1980s, I was very much drawn to the "Signs and Wonders" movement started by the late John Wimber in California. It was very exciting, very heady stuff. But Jesus said that such activity was not the will of God. That was not the way to enter the realm of God. That was not the way to the land of promise.

What then is the will of God? Jesus said, "Everyone who hears these words of mine and acts on them will be like the wise person . . ." (Matthew, 7:24). The will of God is to hear and to act. It is to practice. It is a way of living.

Jesus was in a long line of Jewish prophets who had all begun to realize the same idea. His teaching was in the same spirit as that of eighth century prophet Micah:

> He has told you, O mortal, what is good and what does God
> require of you but to do justice, and to love kindness and to walk
> humbly with your God. (Micah 6:8)

The will of God is about justice, kindness, and humility.

If we reach into the future to that realm of perfection, the realm of heaven (when all will be well), and we pull from that realm the kind of life today that is in accordance with it—what would life look like?

It would be a life of fairness, of loving kindness and humility. To practice those things is to do the will of God. It is that which prepares us for the realm of God.

8. Child of God

When Jane and I were preparing the liturgy for the Lindisfarne Community we were very conscious of exclusionary language. We had long concluded that women had been shut out from many areas of the church's life. Male language reinforced the exclusion each time the liturgy was said or sung. At the highest level of Christianity (the understanding of the Holy Trinity) women were absent. Popular Catholicism had reduced the problem by exalting Mary to a virtual fourth place in the Godhead. A holy family (God, Mary, Jesus) was in the popular imagination as important as the theological Trinity (Father, Son and Holy Spirit).

Yet, our understanding was not Catholic and we had no Mary tradition to militate against the maleness of Protestantism.

God is neither male nor female. For many years, we have called God the Father-Mother and have alternated the personal pronoun, sometimes calling God he and now more often she, as a counterbalance to centuries of exclusion. Some years ago, we decided to refer to God solely in the feminine for three months. The reason, we were told, is that no matter how much we protested that "When we call God Father, we do not mean a male," our imagery of God has been in male terms. It was quite a challenge to see God outside of the male box!

We changed the traditional motif of Trinity from "Father, Son, and Holy Spirit" to "Father-Mother, Child, and Holy Spirit." Why "child" and not "son"? Firstly, for the obvious inclusive language issue. Secondly, for a more nuanced theological reason. There are two schools of thought that say Jesus was a male human being being for good reasons. Males are more suited than females to be leaders. Males are more suited than females to be priests. Jesus is both the archetypal leader and the archetypal priest. As Jesus was male it is clear that only males can be leaders and only males can be priests. However, it seemed to us that the maleness of Jesus was not the issue. The humanity of Jesus was the point. If you understand the notion of conditions, Jesus' humanity was an essential condition of his mission, but Jesus' maleness was only a sufficient condition. Jesus' femaleness would also have been sufficient. (Jesus as a transgendered person would also have been sufficient, though that understanding is new to us and would not have been available to folk in the first century.)

The point of the Christ event is that, in incarnation—the heart of sacramental theology—, the divine is found fully expressed in the human; the human is taken up into the divine. Maleness and femaleness is irrelevant for this foundational theological understanding. Jesus is both child of humanity and Child of God. As the "forerunner" as Hebrews suggests, Jesus is the one who leads all people to that *telos*. In Christ, all of us are children of God, female and male.

Further, in the liturgy, we are concerned not so much with the historical Jesus (though that is part of the Eucharistic prayer) as with the risen Christ, the post-Easter Christ of faith. Theologically, this Christ is no longer bound by a temporal maleness or femaleness, but freed from those material restrictions. The risen Christ is neither male nor female as the Father-Mother is neither male nor female.

Language is always problematical. All we can say about God is ever only by analogy, "It is a bit like this." Meister Eckhart had the profound sense that there is Godhead beyond God. That is, essentially God is truly beyond our language, or imagery or understanding. Yet, language is important for us, and there is a great need to remove unnecessary exclusions.

9. Looking for God

The story of ancient Job has intrigued readers for centuries. Job's was a life of happiness with wealth, success, and a large and loving family. Then it all fell apart. Every conceivable bad thing happened to him. He lost his possessions, tragedy struck his family, and he became desperately ill. In his extremity Job lost any faith in God. His story is an attempt to make sense of it all.

> Oh that I knew where I might find God,
> That I might come to God's dwelling!
> God has made my heart feint;

The Almighty has terrified me;
If only I could vanish in darkness,
And thick darkness would cover my face! (Job 23)

There are many levels of interpretation of the sad story. It seems that when life was smooth and successful, Job had no problems in having faith in God. After all, don't wealth, success, and possessions indicate that God is smiling on you? When you lose them, doesn't that show God is displeased with you, or that God has disappeared, or that God was an illusion in the first place?

Perhaps Job's existential angst was caused by a false belief that there is a connection between the purpose of God and the material circumstances of life. The wealthy and healthy know God's kindness. The poor and sick know God's displeasure.

Perhaps his mistake was to think that there is an overriding purpose in all that happens, an invisible guiding hand that would make all well. It's easy to believe in when life is smooth. It's harder to stomach when life falls apart.

The existentialists in the twentieth century suggested that there is no overarching purpose. There is no point to the universe. There is only angst, only abandonment. The sooner we make peace with the randomness and indifference of the universe, the better for us.

Yet, they did leave us with some hope: our radical, authentic choices. We can't affect the universe, but we can be authentic in our choices. If Job had learned from Sartre, perhaps his life would have been bearable. The stoics had said something similar, "Be concerned only with those things you can affect or change. Be indifferent to the rest." Reinhold Niebuhr's Serenity Prayer has it too, "God give me the serenity to accept the things I cannot change; courage to change the things I can; and wisdom to know the difference."

Missing from Job, missing from most existentialist writings, and missing from the stoics' work is love. Kierkegaard (the father of existentialism) left us with a happier existentialism than Sartre. Though human experience may be angst, our radical choice is to leap into the abyss, trusting that love will catch us. Paul Tillich said, "Faith is being grasped by an ultimate concern" (2011). There is no greater "ultimate concern" than love.

10. Jesus Had Compassion for Her

The way of compassion is a way of living close to the heart of the Lindisfarne Community. Compassion is a facet of love and is closely connected to other virtues: kindness, sympathy, empathy, and altruism. Each of these virtues has a different emphasis, yet each shares a core that is remarkably similar.

What is that core? I found this by Adam Phillips and Barbara Taylor: "the sympathetic expansiveness linking self to other" (2009, 6).

Jesus showed us that the way of true humanity is this linking of people through love.

In my work on love I suggest two ideas: (1) that love is rooted in *desire* for the well-being of the other; and (2) love is *movement* from the self to the other. It is very different to selfishness, which stays locked-in to concerns no greater than "me and my own well-being."

There are always different ways of looking at life. A perennial question about life is: Are human beings fundamentally selfish or cooperative? Let's call these two positions the egoist and the connectivist. The egoist sees the self as the center. Everything resolves to the self. The connectivist sees relationships as the center, that there is something fundamental about being together.

Is the glass half-full or half empty? There is no definitive answer, as both statements are true. You can provide justification for either answer. But the way you perceive the glass, your viewpoint, is deeply psychologically affective: it affects your attitudes; it is a gauge for what matters to you; and what matters to us affects the kinds of decisions we take in life and the choices we make.

Whether the glass is half-full or half-empty is insignificant. But other issues are more significant. Take the question: Are human beings basically selfish or basically cooperative?

Philosophers have given different answers. Aristotle said we are social beings. He favored cooperation. Hobbes said that naturally all are at war against all. Hobbes set the course of a very dismal view of human beings. Later, Rousseau favored cooperation. Hume said we have a hard-wired deep sympathetic nature. Nietzsche and Rand cared little for the cooperative view. Life is the brutal struggle of the individual for power, for self-aggrandizement. I fear Maslow also got it wrong in the middle of getting much right. The goal is not self-actualization, but self in loving relationship with others.

Must we choose one or the other? Egoism or connection? Logicians would have us believe the "law of the excluded middle." It is either raining or it is not raining. It cannot be both raining and not raining at the same time. The truth of one statement proves the falsity of the other. You could say, "Well it is not raining very much." But then it is still raining. You might wax very clever and say, "What is rain?" Is four drops a square foot of ground rain?" "What about one drop a square mile?" What about a certain percentage of precipitation in the air?" But still, when you have disambiguated the statement and have made a decision about what constitutes rain, it is still either raining or not.

Is the question, "Are human beings by nature selfish or cooperative" like that? Does being one exclude being the other? This becomes very complex because we have to disambiguate the words "nature," "selfish," and "cooperative" and in doing so we have to ask whether selfish and cooperative are opposites like raining and not raining.

You may end up by saying that people are in part selfish and in part cooperative, refusing to choose a side. The question then is, how large a part? Are people more selfish, or more cooperative? How much more, or how much less?

In a sense, it does not matter. When the conjuror says, "Pick a card . . . any card," it doesn't matter which you pick. The magician will always win anyway.

So whether people are selfish or cooperative by nature doesn't matter. We can't change that. Yet, in another sense, it does matter. For it is a way of seeing life. It is a way of seeing whether the glass is half full or half empty. It affects what matters to us. It affects what we prioritize. It affects our life choices and our actions. The egoist clings to the self; the egoist protects the self at all costs; the egoist sees compassionate impulses as sentimental, or childish, or annoying. The connectivist longs for relationship with the Other; wants the best for the Other; knows that the self is only found when the self is lost in love's movement toward the Other.

"Jesus had compassion for her . . ." (Luke 7:13_14). What draws us to Jesus? What makes us want to be like Jesus? It is not his supreme egoism. It is not his will to power. It is the vulnerability of compassionate love and kindness. Freud said, "We are never so defenseless against suffering as when we love. (2005, 270)

> Love is vulnerable and risks rejection.
> Love risks all for love's sake.

11. Jerusalem Our Mother—God Our Mother

Today, a passage in Isaiah brought to mind the imagery of Jerusalem. In the scriptures (both Jewish and Christian), Jerusalem is an often-repeated image representing something good (the highest good for human beings on earth, perhaps).

Of course, Jerusalem as a literal, physical place, a piece of land, has seen much violence through human history (ironic as the name contains the word for "peace.") It has been fought over as a supreme holy place by Jews, Christians, and Muslims. It continues to be in the news daily. When you hear "West Bank," that is Jerusalem. Jerusalem is at the center of the West Bank controversy with the city literally divided between Israel and the Palestinians. So, the name has a great deal of pain associated with it. So much so, that I think the history of violence now associated with it overshadows the very positive imagery of Jerusalem in the scriptures.

How to take what has become a symbol of the divisions and violence of humanity and re-think it as a symbol of goodness and hope?

A few thoughts.

First, look at the very powerful female imagery associated with Jerusalem. In this brief passage in Isaiah we are told that we may:

> Rejoice with Jerusalem,
> Mourn over Jerusalem,
> Be nursed and satisfied at the breast of Jerusalem,
> Drink deeply at the breast of Jerusalem
> Be dandled on the knee of Jerusalem.

Jerusalem is portrayed as our Mother.

Second, there is this little shift in the text and the very same things are predicated of God. God is not separable from Jerusalem. Jerusalem is the symbol for God. Jerusalem is God encountered in a place. The invisible God come down to earth. The place where God chooses to dwell. The place of the temple of God. The place where the presence of God is found. And so, Jerusalem becomes a symbol of spiritual well-being/prosperity/*eudaimonia* as human beings encounter God. (In this picture, the well-being of the little child is at the mother's breast.)

Third, what is Jerusalem for us? What does it signify? Can we still use the symbol meaningfully? Or given the now association with violence and division must we reject it?

It cannot for us be the literal place of Jerusalem. I think that is too problematic. I think the literalism of the physical land is too deeply associated with violence to be helpful.

But if the symbol is of that where God comes to us, God dwells with us (we might say God incarnate) then very clearly the person of Jesus is our Jerusalem. In our *Way of Living* (Fitz-Gibbon and Fitz-Gibbbon, 2006), we have a couple of very beautiful canticles of mother Julian that portray Jesus as our mother.

Derived from that, wherever we find a place special to us, where we more readily find God, God's presence, where we find ourselves as little children at God's breast, then that is our Jerusalem. It may be a room in our house, a special chair. A location we are used to going for prayer. A place in the countryside where we drive or walk. Wherever it is, it will be the place where for us God most clearly dwells, is most clearly present. That place is a place to rejoice in. It is also a place to mourn over when we may temporarily lose it. In God's goodness, God will provide such a place for each of us. "You shall be comforted in Jerusalem," says the prophet.

12. Show Me God and I Shall Be Satisfied

One day Jesus was teaching his disciples some deep stuff. One of them, a little exasperated, not really understanding, blurted out, Just show me God and I will be satisfied! Jesus replied, with a great deal of patience, You've been with me for a while now, but you still don't get it! If you have seen me you have seen God. God is in me and I am in God. (see John 14:8-9).

Traditionally scholars have interpreted this in an exclusive way. Jesus is talking about his own uniqueness. "God is in me only. Only I am in God."

But perhaps that is not what Jesus meant at all. Think differently for a while. What if Jesus was saying something revolutionary about God. God is not "out there," separate from all that is, in splendid isolation, "somewhere beyond the blue." God is rather right here, right now. In me. In you. In all that is. If so, Jesus was not making a claim for his own uniqueness, but saying something extraordinarily inclusive. God is in interbeing with all that is.

"Interbeing" is a word Vietnamese Buddhist monk, Thich Nhat Hanh, uses to refer to the idea that everything is inter-connected. Nothing exists in any separate way. I am the food I eat. The food I eat came from the soil.

The soil is made up of decaying vegetation. The process involves water and rain and clouds and wind and sun and moon. All is/are interconnected. You might say, "All things inter-are, therefore I inter-am."

This in not unlike the Christian idea of Panentheism. God is in all, all is in God. God is neither distant nor separate. "The kingdom (realm) of God is among you," Jesus said another time (Luke 17:21).

Two applications:

First, sometimes a friend will say something like, "I will believe in God if you prove to me God exists, but not until." But if God is in interbeing with all things, and all things are in interbeing with God, the question is wrongheaded. There could never be a proof for God. What is required is a different way of seeing.

Second, these ideas are wonderfully practical and profoundly nonviolent. That God is in all changes your relationship to non-human animals, to nature, to your enemies. For here we find God.

13. A Reluctance to Talk about God

I have become reluctant to talk about God. It has been a gradual thing, but looking back over the last decade or so, a very clear development. I also talk much less *to* God. My prayers are more often than not silent—not even words in my head. Prayers for others are most often holding an image of them in the great mystery. (That's for another reflection, another day.)

In the church's calendar, today is Trinity Sunday. Traditionally this is *the* day to talk about God in the way Christians have understood God. So today, I ponder my own reluctance to do so.

Lest anyone think, "Oh dear! Andy's become an atheist," Or else, "Oh good! Andy's become an atheist," that's not the case. It's just that my understanding about God is different. How so?

It's mostly to do with the *via negativa*. Long ago, theologians realized that God, in the very nature of what God is, is beyond any understanding or any human linguistic description of what God is. You cannot say what God is, but you can say what God is not. It was this way of thinking that prompted the mystic Meister Ekhart to speak of the Godhead beyond God. Even so, seriously religious folk often talk a great deal about God, as if they know about God, or that they truly do know God. I make no judgment about that. For me, I have been drawn to the *apophatic* (another way of saying *via negativa*). I seek enlightenment. I am becoming more reluctant to talk about what I do not know.

Still words are important. I am, after all, writing a reflection using words. Words are helpful if we use them carefully. Bottom line: words are symbols—signs pointing beyond themselves. In religion, folks often get caught up in words. Saying the right words. Judging those who use the wrong words. Thinking that the words are literally true. This causes all kinds of problems. As it is Trinity (and just happens to be Father's Day), I will mention the traditional use of Father to denote God. Such can be a useful denotation just as long as we remember that it is a symbol. Language about God has been termed analogous. God is a bit like this, but God is not this, for God is always beyond what we can say or think. Take Father language literally and we have masculinity built into what God is. Males bear a resemblance to God. Females do not. Males can represent God in a way that females cannot. Hence the patriarchy of traditional religions. That is one of the reasons why in the Lindisfarne Community we refer to God as Father-Mother. We have tried to remove sexism from our liturgies. But here's the thing: God is no more literally a mother than she is a father. Words are symbols. It's a bit like this, but not literally this.

This is true also of the primary way Christians have referred to God: Holy Trinity, Father, Son, and Holy Spirit, or as we say in Lindisfarne, Father-Mother, Child, and Holy Spirit. This is deeply symbolic.

So, what does the symbol of Holy Trinity mean? I am tempted to end here. For Trinity is mystery, if it is anything at all. Trinity is also none-sense. In logic it simply cannot be. Three persons who are not three but one, yet cannot be confused. Every attempt at explanation fails. It makes no sense. It's like trying to square the circle. Perhaps, that is the point. Whatever God is, is beyond any sense you might make of her. What is the symbol of Trinity? That God is ultimately mystery.

The symbol also speaks of relationality. Whatever God is, she is not aloof, alone, separate, unconcerned, disconnected, unempathic. The heart of God is relationship of love. There is nothing more profound than loving relationship, nothing more mysterious. Here I do end.

EIGHT

EPISTEMOLOGY, LANGUAGE, AND FAITH

1. What Is Truth?

In the Lindisfarne Community, one of our sayings is that "all truth is God's truth." A friend asked me, "So you think there is such a thing as truth?" It set me wondering. My answer is that, yes, I do believe that there is truth—I would even want to capitalize it as Truth, in the sense of "ultimate truth." Without a belief in truth, I am not sure what education, or indeed, the spiritual quest would be about. Further, I believe with Plato, that truth is fully knowable, but not fully known. The Christian neo-Platonists of the first few centuries spoke of the ultimate realties of "goodness, truth, and beauty." There can be no ultimate explanation of why these are ultimate reality—that is a matter of faith. Faith affords us the courage to live as if these were true.

Yet, the question arises: what is truth? Let us suppose that ultimate Truth (capitalized) we might call the "logos"; and that contingent truth (not capitalized) we might call the "mythos." It is through mythos that we catch glimpses of logos. Pure logos is impossible to explain in human words and human categories, though logos can be experienced. In fact, it is the experience of logos that necessitates the attempt at explanation in human terms, in mythos. Human language tries its best to approximate to that which is experienced as logos. It only partially succeeds. It is why religious language is only ever partially helpful. It can never express or explain the inexplicable.

If, like the apostle Paul's mystical experience of the Spirit, you are "caught up to the third heaven," (2 Cor 12:2) how do you begin to explain that! Yet, the mythoi (the partial truths contained in metaphor, for that is all we have) are necessary as pointers, hints, and guideposts to help us along the way.

The great danger is that having glimpsed the logos we pretend that our mythos is an exact correspondence. At best it is a partial sight. In believing "we have the absolute truth" lies the road of intolerance, hatred and violence.

So all truth is God's truth. Do we truly know it? I suspect not.

2. The Knowledge of Good and Evil

The story of Adam and Eve in the garden is fascinating on many counts: fascinating in itself, and also fascinating in the way the story has been used. Christians have mostly read it through the lens of Paul (Romans 1-8), who uses the story to tell us that when Adam sinned by disobeying God, in some mysterious way all human beings were included in a "species solidarity." Paul also uses the story to tell us why women are inferior to men: the woman sinned first. Poor Eve fairs badly. In Paul's first interpretation, she is ignored: it is the man who sinned and in Christ it is the man who redeems. In his second interpretation the bad results are the woman's fault. Paul's motifs of woman as "ignored because inconsequential" or as "foolish temptress" have shaped Western views of women.

Yet, as I read the story of the garden, I tried to look at it without benefit of Paul's midrash. This is difficult to do, but I tried.

Here is a picture of innocent humanity who does not as yet have the knowledge of good and evil. Nakedness without shame is a sign of that. In the story, when knowledge comes, its first insight is to understand that nakedness is something of which to be ashamed. Fig leaf loincloths are the first essential fashion item! The linking of nakedness, shame, and the need to cover up has given us a very conflicted and distorted view of the human body in Western culture. Whether the myth explains our unease with our bodies, or whether it created the unease I do not know.

Why is the knowledge of good and evil such a problem?

For me, this is quite personal. As a professional ethicist, "the knowledge of good and evil" is my daily work. I spend my time making distinctions, trying to understand, working through problems of human life. So, here is my attempt at a response to the story.

The knowledge of good and evil is the ability to make distinctions between what is good and bad, right and wrong. Childhood innocence makes no such distinctions. It is the pre-rational world of innocent play under the watchful eye of kind parental protection. Yet, innocence lasts only a short time and soon parents give lessons in the knowledge of good and evil: "Don't touch that; it's hot and will burn you." "Share that toy with your sister; selfishness is bad." "Eat your carrots; don't eat that worm." By and large, this parental socialization (primary we tend to call it) is considered a good thing. It helps the little developing human make distinctions between help and harm; it is the beginnings of the moral life—what we ought and ought not to do to live a decent life.

Yet, in the story, this knowledge is a bad thing. It is suitable for God, but not for mortals. For human beings, this knowledge is death not life. In a sense, we know this. The business of living is fraught with difficulties and dangers. Nothing is simple. There are no easy or clear answers. The black and white world of childhood is overtaken by unending shades of grey.

In my introduction to ethics class, I spend the first few weeks deconstructing the simplicities students bring to college. I sometimes feel bad, as I strip them of any last vestiges of childhood innocence—break down, in order to build up. A few years ago, I had a young woman student speak with me after class. The student plaintively asked, "Professor, I have enjoyed the class so far, but when are you going to tell us the right answer?" I smiled, but felt for her plight. "You will have to work this out for yourself," I replied.

Like my student, the story of the garden contains a longing for lost innocence. Take away all this complexity! Make it simple! Make it easy! If only we were back before we knew this stuff!

To change the myth: the genie is out of the bottle. It can't be put back.

Yet, the tree of the knowledge of good and evil is good for food, it is a delight to the eyes, it does make one wise. Mother Eve knew that much. We now live in the tension between the delightful goodness of wisdom (*sophia*, *eros* perhaps) and death (*thanatos*). There is no going back. Enjoy the ride!

3. Ambiguity and Faith

In the letter to the Romans, Paul makes a hopeful confession of faith: "For I am convinced that neither death, nor life, nor angels, nor rulers, nor things present, nor things to come, nor powers, nor height, nor depth, nor anything else in all creation, will be able to separate us from the love of God in Christ Jesus our Lord" (Romans 8:38).

This is a confession about the fundamental, irreducible nature of the universe. For the early Christians, and many Christians since, there is one irreducible reality and that one reality is the love of God. Of course, to say that love is the one reality involves relationship, for love is always a subject in relationship to an object. The Christian understanding of Holy Trinity is the relationship of love, subject, predicate, and object: the Lover, the Beloved, and the Love between them, as Augustine has it.

This understanding of love in reciprocal relationship is a major problem with the neo-Platonism of Plotinus, and his conception of the universe as the One. If there is no differentiation in the One, then there is no love. The Holy Trinity provides such a loving differentiation. In Paul's understanding, because we, and all creation, are "in Christ" (Romans 8:1), then all are enfolded in the love of God. Nothing can separate us from love. "All shall be well," wrote mother Julian of Norwich (Beer, 1998, 44). How do we get to that hopeful confession?

To oversimplify, our understanding of the universe might be like an onion or a peach. Peel away every layer of the onion and you are left with nothing at all. Take away the flesh of the peach and you are left with something solid: the stone.

This is why critical study is a very risky business. It is possible that the more we study, the more we question, the more we debunk silly things, then we may be left with nothing at all. I suspect this is why fundamentalisms of all kinds tell their adherents not to study, not to think deeply, just to accept. Fundamentalisms are often carried along by the fear that they may be wrong. Study only those things that confirm your position or don't study at all. Was Paul's hopeful confession of the love of God like that?

To know anything is quite a complex affair, though we often pretend it is not. Some suggest that the only true knowledge is empirical knowledge. That is, knowledge is gained through experiment and verification. We know that all solid objects fall to the ground when dropped. How do we know? We observe again and again and again. We experiment and the conclusion is always the same. It is so sure we give it the status of knowledge.

Yet, the process of knowing is often more subtle. We know two plus two equals four. How do we know? For most of us, not because we have proved it to be so, but because we have been told by competent authorities. It is also pragmatically useful in everyday life. We can depend on two plus two always equaling four. It never equals five. With the knowledge of gravity and elementary math there is no ambiguity.

But there is a great deal of ambiguity when we approach the great metaphysical questions—questions about the nature of being. When we think about these first order questions (the really big questions) such as, "Is there a God?" or "What is the nature of the universe: good, bad or indifferent?" we are faced with the not provable. Can you prove that God exists? I do not think so, though many have tried. Could you prove that nothing can separate us from the love of God? To try a proof would be futile.

There is ambiguity because the evidence tells us different things. Evidence here does not serve us well in metaphysics. The world is very mixed in all of our experiences. Wonderful, joy-filled events happen. Terrible, agony-filled events happen. What does the evidence say? That nothing separates us from love? Sometimes yes, sometimes no. There are times when some people feel so overwhelmed with goodness that they could burst with joy. There are times when we feel so dejected that we are separated from love and goodness by an unbridgeable gulf. Which evidence would we accept as proof for the nature of all that is?

So, the hopeful confession that nothing can separate us from love is not one based on empirical knowledge. It is a first order faith claim. It is an existential leap in the dark. There can be no proof. It is arrived at more by intuition than evidence; more from a story-formed tradition than by experiment.

Yet, we need to exercise care here. It seems to me that we can make this kind of claim for only very few things. Fundamentalisms make this kind of claim for just about everything. "Simply accept this as true," however absurd the truth claim, and however contrary the evidence. Remember, "The world," the explorers were confidently told, "is flat." We ignore the evidence at our peril; we cannot cease to question.

Yet, for the big questions, the evidence is always mixed. No one clear answer can be reached. Here, we simply trust. Nothing can separate us from love. The evidence is mixed, but we trust it to be so and live as if it is so.

4. Water, Fire, Spirit

I have been mulling over the idea of "language games" suggested by philosopher Ludwig Wittgenstein. It is not altogether clear what he meant, and there have been many interpretations. In brief, a language game is the way language is used in a particular social context that gives sense to the users of the language in communicating their common experience. To those unschooled in any particular language game, the way language is used often makes little sense, if not nonsense.

Religious uses of language are particular language games. When you first read a religious text (or hear a conversation) from a tradition unfamiliar to you, it can be very difficult to understand. It is not what the words mean, but what the words mean in a particular context of mutual experience and understanding.

Early anthropologists worked this out in studying new cultures. It was necessary to "go native"—to immerse yourself in the new culture and shared experience before language begins to make sense.

Often, religious language gives us richness and mystery in its imagery.

> When you pass through the waters, I will be with you; and through the rivers, they shall not overwhelm you; when you walk through fire you shall not be burned, and the flame shall not consume you. (Isaiah 43:2)

> "I baptize you with water; but one who is more powerful than I is coming; I am not worthy to untie the thong of his sandals. He will baptize you with the Holy Spirit and fire." John the Baptizer. (Luke 3:16)

> Then Peter and John laid their hands on them, and they received the Holy Spirit. (Acts 8:17)

Water and fire are vivid images. In Isaiah, the promise is that though the floods of water come, God's people will not be overwhelmed; when fire ravages, God's people will not be burned. Clearly, water and fire are imaged as powerfully destructive elements that cause fear and from which we must be rescued.

Yet, John the Baptist promises that when the Christ appears, there will be a baptism in fire—an unquenchable fire! This baptism in fire was connected with both a baptism in water and the coming of the Spirit of God. So good was this to be that, later, the apostle made extra sure that the people of Samaria who had been baptized also experienced the coming of the Spirit.

New Testament scholar James Dunn makes the point that it is clear that the coming of the Spirit of God is something quite tangible, something felt, that could even be seen by others. Why? Because it was clear to the apostles who had, and who had not, received this extraordinary experience. Put simply, the coming of the Spirit of God to a person is not only something felt on the inside, but also has an outward, visible, physically embodied expression. Others can see it. Others know it to be the case or not.

The experience of God as Spirit is connected in the passages with material elements. Not only is the Spirit described by water, fire, and embodied in a bird, but is passed on from person-to-person through the experience of bathing in water and by the touch of the hands of the apostles. In other words, these are very sacramental passages. The visible and the invisible are closely connected. The worlds of the natural and supernatural are united in water, fire, in the presence of a simple bird, and through human touch.

I think this shows us the interconnectedness of all things. W.R. Inge (Dean of St. Paul's in London in the first part of the twentieth century) said:

> A mystery, for the ancients, is not something inexplicable; it is
> something revealed, truly though inadequately, in a lower medium.
> Earth is the shadow of heaven (1947, 75).

For me, this suggests that we can arrive at no definitive interpretation of religious language. Religious language contains a richness to be savored. Is the imagery of water good or bad, destructive or comforting? Is fire the very essence, the verve of life or is it fearfully destructive? How was Spirit embodied in the physical form of a dove? What does Spirit look like when it is given by human touch from one to another?

All of this I think is to be pondered. Let's take the language and meditate. Take the way of the Benedictine *lectio divina*. That is, to use language not as a source of things to know about, but as a way of divine knowledge; a growing into God as the Spirit does her work of slow change and transformation.

5. This I Believe

Yesterday, I gave a very brief talk to a gathering of the Protestant community at my college. The talk was in a series called: "This I believe." Preparing what I would say proved to be an interesting experience. It raised a number of questions: Actually, what do I believe? What is belief? Are my beliefs justified? Does it matter? I had only a couple of minutes to say it, so I couldn't say much. I decided that I would try to work out what my core beliefs are. When I did, I realized that a few words cropped up a number of times and seem important to me. I have italicized them.

This is what I said (with a few brief comments on each in the telling):

> Religion is a human attempt to make sense of the experience of *transcendence*.
>
> All religions, at their best, bear witness to the way of *love*, compassion and nonviolence.
>
> GGod is *love*, and wherever we find *love*, there we find God.
>
> Jesus—in his life *practice*, teaching and in the way he died—is an exemplar of the way of *love*.
>
> Orthopraxy (right *practice*) is more important than orthodoxy (right belief).
>
> Our *practice* we can become more *loving* and so change the world for the better.

So! An interesting experience. Try it for yourself!

6. Chasing after the Wind

I have often returned to the ancient Jewish wisdom book of Ecclesiastes. The book purports to be written by the great king Solomon, but for a long time scholars have thought the book merely uses Solomon's name. Nonetheless, it is a helpful element of the Jewish wisdom tradition.

Its content is quite simple—and quite disturbing. The great king, being very wealthy and very wise, has tried everything under the sun to find some meaning in life. Nothing has been denied him. His answer? Everything is meaningless. It is like chasing after the wind. You will never catch the wind so why bother? Life is quite literally a waste of time. (There are a few brighter passages in the book, like the poem about everything having its own time, but not much beyond that). I have found the book depressing, but also inspiring.

I think "the Teacher" (as the king calls himself) says things I have felt often. Life has a drudgery about it—the daily round of getting up, going to work, coming home, most days of most weeks of the year. The drudgery is interspersed with brighter weekends and occasional vacations. Holidays promise hope, but often don't deliver. Meaningless. According to the Teacher we tend to surround ourselves with pleasures that act like a drug that soon wears off.

Is the Teacher right?

It depends on the way you look at life. The great mystical traditions tell us that there is a deeper way of looking. A looking into rather than a looking at. It is a seeking the *Dao*, a way that is always there, yet always hidden. The *Dao* does not reveal itself to the casual observer, but to the careful seeker. Glimpses of the *Dao* dispel the gloominess of the Teacher.

Philosopher Irving Singer wrote a trilogy called "Meaning in Life." He suggested that though a "meaning *of* life" is impossible to find, everyone can find "meaning *in* life." The trilogy is worth a look if you have time. Singer's point, that I want to emphasize, is that meaning can be found in the ordinary lives we lead. Meaning is found in the daily round of "work, rest, and play" (as the old British Mars Bar ads have it).

Meaning is found in the Way that permeates all things. Look for it yourself. It will likely have something to do with value, and with love and with the Spirit.

7. To Work or Not to Work

When the New Year turned in 1517, few would guess that Martin Luther would cause a revolution in thought and practice in European Christendom. On October 31, 1517 Luther posted his 95 Theses to the door of the Castle Church in Wittenburg. This was the formal beginning of the Protestant Reformation—some would even say the beginning of modernity, as the hegemonic grip of the church was challenged for the first time in several hundred years.

Luther's theological genius was in bringing to light a long forgotten idea—the idea of grace. Working for salvation would not, well, work. Salvation was about the action of God, not human striving. This remains a very important idea. In the spiritual life mere striving produces nothing of much value. Luther's emphasis is echoed in Daoism in the concept of Wu Wei—action through non-action—and the Buddhist practice of stillness. Of course, the ideas are not the same, but they share the same emphasis that mere activity is ineffectual. Luther's grace, Laozi's Wu Wei, and the Buddah's stillness are necessary corrections to the incessant activity and busyness of contemporary life.

But there is always another story to tell. A sad side effect of Luther's great insight was a religion that said that nothing at all was needed by the seeker—no effort required at all. One expression in the following centuries was revivalism, which promised the hearer that all is accomplished, simply and easily by "walking to the altar," "raising a hand," or "signing a card." I am not doubting for a minute the sincerity of folk who respond that way. In time past I was one of them and the moment is often deeply and intensely spiritual, and can be transformative. The problem is the packaging. The respondent is told that having walked forward everything is now changed. All is different. Nothing more needs to be done. Things are changed for a day or two, but the respondent soon realizes that nothing much has changed. Before too long the seeker needs to walk forward again, when all will be fixed once and for all. Again. For too many people the process leaves mere guilt, "There must be something wrong with me."

The truth is that the spiritual life is grace and work, stillness and practice, being and doing.

In Ancient Chinese philosophy, the twin ideas were expressed as Wu Wei and Gongfu. Wu Wei is action through no action. Gongfu is skill developed though long and consistent practice. Wu Wei is no effort. Gongfu is great effort. Which is the right path? Both. Take the way of Wu Wei and you will find a life of Gongfu. Walk the path of Gongfu and you will be led to Wu Wei.

I finish this reflection as I wait for folks to come to our New Year's Eve party. We welcome the New Year with pundits on all sides predicting gloom. Some seriously fear the world's end. Economists fear the collapse of the European Union, and global economic collapse (again). Many fear Iran's blustering about oil and nuclear power.

Just like the turn from 1516 to 1517, who knows what the year will bring. Perhaps another Luther may arise to bring a paradigm change to the way we think. Likely not.

For me, I am looking forward to developing my Gongfu, deepening my practice through consistent hard work, while realizing that all I do is as nothing, content to rest in Wu Wei, to enjoy Grace upholding me through all.

NINE

RELIGION AND SPIRITUALITY

1. True Religion, Karma, and the Deeper Magic

My thoughts today arise from the prophet Isaiah, who issues a prophetic and scathing attack on religion. He considers the trappings of religion as nothing before God. What were the religious practices of his time? Sacrifices, burnt offerings, the shedding of the blood of animals, incense, solemn assemblies, various religious festivals, and prayers. According to the prophet, God does not delight in these things, but finds them an abomination. They are unendurable, they are a burden to God, and God will not listen to those who practice them! This is a far-reaching critique.

For us, I think we might get out of the criticism by saying something to the effect, "Well, that was then. It doesn't refer to us. We don't sacrifice animals." In other words, a neat "get out of jail free" card! But I am not happy with that at all. It still niggles me.

What if the prophet were here today and made the same criticism? Perhaps, he did not mean a particular kind of religion, but any kind of religion. What if all religion is futile? Instead of sacrifices, the prophet might say "your church services, your daily devotions, your prayers." It might be that God, the Ultimately Real, doesn't need any of our religious practices, in any of our traditions. In fact, one understanding of God holds that for God to be God, God has need of nothing. To need something is a characteristic of imperfection not perfection. The ultimately perfect needs nothing. So, it might be the case that even our very best religion and worship and practice is a futility—if we think that God needs us to do it.

Does this mean, then, that we should abandon all religious practices? I think not. Spiritual practice, prayer, and ritual all are for our sake not God's sake. Spiritual practice (at its best) is what shapes us and helps make us more balanced.

I have written a book chapter entitled, "Spiritual Practice as a Foundation for Peacemaking." In researching to write the chapter, I found out that most people, throughout history, who have been committed to peacemaking or to social justice were rooted in a spiritual practice. I concluded that it is spiritual practice that sustains folks in their work for peace and social justice. So yes, I think we cannot live as well as we might without religious practice.

Yet, listen to the prophet's critique. When religion is an end in itself, when it turns only inward, when there is no outworking of it, then it becomes an abomination.

Listen to what is needed: cease to do evil, do good, seek justice, rescue the oppressed, defend the orphan, plead for the widow. In other words, true religion has a very strong ethical component. And here we need to rescue ethics from being merely about "sexual sins." Ethics is about the way we live our lives. It is about goodness and social justice. If religion does not lead us there, then it is truly futile. "You say you have faith," said St. James, "then show me your faith by your works" (James 2:18). He was restating the words of the prophet in a different context.

The next thing that struck me from the prophet Isaiah is the idea of karma. "If you are willing and obedient, you shall eat the good of the land" (Isaiah 1:19). The idea of karma is in simple terms, "what goes around comes around." What you do has a consequence. Every cause has a related effect and every effect has a related cause. You might say, "You get what you deserve." Though the word karma comes to us from the Eastern tradition, it is there deeply rooted in our Western understanding. It is the root idea of responsibility. We each must take responsibility for our actions because actions always have consequences.

Karma is found everywhere. Take preventative medicine. We now know that if we do certain things to our bodies, the effect will be for good or ill. If we eat sensibly, exercise regularly, avoid the over-use of drugs of various kinds, then we can expect to be fairly healthy. If we overeat, abuse alcohol, never exercise, smoke cigarettes, then we can expect negative consequences in our bodies. Those bits of conventional wisdom are quite obvious. Less obvious, but equally true, is that if we are constantly verbally abusive to people, then we will find that people become verbally abusive to us. If we show kindness, then kindness will be shown to us. (There are exceptions to this rule, but generally it seems to hold true.) It is a useful rule to keep before our minds. What kind of karma am I producing today?

I had another thought. It is in the words of C.S. Lewis in *The Chronicles of Narnia*, about a "deep magic" (2004, 172). I think the revelation of God in Jesus is to say that even though there is such a law as karma, that actions have consequences, there is such a thing as grace. Grace is a deep magic. I would go so far as to say that grace trumps karma. By this I mean that if God acted toward me as karma dictates, then I would be in a sorry mess. I am just not that good. Thankfully, Jesus shows me that I do not get what I deserve. In his dying moments Jesus said, "Abba Amma, forgive them. They do not know what they are doing." Karma dictates that they get what they deserve. They are executing as a criminal an innocent man. That is bad karma if ever there was. They deserve to suffer the consequences. Yet, grace says, "forgive." Grace trumps karma. Thank God for the deeper magic!

2. A Finger Pointing at the Moon

Recently, I came across someone who was very angry at religion. I do not know the details or the reason for his anger. But it was intense and heartfelt. He said he wants nothing more to do with religion of any form. Like many folks, this young man was seeking truth and had looked to religion to provide it. Religion had failed him. Religion had promised much, yet failed to deliver. It is not an uncommon experience.

Perhaps we expect too much from religion. After all, religion is merely a sign pointing away from itself toward a greater reality. Our trouble arises when we mistake the sign for the thing signified.

Many may find this beautiful little Zen story helpful:

> The nun Wu Jincang asked the Sixth Patriarch Huineng, "I have studied the Mahaparinirvana sutra for many years, yet there are many areas I do not quite understand. Please enlighten me."

> The patriarch responded, "I am illiterate. Please read out the characters to me and perhaps I will be able to explain the meaning."

Said the nun, "You cannot even recognize the characters. How are you able then to understand the meaning?"

"Truth has nothing to do with words. Truth can be likened to the bright moon in the sky. Words, in this case, can be likened to a finger. The finger can point to the moon's location. However, the finger is not the moon. To look at the moon, it is necessary to gaze beyond the finger, right?"

Religion, like words, is merely a finger. If I could talk to my young friend I would sympathize with him and tell him I have often shared his disappointment with religion. Yet, religion isn't "it." Religion will always disappoint if we mistake it for Reality. It doesn't help that religion often makes a claim to be truth. It is an arrogant claim that has caused a great deal of suffering.

The mystics have told us that once we know Reality we can dispense with the sign. I long for that day. As it is, I suspect most of us still need the sign to point us in the right direction. But let's keep the sign in its place!

3. The Ambiguity of Religious Passion

This week, I read an account from the United Kingdom of a taiji group being told they could no longer practice on church premises. The teacher of the taiji group practiced with patients in a local hospital as part of their wellness program. After one of her clients in the hospital read the story in the local newspaper, he refused to have any more taiji therapy, believing it to be bad.

The minister of the church said, "Our understanding is that the basis of taiji is an Eastern religion, and from the church's point of view, that isn't something that we want to be involved in."

It is often the case that reasonable, highly religious people, full of religious zeal persecute others who follow a different way. In the New Testament, Saul of Tarsus was one such man. It says:

Meanwhile Saul, still breathing threats and murder against the disciples of the Lord, went to the high priest and asked him for letters to the synagogues at Damascus, so that if he found any

who belonged to the Way, men or women, he might bring them
bound to Jerusalem. (Acts 9:1-18)

Persecution is a strange word—it is not a part of our everyday language.
It means to be hostile to someone, to subject someone to ill treatment.
Usually it is because of their religious or political beliefs, or because they
happen to belong to the "wrong" race or ethnicity. It is often out of pure
spite, prejudice or hatred. Yet, at times because the one persecuting seeks
the best for the other. Their beliefs or lifestyle are considered so wrong that
they must suffer hostility in order to change their ways. In the long run, the
persecution is for the person's own good. So the script reads!

My thoughts turn to the ambiguity of religious passion. In the world
in which we live, I think it is hard to be a person of faith. Not because
believing is difficult to do per se (though belief has its issues now as it has
always), but because the practitioners of religion in the contemporary world
are so often violent, so often persecutors of others. Their religious passion
leads them to do harm—harm now that good may come in the future. I
do not want to pick on any one religion. In this regard, all religions are the
same: all have their religious zealots. It seems the world has more of them
now than at any time. If you thought the wars of religion ended with the
Peace of Westphalia in 1648 after the Thirty Years War, think again. Take
a look at what is happening in Nigeria and a score of other sub-Saharan
African nations. Listen to the rhetoric of the "clash of civilizations"—Islam
against Christian Western democracy. Even in Tibet, despite the pleas of the
Dalai Lama, passionate Buddhists have taken up arms. Think, too, of the
internecine religious struggles in Northern Ireland (where, thankfully, we
are beginning to see some positive change). And finally, since the death of
Ghandi and Indian partition, Muslims and Hindus have been continually
hostile to one another. It is often because of religious passion. They even
threaten each other with nuclear weaponry. Truly, religious passion has no
bounds!

Like religion itself, religious passion can be very good or very bad. It
can also be very irrelevant (in terms of effect on others) when religious
passion is a purely private affair, with no social outworking.

Religious passion is ambiguous. Without religious passion, would we
have seen the end of the slave trade? Without religious passion, would
Martin Luther King Jr. have pressed for integration? Without religious
passion, would we have seen the advancement of medical care, the care for
the poor?

Saul of Tarsus in the New Testament is just one example, on a small scale, of where religious passion often leads. Threats, murder, seeking the imprisonment of the offender. Can a leopard change its spots? Can the religiously inspired hurter become a religiously inspired lover?

I think so. Saul is one example to give us hope. His is, perhaps, not the best example, but a good one. From a persecutor of others, he becomes, in the words of F.F. Bruce "the apostle of the free spirit" (2000). His passion turned from persecution to love, from law to grace, from religious conformity to the freedom of the spirit. He worked hard at breaking down religious and ethnic differences. He opened the way for women to lead in the communities he created. In a limited way, he presented a new way of looking at slavery—not yet a liberationist, but saw all as slaves of Christ. Of course, we can point to areas where Paul still adopted the old patterns. I suspect he would still have hostility to those he perceived as sexually aberrant. Yet, by and large, the change is amazing, the leopard changed its spots (or at least, quite a few of them).

Back to my story of the taiji group being asked to leave a church. I am sobered to think that thirty years ago I would have agreed with the minister.

What then can we say about religious passion? Should we avoid it like the plague, or embrace it in the hope that some good will come. I am tempted, to be brutally honest, to opt for the former. I have seen so much damage caused by religious passion. Aristotelian balance is quite appealing to me! Yet, here is an idea: religious passion can be a good thing when it is grounded in the kind of love that seeks only the well-being of the other, seeks to do no harm and respects the personal integrity and autonomy of everyone. It needs to be rooted in nonviolence, both as an internal discipline and an outer practice. Without this, religious passion quickly becomes destructive and a travesty of love. Even when love is defined as, "to seek the neighbor's good," without a commitment to nonviolence, to no harm, "the neighbor's good" can become an excuse to harm. "I torture you now, so you will go to heaven later," says the Inquisitor.

My final thought is this. In the story of Saul the persecutor, in a vision the Christ says to him, "Saul, Saul, why are you persecuting me?" (Acts 26:14). The Christ is always the one persecuted, never the one persecuting. Wherever harm is done, the Christ is the one harmed, incarnate in the other. My desire is to be found as a person of nonviolence, of love, and not to be confronted as a persecutor of others.

4. Religion or Spirituality Redux?

A difference between spirituality and religion expresses a deep intuition. Whatever spirituality is, it is a good thing—something we ought to embrace as it speaks to us of something foundational about being human (and I suspect being animal). But religion . . . religion is a very mixed bag! Dabble in religion and you may well get your fingers burned! My friend is happy to be associated with spirituality, but not with religion. I have some sympathy with my friend.

However, to make this distinction is quite tricky. In many contexts the words religion and spirituality are used interchangeably. A religious tradition is a spiritual tradition. A religious experience is a spiritual experience. In usage the words are often the same. So, William James' classic, *The Varieties of Religious Experience* is a book about spirituality. When we make a distinction, then, it is helpful to say, "When I say religion I mean this . . . and when I say spirituality I mean this . . ." It will help in communicating more clearly what you mean.

I suspect that my friend is saying something like:

> This deeply important aspect of being human—let's call it *p*—has very helpful and beneficial elements for well-being and wholeness. I identify with those. But aspect *p* also has elements that are unhelpful and work against human thriving and wholeness. I do not identify with those.

Human aspect *p*—religion and/or spirituality—is that human grasping for, and seeking to understand and give meaning to, the experience of transcendence, Freud's "oceanic feeling."

Religion is both friend and enemy of spirituality.

As friend, religion provides a framework in which spirituality can grow and blossom. It gives spirituality shape in texts to ponder and from which to gain wisdom. It provides a living tradition with a sense of belonging and community and accountability and order. Religion gives spirituality its rituals and practices—essential for healthy development. Anyone claiming to be spiritual who finds no use for text, tradition, ritual, and practice deceives themselves.

Yet, when religion ossifies, it becomes the enemy of spirituality. Then religion, rather than being the finger that points to the moon becomes merely a finger pointing—and usually pointing in an accusing way at someone else. It is a grave danger to mistake religion for spirituality. People fight each other over religion, but not spirituality. There is such a thing as religious hatred, but not spiritual hatred. There is religious intolerance, but not spiritual intolerance.

Finally to separate religion and spirituality is impossible. As *yin* and *yang*, spirituality and religion need each other, are contained in each other, mirror each other and balance each other. Spirituality needs the vehicle of religious text, tradition and ritual for healthy growth. But when religious text, tradition and ritual lose the core of deep and lively spirituality, then religion becomes mere husk. A dry and hardened husk with no kernel may be—perhaps ought to be—discarded without worry or grief.

5. What's in a Name?

What's in a name? that which we call a rose
By any other name would smell as sweet
　　　　—Juliet in William Shakespeare's *Romeo and Juliet*

I have been struck many times of the confluence of the really important ideas in all the world's great traditions. If something is very important, it seems the idea arises in different places over time in different cultural guise.

This is so clearly with ethics. The "golden rule"—do to others what you would have them do to you—is everywhere present as a foundational, and practical, way of living. Love, too, as compassion, kindness, *ahimsa* (no harm), or benevolence is a common theme. Whatever it is called, a rose by any other name would smell as sweet. It is not the words we use about the rose, but the experience we have of the rose that counts. I think this is much the position that philosopher of religion John Hick suggests. There is the "Ultimately Real," known only by experience, that defies categories. Our wordy attempts are fine, just so long as we realize that the Real is beyond our attempts at explanation. That is why we have so many different explanations of the Real in the different traditions.

At this point the cry usually arises, "Relativism! If all is relative, then nothing is absolute and we can know nothing about anything with any certainty!"

This is partly true. For myself, I have abandoned any search for absolute knowledge. But that is not the only game in the playground. I prefer to play a pluralist game. If absolutism says, "We have the truth and you don't!" and relativism proclaims "There is no such thing as truth!" pluralism says, "Let's see if by dialogue we can all approach the Truth!" When plural positions make contact, though the words differ, the rose smells the same, if you have a nose for it. I am convinced (as convinced as a pluralist can be) that this is the case in ethics.

It is true also in other areas. In the Lindisfarne Community, we have a number of good bloggers. In the blog *Celtic Odyssey* my good friend, and member of our community, Jack draws attention to "centering prayer" (http://odysseusjak.blogspot.com/). This is a form of contemplative inner silence, a "resting in God." In this iteration it was the genius of Fr. Thomas Keating from the 1960s onward, who, through his writings, gave this practice to the world. Of course, Keating was only one among many and there were other bright lights, notably Thomas Merton and Basil Pennington, who discovered the same.

Perhaps, I should more correctly have said "rediscovered," for the practice of inner silence is an ancient one shared by all the great spiritual traditions of the world. It has gone by the names "meditation," "contemplation," "silence," "stillness," and in practice has sitting, and standing and walking, and moving forms. It has Hindu, Buddhist, Christian, Jewish, Islamic, Daoist, and secular forms.

There are different explanations of what goes on psychologically, or metaphysically, or physiologically during meditation. My suspicion is that all the traditions have discovered the same thing. There is a way to the Ultimately Real and the Way feels much the same. It's only a suspicion based on smelling the rose in different traditions. I confess to never having tried kabalistic meditation, or sufi dance, or tantric yoga. I have experienced Buddhist meditation (*zazen* sitting and walking), Doaist meditation (*qigong, taiji*) and Christian contemplation and centering prayer. Tentative conclusion? Smells like a rose to me.

6. Without Buddha, I Could Not Be a Christian

A few weeks ago, on our annual retreat, Fr. Scott, in his talk on Buddhist monasticism, mentioned Paul Knitter's book, *Without Buddha I Could Not Be a Christian* (2009). What an intriguing title! With the wonders of technology I had the book on its way before Scott reached his next point.

Without Buddha became my beach reading last week when we camped at the ocean (along with *The Book of Chuang Tzu* (1996), and an oral history of the Dambuster's Raid in 1942.)

Knitter's book is very heartening. For me, it is one of those books that has such resonance that on page after page I was mentally saying, "Yes! I feel that too. Yes! I understand it that way!"

Now a professor at Union Seminary in New York—he came out of retirement to take the job—Paul Knitter was a Roman Catholic priest from 1966 to 1975. He left the priesthood, became a theology teacher and peace activist, married and had a family. In the early 1980s, he began to study Buddhism. Through a gradual process, it became his practice. In 2008, he became a card-carrying Buddhist by taking his Bodhisattva Vows. In his words, "In 1939 I was baptized. In 2008 I took refuge." He identifies himself now a "Buddhist Christian," something he realizes he has been for some decades. (Fr. Scott in the Lindisfarne Community also embodies this.)

In his journey, Paul Knitter exemplifies an understanding dear to my heart, and which we try to practice in the Lindisfarne Community, that all truth is God's truth. What is helpful about this book is the way Paul examines his Christian understanding (and his worries about some of it), makes a journey into Buddhism, learns from it, and passes back to his Christian understanding. The two religions have much in common. There are disagreements—at times substantial ones—which he doesn't merely brush under the carpet, but lives with the tension. A living synthesis of Buddhism and Christianity is not neat and tidy. But it is profoundly creative.

In *Without Buddha* there is much about mysticism, much about practice, much about silence, much about mindfulness, much about symbol and myth, much about "being peace," much about what God might be and who Jesus is. It is a very honest book and Knitter wears his doubts about traditional Christian teachings on his sleeve. He voices worries that I suspect many people have, but can't quite bring themselves to admit it. That in itself is quite helpful. I learned a great deal.

Here's a couple of gems. On love:

> To love is to move out of self, to empty self, and connect with others. Love is this emptying, connecting energy that in its power originates new connections and new life.

On the Holy Trinity:

> God's very being, or existing, or identity consists of relating, or inter-existing, or InterBeing . . . It's the most basic, and the simplest, thing we can say about ourselves and about God: we exist through relationships of knowing and loving and giving because that's how God exists.

I am not suggesting that we all become Buddhist Christians, as Paul Knitter has. I am saying that we continue to seek truth, be fearlessly honest with what we find, practice courageously, and follow the Wild Goose wherever she leads.

TEN

OTHER REFLECTIONS

1. The Feast of St. Aelred

Today, January 12, is the feast day of St. Aelred of Hexham, Abbot of Rievaulx. Aelred is close to my heart. His birthplace is the birthplace of the Lindisfarne Community. The community had tentative beginnings in Hexham, Northumberland, in in the home of our good friends, Stuart and Jenny Raistrick. Aelred's heart is our heart—to be friends of God and friends to each other—to be *Celi Dei*. "Friends of God" was used of the early Irish and English saints, of Celtic spiritual renewal and of the later English mystics (*The Cloud of Unknowing*, 2002, etc.). In Lindisfarne we seek to emulate that simple idea. This is the collect for St. Aelred's day:

> Almighty God,
> who endowed Aelred the abbot
> with the gift of Christian friendship
> and the wisdom to lead others in the way of holiness;
> grant to your people that same spirit of mutual affection
> so that, in loving one another,
> we may know the love of Christ
> and rejoice in the eternal possession
> of your supreme goodness;
> through Jesus Christ your Son our Savior,
> who is alive and reigns with you,
> in the unity of the Holy Spirit,
> one God, now and forever.

One of Aelred's prayers reads:

> O Good Jesus, let your voice sound in my ears so that my heart
> and mind and inmost soul may learn of your love, and the very
> depths of my heart be joined to you who are my greatest delight
> and joy. What is the love I desire, O my God? What is this
> wonderful delight in my soul? May I call love the heart's own
> sense of taste since it enables us to feel your sweetness? May we
> call love the eye through which we can see that you are good?
> When we love, O God, we join ourselves to you because you are
> love. Love is your rich banquet which deeply satisfies us when
> we eat at your table and drink deeply from you. In your love
> we can forget ourselves and lose ourselves only to find ourselves
> in you. I beg you, Savior Jesus, let even a touch of this delight
> penetrate my soul. It is my heart's desire to seek you day by day
> by loving you.

> In love: forget ourselves, lose ourselves, and find ourselves.

That is the heart of the mystical experience. That experience is close to
all of us. It is there in the wonder and beauty of creation. It is there in the
love and affection for children. It is there in the lovers' embrace. It is there
between close friends. The first book Jane and I wrote together was called
The Kiss of Intimacy (1995). It was a book about the mystical experience
available to all of us. Our third book was *Prophetic Lifestyle and the Celtic
Way* (1997), in which we were moving toward these things: finding God in
the ordinary things of life.

What is needed for God to be made real in the ordinary? Awareness:
openness to the possibility that we may find God in all things; awareness
that enlightenment is not some far off event, but the coming of the light
of God today.

2. Unity, Strife, and Conformity

Psalm 133 is a sweet little poem that celebrates unity. It is very nice when we
see a family together with no strife, bitterness, or divisions. That "family"
may be the traditional family of parents and children and others who are

part of the household, but by analogy could be any grouping of people: a church, a nation, the whole "family of humanity."

Unity is good and pleasant. By inference, disunity—strife, conflict, bitterness—is bad and unpleasant. For ease, I will refer to the couplet as unity and strife. In a marked way, this little couplet summarizes the deep psychological drives of humanity. Freud called them *eros* and *thanatos*—the life and death instincts. We know them pulling away at each other in the fabric of our own psyche. We see human history as the great aspiration for unity, and the lived reality of strife.

Instances of strife are extremely easy to find. Over the last couple of weeks, a few have occupied more than their share of my thinking. The Anglican Communion is threatening to tear itself apart because one of its dioceses consecrated a gay bishop. Aspirations for unity seem a long way away there. Here in the United States, the upcoming elections are gaining momentum, as are the invectives of the parties one for the other. What would good and pleasant unity look like in American political culture? Then there has been the brief but destructive war between Russia and Georgia, with echoes of cold war rhetoric, as the West condemns Russia and Russia answers back in kind. Just this week, large parts of the Christian church are raging against each other because of the strange goings on of a Pentecostal revivalist in Florida. The revivalist had been gathering a worldwide following of unprecedented size, with massive exposure on television and the Internet. Now he has resigned in disgrace and the knives are out. Unity amongst Christians? The impossible dream! Unity in any area of life seems whimsical. Yet, when we see it, it is truly good and pleasant.

Two thoughts about unity. First, unity is not conformity. Conformity is often mistaken for unity. Conformity has the feeling of "being forced to" about it. Unity is the harmony of diverse members. Unity is the enjoyment and acceptance of the beauty of differences. Unity is the refusal of violence in actions, speech and thoughts. Unity is love enacted.

Second, unity is modeled in our notion of the Holy Trinity. Here we have trinity in unity; unity in trinity. Let me suggest it this way: unity in community. The historic debates of the church about the Trinity are interesting and complex. At times, they seem obtuse in the extreme. Yet, the whole debate was intended to ensure that the Christian orthodox view would be that the three persons of the godhead (and how they argued bout the term person!) were three and, therefore, distinct, yet at the same time were one. The conclusion was that the Ultimately Real (to use John Hick's term) was the reality of unity in community. There is the model for humanity, created in the image of this ultimately real. Different, yet together. Neither conformity nor strife.

So, I am going to take an Aristotelian twist and say that rather than a couplet, "unity and strife," it might help to think of a golden mean with unity as the virtue. The deficiency of unity is strife; the excess of unity is conformity. Neither strife nor conformity is our aspiration, but unity that loves the other as other and rejoices in the difference. How good and pleasant would that be!

3. Contemplating the Beautiful

Whatever is true,
Whatever is honorable,
Whatever is just,
Whatever is pure
Whatever is pleasing,
Whatever is commendable,
If there is any excellence,
And if there is anything worthy of praise,
Think about these things.—St. Paul (Phil. 4:8)

It seems to me that at the heart of theology, philosophy, spirituality, and religion is the idea of a life well lived. In different ways, each discipline tries to find an answer to that perennial human search. What does a well-lived life look like? What would make us decent human beings?

Just over 100 years ago, British philosopher G.E. Moore, in his *Principia Ethica*, reached his conclusion about the life well lived (1903). It consisted of two things: friendship and contemplation of the beautiful. These, for Moore, were what made life worth living. His was not a novel suggestion. I think you can find very similar thoughts in Plato and Aristotle. Nonetheless, I find Moore's conclusion very appealing.

Moore's idea is subject to the criticism that both friendship and contemplation of beauty are luxuries for those who already have their basic human needs met. If you are poor and have no food or decent shelter, then what need of friendship and beauty? So goes the argument. However, I could make the argument—but not here—that for all human beings, in whatever physical condition, friendship and beauty are what make life tolerable.

Friendship is close to my heart, but it is the contemplation of beauty I want to think about today. It is in that poetic passage of St. Paul where he urges us to think about beauty—the true, honorable, just, pure, pleasing, commendable, excellent, and worthy of praise. These things are nourishment for the human spirit (Philippians 4:8). Deprived of beauty, we wither and die.

Paul's little poem leads to expansive ideas of beauty and what it might mean to think about beauty. Every conceivable thing that is true, honorable, just, pure, pleasing, commendable, excellent and worthy of praise is beautiful. Physical objects, works of art, nature, people, music, activities, non-human animals, crafts, and engineering—the list goes on. Beauty is expansive, if we have eyes to see.

Thinking too is expansive. It is not merely the rationality of the calculation. In the Post-Enlightenment world, we have tended to separate thought from feeling in a severe way. If one is feeling, then one is not thinking. Yet, surely to think involves both reasoning and feeling. Reasons and emotions are all part of the complexity of thinking. This is important when we consider contemplation of the beautiful. It is not a calculating analysis of a sunset or thinking about the meaning of a walk in the woods. To think about—to contemplate—the purely sensual delight of walking in the woods is to be there, to experience, to feel, to be swallowed, to be overwhelmed. That is to contemplate beauty. To think about the beauty of music is not to analyze the notes, the melody, the rhythm, the harmony (though for some folk that is contemplation), it is to feel the music, to be taken up by it, to be absorbed in it. That feeds the soul.

I do not think that Moore has the last word on a life well lived. But I think he was on to something. So was St. Paul.

4. A Delightful Little Gem

I have been enjoying a delightful little book by the stoic philosopher Epictetus. The book is the *Enchiridion*, or the *Manual* (2008). It is a little guidebook for living. Epictetus was one of a handful of "pagan" writers who were approved reading in the early Christian church. Origen loved him and the *Manual* became an important resource for many monastic communities in the medieval period. It consists of fifty-three very short chapters full of wisdom. Here's one little snippet from chapter five:

It is not events that disturb people, it is their judgments concerning them.

Another from chapter nine:

Sickness is a problem for the body, not the mind—unless the mind decides that it is a problem.

The *Enchiridion* is available in many editions. Find a copy and enjoy!

5. Three Unrelated Things to Ponder

A Slave Girl . . . Reading Against the Grain

> One day, as we were going to the place of prayer, we met a slave girl who had a spirit of divination and brought her owners a great deal of money by fortune-telling. While she followed Paul and us, she would cry out, "These men are slaves of the Most High God, who proclaim to you a way of salvation." She kept doing this for many days. But Paul, very much annoyed, turned and said to the spirit, "I order you in the name of Jesus Christ to come out of her." And it came out that very hour. But when her owners saw that their hope of making money was gone, they seized Paul and Silas and dragged them into the marketplace before the authorities. (Acts 16)

Over the years, I have tried to learn from Jane and from the feminist theologians who read the scriptures against the grain. To read against the grain is to find the women in the text (or the absence of women) and to ask questions of the text in the light of the women in or outside the text. Jane is very creative, and most of the readings against the grain that she shares with the Lindisfarne Community are her own. I find them very insightful and I have tried to learn from her. I am not very good at it, and I am often surprised when Jane brings her readings of the text. Today I have tried, and to read against the grain is to find in the Acts passage a slave girl.

As with so many of the women in the scriptures, she is unnamed. To be unnamed is to be inconsequential, of no account. She is a mere prop in the story. And she is a prop for the main characters who are men.

She is used by:

(1) The spirits who afflict her
(2) The slave owner who profits from her gift of fortune telling
(3) Paul who casts out the spirit, not for her sake, but because he is annoyed that the girl is disruptive.

Once the spirit is cast out, we hear no more of the girl, and the story returns to the main theme of men bickering over making money, civil disturbance issues, and squabbles over religion.

What happens to her? Does she place trust in God? Does she become Paul's friend? Is she still a slave? How does her owner treat her? How does she feel? All is passed by in silence.

To read against the grain is not to arrive at conclusions: it is to ask questions and so I leave you with the questions to ponder.

The Household and the Individual

> The man said, "Sirs, what must I do to be saved?" Paul answered, "Believe on the Lord Jesus, and you will be saved, you and your household." Paul and Silas spoke the word of God to him and to all who were in his house. At the same hour of the night he took them and washed their wounds; then he and his entire family were baptized without delay. He brought them up into the house and set food before them; and he and his entire household rejoiced that he had become a believer in God. (Acts 16)

This passage is a favorite for Baptists and non-Baptists alike. The debatable issues are "household salvation" and "infant baptism." The text suggests that if the jailer believes then not only he will be saved but his household as well. It also suggests that as a result of his new faith his entire family is baptized. Presumably, that included the children.

Many years ago, when I was animated about such things and thought they mattered, with other Baptists, I argued that the text should be read as "Believe on the Lord Jesus and you will be saved, you and your household [all of you believe on the Lord Jesus, if some of you do not you will not be saved.]" If it is read the other way, that because of the jailer's belief the whole family is saved—oh my! It undermines the whole evangelical scheme of salvation! That would never do, so it could never be a correct reading.

The second part was even more difficult to deal with (if you are convinced that Christian baptism is for believers after a conversion experience). The Baptist take is that the whole family must have become believers based on the jailer's testimony. When it says "family" is does not mean children, only those who could make "a decision for Christ"! The infant baptizers at this point merely raise their eyebrows.

What do I make of it now? Well, I think the Baptist reading is a fairly clear case of having a conclusion at hand before evidence is presented. On the evidence of the story, it would seem reasonable to conclude that when the passage was written, when a household patriarch believed (changed religion; was converted), that all in the family changed religion as well. To become a Christian meant to be baptized, so everyone in the family was baptized.

This tradition is difficult for us to grasp because of our understanding of autonomy (that each person has a right to make their own decisions about such things as religion), but less difficult in societies and cultures that have not been influenced by the Enlightenment of the West and its understanding of the individual. Of course, it is still there in our rights of passage, be they infant baptism or blessing, or male circumcision: the parents are introducing their child to religion without the child's say so. When the child is "old enough" the child makes its own decisions about religion. Yet, based on the passage it would seem reasonable that should a father in a patriarchal family change religion, all in the family do, or even further that in a patriarchal village, when the chief changes faith, the village does too. When the leader of a nation changes faith, does the nation follow suit? Does a Christian king or president mean the country is Christian?

I think we would struggle with that. But perhaps the seeds of the Western understanding of individualism were sown by early Christian theologians who struggled with the ideas of social solidarity and personal faith decisions.

Christ Mysticism

> I in them and you in me, that they may become completely one,
> so that the world may know that you have sent me and have
> loved them even as you have loved me. (John 17:23)

My third unrelated thing to ponder is the Christ mysticism of the Johannine community. Here there is the interdwelling of divine and human and the encompassing of the believers into this divine oneness. "I in you, you in me, they in us." The first part of this was taken up in the nascent understanding of Trinity. The passage has been used as a basis for a Holy Trinity of perfect interdwelling of Father and Son (the Spirit being added at a later date, an afterthought perhaps). In the discussion of Holy Trinity—what is orthodox and what is not—the other side of the passage was lost: that all of us are to be taken into that mutual interdwelling of God and Christ.

Of course, the mystics were not slow to see this and you will find it becomes the bedrock of their understanding of the spiritual life: that human beings can be taken up into the life of the divine. But the mystics in their time were more often than not considered heterodox. Only after their deaths (like most great artists) were they revered for their creativity.

So what do we have here? A remembrance of Jesus who had such a relationship with the divine that it was perceived as oneness. Yet, this oneness of divine and human was not for the one alone but for all. And the promise remains for us: "I in you, you in me, they in us" the interbeing of all that is.

6. Refocus on What Matters

A great deal of life is spent in pettiness. It's not that the little things don't matter. It's that when we attach to the little things, in such a way that we block out the light, life is poorer. This is particularly so when we focus on what we can't change—and there is much in life we can't change! Often, it is those very things that become the subject of our worries, frustrations, anger, and disillusionment. One of the great secrets of a fulfilled and happy life is to know how to let go.

Be in charge of those things you can change. Let the rest go by. I wish I had learned this many years ago. It would have saved so much energy wasted on the futile. (I wish I lived it more consistently now.)

Besides internal disturbance, focus on the things we can't do anything about prevents our enlightenment. When we say, "The sun's not out today," we really mean that a cloud has hidden the precious rays of the sun from us. Our enlightenment is always there, just as the sun is always there. Our preoccupation with the petty becomes the cloud.

Here's a little something from the philosopher Epictetus in the lovely little piece the *Enchiridion*:

Some things are in our control and others not. Things in
our control are opinion, pursuit, desire, aversion, and, in a word,
whatever are our own actions. Things not in our control are body,
property, reputation, command, and, in one word, whatever are
not our own actions.

The things in our control are by nature free, unrestrained,
unhindered; but those not in our control are weak, slavish,
restrained, belonging to others. Remember, then, that if you
suppose that things which are slavish by nature are also free,
and that what belongs to others is your own, then you will
be hindered. You will lament, you will be disturbed, and you
will find fault both with gods and men. But if you suppose that
only to be your own which is your own, and what belongs to
others such as it really is, then no one will ever compel you or
restrain you. Further, you will find fault with no one or accuse
no one. You will do nothing against your will. No one will hurt
you, you will have no enemies, and you will not be harmed.
(Epictetus, 2008, chap. 1)

It interests me that Epictetus has "the body" as one of those things
outside our control. This is only partly true. For Epictetus, as for many
in the Western tradition, there is too firm a dualism between body and
mind—the body is seen and experienced as something other, something
alien. Much that happens to and in our bodies is truly beyond our control.
Yet, a more helpful practice brings body, mind and spirit into holistic
balance. But that is for another day. I find myself often having to refocus
on what matters. Epictetus is a helpful friend.

7. It's Beyond Me, So I Think I'll Just Let Go

I've been thinking. A lot. Probably more than usual.

Perhaps strange to those outside the academy is the idea that every
seven years or so you get a sabbatical—a period of release from your normal
round of teaching and administration to give yourself to research and
study.

I am in the middle of a sabbatical just now. From 7:30 a.m. each day,
I think, read, meditate, and write. After Jane and the kids leave for work

and school, the house and garden are quiet until 3:00 p.m., when we all gather to discuss the day. Mostly its just me and the pugs. That's why I've been thinking a lot.

My thoughts have ranged from the philosophy of love, to sentimentalism and morality, to nonviolent (re)parenting, to the First World War, to secular monasticism, to the constitution of the United States and freedom of religion, to Chen style taijiquan, to the abolition of prisons, to juvenile delinquency.

My provisional conclusion is that it's all beyond me, so I'll just let go. The issues and problems of life (not my own, somewhat insignificant life, but life as a whole, the big picture) are so intractable that there is no big solution.

I've been thinking too about the self, and self-interest, and self-love. Jesus said, "Those who love their life lose it, and those who hate their life in this world will keep it for eternal life" (John 12:25). This too is beyond me. But I think I have a clue to its possible meaning that takes me back to the Buddhist notion of non-attachment (which also is beyond me).

It is human nature to grasp hold. Think of the tiny baby who grasps your finger and doesn't let go. It's one of the first signs that all is well. "She's got a good grip!" says the doting parent. All shall be well. That grasping stays with us for much of life. We hold on to life and don't want to let go. We take on ideas and concepts and images and understandings and we hold on to them tightly—as if life itself depended on our being able to hold the whole thing together.

Then we hear Jesus say, "Simply lose your life." It is to let go of attachment to your self-image. Let go of self-importance, power, correctness, wit, intelligence, skill, sharpness and independence.

The inner urge is to hold on. The fear is that letting go will be worse than keeping hold. Think of the baby. Her little grasp is not keeping her from falling. She is held in more secure arms than her feeble grasp.

The perennial philosophy responds, "Let go! For in letting go is release, freedom. Joy doubled."

For me, in the midst of all my thinking it is to let go of the idea that I might find the solution to the intractable problems of life. Perhaps in letting go I will find.

Perhaps.

PART TWO

SEASONAL REFLECTIONS

ELEVEN

SAMHAIN/ALL SAINTS

1. Samhain Thoughts

The Celtic year begins with the coming of the dark. The day begins in the evening, not the morning. Leaves are fallen. Days are getting shorter. We ready ourselves for winter. Samhain (pronounced SOW-when) was for the Celts the thinnest part of the year, when the veil between time and eternity is most easily traversed. The dead are closest to us.

In the Western church calendar, we celebrate All Saints on November 1 and All Souls on November 2. Halloween is the eve of All Hallows. Those who have gone before us are with us now. Halloween, All Saints, All Souls, and Samhain give us a wonderful merging of many traditions. All speak truth to us. All give us a glimpse of mystery.

> That which is called the Christian religion existed among the Ancients, and never did not exist, from the beginning of the Human race until Christ came in the flesh, at which time true religion, which already existed began to be called Christianity. (St. Augustine in the *Retractions*, 426 CE)

I recommend Shirley Toulson's book *The Celtic Year* (1993). It is a handy companion to use alongside the Daily Office. Much food for thought. It may not still be in print, but used copies are easy to find.

For the ancients, Samhain was a season to feast before the austerities of winter. To my Christian and Pagan friends: Enjoy the feast!

2. There's Magic in the Air

I love this time of year. The smell of the fall, dry leaves rustling beneath my feet, a crispness to the blue of the sky, the first morning frost giving the green grass a white fringe, squirrels frantically collecting pine cones in preparation for the winter to come. Since being a kid I have always felt there's magic in the air at this time of the year.

There is a spiritual change in this season that is clear for those with eyes to see and sensitivity to feel. The Celtic people knew it. The New Year begins with Samhain, the eve of which we celebrate as All Hallows (Halloween—the Christianizing of pagan ways).

It's a new beginning. But strangely the new beginning doesn't start with the coming of the light, but with the drawing in of the light, the "shutting down" of nature. The new begins with "it will get far worse before it gets any better."

I have been stacking wood. More will be delivered today. I will be stacking again. It's quite hard work! Constant bending and lifting. I enjoy the ritual of it. A Samhain ritual of getting ready. Winter is coming. Change is happening. Be ready! I am one with the squirrels as we work side by side.

The Church's calendar changes in a few weeks with the beginning of Advent. It's a month too late! In 1978, the Joint Liturgical Group—an ecumenical gathering of scholars in the United Kingdom—produced a revised Daily Office. It was the version of the Office to which I was introduced in 1981, and was my daily practice for many years. I have the very beat-up copy in front of me, page edges darkened through thumbing through. This version of the Office begins the ninth week before Christmas. In other words, it begins roughly at Samhain. It starts with the Celtic New Year. In 1980, the Church of England published its Alternative Service Book, and also began the year nine weeks before Christmas. In its 2000 revision of liturgy, the Church of England returned to the Advent beginning of the year. I preferred it the other way. Advent feels just a little late. The party begins on Halloween, replaced quickly with preparation.

In more recent years, I have reflected more on the nature of change in traditional Chinese philosophy. The constant movement of yin and yang. Autumn is yang turning to yin. Winter is fully yin. This season is the beginning of withdrawal.

Spiritually, there is a drawing in, a contracting—the expansive openness of summer is giving way to a smallness, fewness, rareness, gentleness of approaching winter. Between the two we prepare. When we came to the United States, we were introduced to a new phrase: "winterize." Generally, I resist turning nouns into verbs with the addition of "ize," but this one is useful. It speaks of getting things ready for the cold to come.

Chinese philosophy reminds us that neither yang nor yin are bad. They complement each other and fulfill each other. The coming of the cold is not to be feared, but to be embraced. Of course, it's difficult to embrace if you are not prepared. There is a season for preparation. The season has begun. There's magic in the air.

3. Christ the King [*sic*]?

In the church's year the season of the Reign of Christ starts on November 1 with All Saints and ends today, on the Sunday traditionally called Christ the King. In the Lindisfarne Community liturgy, we have changed the name of the season from Christ the King to the Reign of Christ. We did that to avoid the problems associated with patriarchy (the domination of the male). Yet, in staying with the idea of reigning we have not avoided another difficulty: what Elizabeth Schüssler Fiorenza calls kyriarchy (a domination system of any kind, 2001, 118). We would face this problem still if the one reigning were a queen.

Pause and think about the idea of reigning, of the domination of the one over the many. It is a strange idea when in our culture we so laud the idea of democracy. Rule of the people by the people (even in its not so pure form of representative and hierarchical democracy we practice in the West). Dictators (even benevolent dictators) are frowned upon. As I write, many of the Pakistani people are clamoring for democracy. In response, President Musharraf has declared a state of emergency and has taken even more power to the executive. The Commonwealth of Nations (53 sovereign nations, two billion people, formerly the British Commonwealth, but still with the Queen of England as representative head) has suspended Pakistan. Dictators are no longer welcome at the table. Even friendly ones in the "war on terror."

Yet we still have this metaphor of "Christ the King." The ultimate dictator? As benevolent as could be, but still a dictator?

Marcus Borg in his book *Jesus* (I recommend it as the best single book about Jesus available today) is very helpful in looking at domination systems. He says about domination systems that they are the "political and economic domination of the many by the few and the use of religious claims to legitimate it" (2008, 85). Jesus was born into such a system that had the added feature of being an imperial domination system. The domination was by Rome, one of the world's great imperial powers. As people in Pakistan are clamoring for democratic change and the end of dictatorship, many in Palestine in the first century wanted to see the end of Roman imperial domination. Some tried noncooperation, some collaborated, some sought political violence as the means (we call it terrorism today), some turned inward on the spiritual quest.

In the middle of this ferment, Jesus taught a subversive message of the end of domination systems in the realm of God. It is clear that in sayings such as those gathered in the Sermon on the Mount, Jesus radically undermined domination. His message was radical love. Love does not dominate. Domination and love are antithetical. If I love you, I cannot exploit you. Love is opposed to violence. Wherever there is violence is a failure to love. Domination systems thrive on violence. They grow stronger when flexing muscles against futile violent resistance by the weak. Domination systems are birthed in violence in the great social upheavals of war.

The message of love has always been subversive. At a conference a few years ago, in a hallway after a session, a participant shook his fist in my face protesting, "The trouble with you pacifists is that you are dangerous. Think what would happen to the world if everyone was like you, if everyone refused to fight!" I have thought about it!

It is puzzling why, on this Sunday, the gospel reading is from the crucifixion story (Luke 23:33-43). I think it must be because in the story there is a sign affixed to the cross that said, "This is the King of the Jews." There were rumors. Some said that this Jesus was the coming messiah who would overthrow the hated Romans. Some political extremists (the Zealots) joined his group. It may have been because of that kind of expectation. On more than one occasion, the crowds who listened to him wanted to make him king. Jesus always refused. On a day when there was an imperial procession displaying all the might and power of triumphant Rome, Jesus staged an alternative procession. He went into Jerusalem by the back route on a donkey. His message and his actions were subversive. He was executed as a subversive criminal. The sign "King of the Jews" mocked him, gave his followers a very clear message not to mess with the domination system.

So, today is the Sunday of "Christ the King [sic]." I think we can still use the idea if we remove the ideas of domination—if we rethink the idea of "king" or "ruler" in such radical ways that the concept is robbed of any kind of domination—if we remember that Jesus taught us to love, and love does not dominate others, not even the love of God.

TWELVE

ADVENT

1. A Poem for the Beginning of Advent

This poem is so like New York in November. A magical time of the year: full of mystery, a little sad, pregnant with expectation.

Scel Lem Duib

Here's a song—
stags give tongue
winter snows
summer goes

High cold blow
sun is low
brief his day
seas give spray

Fern clumps redden
shapes are hidden
wildgeese raise
wonted cries

Cold now girds
wings of birds

icy time—
that's my rime.

Ninth-century, version—Flann O'Brien (Toulson, 1993, 43)

2. Waiting for and Preparing for the Coming of God

For almost thirty years, at this time of the year, this has been the refrain heard in our house: "I can't wait until Christmas!" "Christmas is never coming!" Our response? "Christmas is coming. Have patience. Wait for it." Christmas always comes.

More so than any other time of the year, this is the time of getting everything ready. We get the house ready. We decorate. We clean. We think about presents for folks. We buy presents for folks. We send presents for folks all over the world. We get ready to feast. We prepare for a few days off from the regular routines of life. The waiting and preparing go hand in hand. Our getting ready and waiting in the season of Advent mirror spiritual realities: waiting for and preparing for the coming of God.

The coming of God is the longing and hope of humanity. In Isaiah, it is when the wilderness and dry land will be glad. It is opening blind eyes, unstopping deaf ears. Singing, joy, and gladness. In Mary's song, the Magnificat, it will be the lifting up of the lowly, the filling of the hungry with good things. In the gospel, the blind receive sight, the lame walk, the lepers are cleansed, the deaf hear, the dead are raised, and the poor have good news brought to them. The blessing can only be the end of their poverty. That, and more, typifies the longing of humanity. The righting of wrongs. The coming of all that is good. All will be well when God comes.

Yet, the coming of God is elusive. We have no reason to think it will be so other than hope and glimpses. There is little reason to be a "progressive." The track record of humanity has not been a good one. The great advances of civilization in the last two hundred years have also been matched by terrible devastation and destruction. The glimpses that give us hope are the signs of the coming. The signs are in all those good things that show us a better world. Every healing of disease is a sign. Every poor person who is fed and given decent shelter is a sign. Every child born in hope of a bright future is a sign.

Our greatest glimpse is in the person of Jesus. Here is the coming of God in human form. What will the coming be like? It will be like this person Jesus. Yet it is still hope delayed. Two millennia have passed and still we wait for the coming of God.

Our waiting for is also a longing for. It is the deepest yearning of human hearts for a better world. And in waiting and longing we prepare. Advent gives us a yearly reminder to prepare for the coming of God.

There is a beautiful mediation in our *Way of Living* (Fitz-Gibbon and Fitz-Gibbon, 2006), Day 8:

> People love feasts. They love to prepare huge amounts of rich food, and to choose the finest wine; the excitement of preparing a feast is an important part of its pleasure. Then on the appointed day they love to gather in a great crowd, to sing and dance, and then to eat the food and drink the wine. When a child is born people hold feasts; when a young man and woman get married their families hold a feast; when a person dies, his or her children hold a feast . . . And there are feasts to mark all the great religious anniversaries. It is good and natural that people should enjoy feasts, because they are a sign of the greatest feast of all, to which God invites us: the feast in his heavenly kingdom around his throne. There the singing and dancing, the eating and drinking, will last for all eternity. But we do not need to prepare food and choose wine for this heavenly feast; we need to prepare ourselves by learning always to choose righteousness." (Pelagius)

So in Advent, we wait, we yearn; we prepare ourselves for the coming of God. Christ is our hope. All will be well in the coming of God.

3. At the End of the Day, What Counts?

Jesus was a master communicator who spoke to the people of his day in popular language. One way was the language of apocalyptic, In his stories, Jesus uses the then popular image of the Son of Man. Better translations are the Human One or the Child of Humanity. In Hebrew, the phrase is "ben adam." It originally was a phrase simply meaning human, but in the apocalyptic genre following Daniel (mid-second century BCE) it became a title of the messianic figure who would end history as we know it and bring in a reign of goodness and peace. Jesus uses this popular story telling to paint a picture in apocalyptic terms. It would connect very well with his hearers.

Apocalyptic is a strange and wonderful genre. It is at once terrifying and hopeful. It developed in a context of great repression, by a subjugated people who needed to hope for the future. It deals with the justice of God and human suffering. It sees the present world as an awful place beyond redemption where the people of God, the minority, find no respite from oppression and terror. What hope could there possibly be? Enter apocalyptic. It tells of a coming world of justice where the oppressed will be freed. This new world will be brought about by a messianic figure that will terrify those who terrify others and show kindness to the oppressed.

The apocalyptic genre is told in Technicolor—it is vivid, imaginative, gruesome, violent, and very frightening. For those who suffered it was a hopeful imagery. In later Christian tradition, we have equated Jesus with the Child of Humanity, so much so that it is very difficult to read the phrase without thinking that it represents Jesus. Still, I do not think that necessarily follows. Did Jesus see himself as the Child of Humanity? I think it can be argued that he is merely using the then popular apocalyptic genre to make a point. I do not think we can derive doctrines of heaven and hell from a popular story. It is story telling, not metaphysics.

Jesus uses parables to make points to his hearers. By using the familiar phrase the Child of Humanity, his hearers hear the code of apocalyptic. He is speaking of the end of the things we know and the beginning of the new things. His story has the imagery of the apocalypse: the Child of Humanity, the judgment throne, the gathering of all the peoples of the world, the judgment pronouncement by the messianic figure, eternal punishment for the ungodly, eternal life for the godly. All is made right, and justice prevails. It is a familiar story to his hearers. It is comfort for the oppressed. It is terrifying for the oppressors.

But Jesus gives it a twist. In the usual apocalyptical visions, the world as we know it is beyond redemption, fit only to be destroyed, consumed by fire. There is nothing for it but to wait out the horrors and long for the Messianic One. Yet, Jesus says that something does count. It is not simply a time to wait. What counts is feeding the hungry, providing water for the thirsty, welcoming strangers, clothing the naked, caring for the sick, and visiting those in prison. At the end of the day, that is what counts. In those activities is blessedness. In apocalyptic language, that is what separates the sheep from the goats. In our modern parlance, we would say what counts is social justice.

Let me paraphrase the message of the story. "You are all concerned about issues of justice. You think that justice will come at the end of all things. You wait for a messianic figure to make the bad go away and to bring in something better. But look around you. Look at the hungry, the thirsty, the homeless, the sick, and the imprisoned. You nourish them, you clothe them, you welcome them, you care for them, and you visit them. That is what counts at the end of the day."

In other words, to take the story as a literal tale of the end of the world is to miss the point. The point is not the end, but what we do in the present. What counts now? How shall we live now?

4. Desire

The season of Advent is that time in the church's calendar when longing is the central emotion. A longing is a strong desire for something not yet received; not yet consummated. The longing of Advent is a longing for the coming of God. Things are not as they should be. All will be made well in the coming of God.

This week, I have been reflecting on the sentiment of desire and I have expressed my thoughts in the form of a sonnet. Before I share the sonnet, a few musings on desire.

Emotion has generally a checkered history in Christian thought. Desire has received the roughest ride. Under the influence of Greek thought, particularly elements of Platonism, desires have been considered unruly. Desire, a wild horse, needs the sense of reason as a master charioteer to keep it in check. Ultimately, desire will be left behind as childish as the mature soul contemplates the beauties of perfection. Further, desire is the root of the deadliest of all sins, lust, and most effort has been expended in trying to control its powerful contamination. Lust, we know, is most closely associated with sexuality and so the church has been constantly troubled with how to deal with this truly human complex of emotion and behavior.

Yet, as Augustine knew well, desire is at the heart of love. God is love, and we are to love. Remove desire and love becomes mere form, mere shell with no content. The mystics knew this too and expressed their mystical ecstasies in the language of love's strong desires. In the Enlightenment, David Hume, British philosopher who was no friend to religion, rooted the whole of morality in the passions. Desire is the wellspring of all moral sentiment. He went so far as to say that reason is and ought to be the slave of the passions.

There is truth in both traditions. Desire corrupted becomes lust. Desires misdirected can cause great suffering. Yet, human life in the world as we know it has at its heart a longing for God, a longing for goodness. It is a longing because never fully satisfied; never truly fulfilled. The emotion of longing is also the motivation for a better life. It is deep desire to see the poor helped, the sick healed, the oppressed freed that leads to ethical action. It is longing for connection that leads to deep friendship. It is the deepest desire for the well-being of the loved one that produces all the care in the world.

And so a sonnet:

A Sonnet

There is in human hearts a desire so
Profound, yet goes by but one name. A sage
Long gone said, "Our hearts are restless," (we know)
"Until they find their rest in you." Old age
May tell its truth; yet, with no words to form
A meaningful account. A gaping hole
Too vast to fill. Religion, to perform
A function necessary, a good role,
Tries its best. It fails; the labor too great.
A chasm filled with child's bucket and spade!
No wonder, tender souls soon learn to hate
Its pretenses. A game so badly played
Is abandoned as futile. The end of
Longing is still to long in hope for love.

5. Prayer Reflections

Advent, like Lent, provides a period of introspection and self-examination. It is a period in the Christian calendar when we allow ourselves a "tune up." If Lent is a major service, Advent is at least an oil change and tire rotation! We see how we are doing and make a few minor changes.

For many reasons, this has not been an easy Advent for me—physically, psychologically, or spiritually. Toward its end, I have been more introspective than usual. The little cycle of prayers in our *Way of Living* (Fitz-Gibbon and Fitz-Gibbbon, 2006) have been helpful.

The prayers are these:

> That all people will be ready for the coming of God
> That all nations will know the realm of God
> That the broken will find healing from God

I have been struck by these requests and, this week, I have turned them toward myself. It has helped me look at my own readiness, my own apprehension of the realm of God, and my own need for healing. In all three areas, I have realized a great lack. In other words, it has been very challenging as I have daily made these requests for others, to realize that I have the same needs.

Readiness for the Coming: The coming of God is an extraordinarily rich idea. It is one of those word pictures that contain so much. It speaks of something not yet but soon to be—like the birth of a child. It is something of the greatest importance—like the visit of a sovereign or president to a lowly village. It suggests that great change is on the way—like the coming of spring after a hard winter. For all of these "comings" preparation is essential. The coming of God is like this only more so. What that coming is or may look like I have no idea. Yet, this week it has felt to me near and very real. I wonder if this is what St. Benedict meant when he urged his monks to "keep death daily before one's eyes"? Surely, in death is one of the ways of the Coming of God. Benedict urged preparation, readiness, for who knows when that will be. As I thought about this in this fourth week of Advent I had a stark realization that perhaps I am not ready for the Coming.

Apprehension of God's Realm: The realm of God is the realm of love, for God is love. Where we find love we find God's realm. Hell is the absence of the realm of God. Hell is where there is no love. Hell does not exist in itself; it is mere negation of love, a deprivation of love. Hell, evil, and the devil have no positive existence. They are ways of speaking of the absence of love. (This was Augustine's great insight.) To know the realm of God is to know love. This speaks to me of the apprehension, or realization, of love as the knowledge of God's realm. During this Advent I have become aware of how little I have apprehended love. To know more love is my prayer.

Brokenness: Part of the difficulty of this Advent season has been my own realization of brokenness. I am not whole and desire to be so. The promise of Advent (longing) to Christmas (birth) to Epiphany (the fullness of light) is held before us each year. It is a promise of healing, of becoming whole. We are all broken. We all need to be healed. As I have prayed this for others, I have turned it inward and it too has become my prayer.

6. Purity and Preparation for the Coming of God

I am grateful for Advent when the lectionary helps us to look forward to the coming of God. The world in which we live is open to God's future. The universe is ultimately hopeful, despite what the news says, despite the way human beings are disrespectful and abusive to the planet.

Advent themes help us by the focus on the way our forebears looked forward, longingly and hopefully to the coming of God. The lectionary passages today remind us that there was a strand of Jewish thinking that looked for the coming again of the prophet Elijah. The early Christians picked up the theme and saw in John the Baptist a messenger from God who was either Elijah come again (in parts of the tradition) or one who came in the spirit of Elijah (less literally). Either way does not matter much, for the content is the same: here was one who came as messenger to prepare the way for the coming of God. Because the future is open to God, God comes to us in many ways and at many times in our lives. A message of preparation helps us to see those comings and not to miss them. To miss them is easy for the unprepared.

Today, it was the image of purity that struck a note for me. It is there in Malachi as the refining process of metal; it is there in Philippians as purity and blamelessness; it is there in the Gospel in repentance for sin and in the image of making level and straight paths to walk on.

Unhelpful views about purity: Yet, I must express diffidence about purity, for I think the idea has been much misused. What might purity mean for us as we prepare for the coming of God in our lives?

I can think of four ways in which the idea of purity has been used, but which are less than helpful:

(1) Religious purity. I am thinking here of ritualistic purity, where what we do, what we wear, the outward things of religion, seem to matter a great deal. A great deal of religious zeal is directed here to getting religion "right." Much denominationalism is about getting the form of religion right, more pure, closer to the Bible or closer to tradition.

(2) Doctrinal purity. Here the direction is to get what we think or believe correct. It seems to me a great many Christian live in fear of this. Or rather, in fear of being found holding the wrong doctrines. In my earlier years the worst thing anyone could say of me was that I was unorthodox, or, God forbid, a heretic! I tried extremely hard to have all my little doctrinal ducks in a row! I know of Christians who when they think deeply about an issue, or look closely into their own hearts, do not hold to some of the orthodox ideas (things like eternal hell as a literal place of flames for non-Christians), but who dare not say so for fear of being doctrinally impure.

(3) Sexual purity. This is a difficult area and I cannot spend much time with it. In Christian history, sexual purity has often been associated with the cult of virginity. The sexual ideal has been "no sex." The virgin is the purest Christian of all (hence enforced celibacy for priests and monastics). My view is that it has given us an inherited tradition with a very distorted view of human sexuality that has brought untold inner misery to millions of people who have grappled with interminable guilt over something that is God given, normal and quite healthy.

(4) Racial and ethnic purity. Of all the purities this is the most pernicious. We have seen in recent history what happens when groups of people seek this kind of purity. It is invariably destructive.

I say all the above are unhelpful because they all have a tendency to become exclusive and divisive. Where there is an emphasis on purity of those kinds there is also a tendency to exclude and to hurt other people who do not fit the notion of purity.

A better understanding of purity as preparation for the coming of God?

(1) With regard to our selves, I think we need to make it an inner matter. It is more to do with attitudes of heart and mind than conformity to a standard of purity derived from a social and religious context. It would be to seek something like Paul's fruit of the Spirit in Galatians. "Love, joy, peace, patience, kindness, generosity, faithfulness, gentleness, and self-control." In other words, purity is a matter of inner disposition. It is about character.

(2) With regard to others purity is not about exclusion. In the Philippians passage, Paul is a model of three things. (a) Prayer for others (b) holding others in his heart (c) compassion. Purity of the inner focused kind will bring with it these attitudes toward others that will initiate inclusiveness rather than exclusiveness; good toward others rather than harm.

7. Love Came Down at Christmas

We have decorated for Christmas early this year. It is a break with strict tradition that says "Don't put up the tree until Christmas Eve. Celebrate Advent properly. Advent is a more solemn season." This I know, and I do want to take Advent seriously and not let it get swallowed by Christmas. It may be that we have simply given in to cultural pressures. In our culture, Christmas ends on Christmas Day and the twelve days of Christmas have been lost to the pre-Christmas commercial binge. Advent means shopping not solemn reflection. Yet, I hope our early beginning of celebration is more than that. If the Christmas season has been taken from us after Christmas Day, then we might as well enjoy Christmas before. I have made suitable adjustments to my iTunes play list! (Five hundred and four tracks and counting. Check out Bob Dylan's "Christmas in the Heart," Delightful!)

Over the last couple of days, I have had in mind the words of Christina Rossetti's poem "Love came down at Christmas." She sees the meaning of Christmas as love, and the effect of Christmas to love God and all people. This for me, too, is the meaning of Christmas. Christmas is the sign and symbol of universal love. Love as practice. Love as hope. Love as aspiration. Love as longing.

Love is in the universal experience of nurture and care. None of us would be here without it. Love is in the universal ethical aspiration of all the world's great traditions and religions—Confucian benevolence, Buddhist lovingkindness, Jewish and Christian love, Muslim compassion, Kant's categorical imperative, feminist care . . . the list goes on. As it says in the *Daodejing*, "Thirty spokes share one hub" (XI, 27). Love is how we would like to see the world.

In our ongoing discussions as a community we have been pondering love. This is our understanding:

> Love is to be at the heart of the Lindisfarne Community. "Love your God with all your heart, mind, soul and strength. Love your neighbor as yourself. Love your enemies." The immensity of the task makes it naturally impossible! Yet we are called to be a community of love. We need to remember, it is God's love, not ours; perfect, eternal, constant. With God's love there are no strings attached, no conditions to be met, no favoritism. Yet it is not sentimental nor romantic, for love is not merely a feeling, it is an act of will; the "naked intent" of the heart to

love God, neighbor and enemy. There is the deepest of all joy
in the love of God. We seek to learn to love, to walk in love,
to exult in love, to make love our highest aim, to let God's love
fill us completely. Our desire is to be free within the love of our
heavenly Father-Mother—to know God's passionate love for us
and to live our lives from within God's acceptance of us. This
love of God is reflected in our love for all, even those who are
considered our enemies. It is a reconciling love; a love that seeks
peace. It is a love for the whole of creation.

Our written understanding is only the beginning, imperfectly expressed,
but giving us a direction. To name love is not to know love. To know love is
to experience love. The gateway to experience is the door of practice. The
door of practice is found in the mundane. Love came down at Christmas.
Love was found in a stable, in the profundity of birth and parental love, in
everyday life.

THIRTEEN

CHRISTMAS

1. We Are Too Busy

I am too restless to watch long; I am too Occidental for a long vigil. I could work at a problem for years, but to wait inactive for twenty-four hours—that is another matter.—The Time Traveler in H.G. Wells, *The Time Machine.*

Over Christmas, I read H.G. Wells *The Time Machine* (1895) as a light distraction. I came across the above quote that summarized for me one of our central problems: we are too busy. The malady is deeper in that, while we complain about our busyness, in truth we like it. Given space we want to fill it. "What ought I to be doing now?"

In Epiphany, we consider each year the Magi from the East who come to worship the Christ child. Those from the Orient each year remind those in the Occident that there is another world. East meets West.

Clearly H.G. Wells considered the Western drive to plan, fix, invent, and change things to be virtuous. Yet, perhaps Thomas Merton was right. Is it time that we learned from the East? Perhaps it is time to wait.

2. The Birth Again of the Sun

Today reminds me of almost every Christmas when I was a child in Manchester. It is overcast with a hint of cold drizzle in the air. The grass remains green. At 10:30 a.m. it is still not really light, and I do not expect it will get light today. For the last three years, we have had a "not white" Christmas.

Some time ago I had a conversation that went something like this (in the middle):

> "Of course, Jesus was not actually born on Christmas Day," I said with a smile.
> "So, when was he born?" my friend replied, clearly puzzled.
> "I think most scholars think sometime March or April."
> "Really? Then why do we celebrate it on December 25?"
> "The early Christians picked it because it was already a festival: the winter solstice. Christians have done that with just about every major feast. They took over a pre-Christian festival and Christianized it."
> "What a waste of time, then. We celebrate Jesus' birthday on the wrong day, and it's really pagan, not Christian!"

My friend, I think was a little disappointed, but it set me thinking.

During the Christmas season we make much use of the canticle we call "the Song of the Messiah" from Isaiah 9. It is very familiar to us through Handel's *Messiah*. There are allusions to it in many Christmas carols.

> The people who walked in darkness have seen a great light;
> Those who dwell in a land of great darkness, upon them the light has dawned . . . For to us a child is born and to us a child is given.

The great season of Advent-Christmas-Epiphany is about the light of God coming to a darkened world. Jesus, the light of life; Jesus, the light of the world. A light for our path. The one who makes sense for us. It is a story that tells us there is a way through the darkness. There will be light.

I think it is no coincidence, then, that the Church chose the darkest part of the year (for us in the Northern Hemisphere) to celebrate the coming of Christ our light. It is, of course, much the same reason that the winter solstice is celebrated in other than Christian ways. At the very darkest time, when the sun rarely visits for more than a few hours, there is the promise of lighter days. The very darkest day gives way to a lighter day. That day, in its turn, gives way to a lighter day still.

It is fitting to make this the time of great feasting, of food and drink, and families gathered. A great festival in the deepest darkness with a promise of the coming light.

My prayer for all of us is to know again the rebirth of the sun, the rebirth of the light of Christ. Whatever has been dark to us, may God bring again the light of love.

A blessed Christmas to all!

3. Nine Lessons and Carols

Yesterday morning (Christmas Eve) I enjoyed greatly listening to the service of nine lessons and carols broadcast live from King's College Cambridge. There was a comfortable familiarity about it. I knew the words to all the congregational carols. The choir pieces were mostly familiar to me, and the readers reassuringly somber enough. The readings from the King James Version have a magic of their own—wisdom from another age telling the story of human foolishness and sadness, followed by promise and fulfillment. The reassurance was in the changelessness of it all. It could have been the first service from 1918, in the aftermath of the First World War.

Comforting—that was the primary feeling. Nothing changes.

Perhaps that is why we like traditions and rituals. They perform a useful function of anchoring us in the constantly shifting tides of life. The Christmas story is a stable one. (Pun intended!)

Yet, as I listened with fondness and enjoyment I was struck also by the patriarchalism of it all—one female voice in the production, one male voice that was clearly none standard educated upper class white male. The story itself, though with a woman in an almost central place, has the woman in subservient role. A story of the marginalized and poor being rehearsed by the privileged. Here was dissonance. This made me uncomfortable. I was a little shaken.

So, there I was . . . Outside meditating in the first snow of the year, listening to the familiar service, comforted and disturbed. It was for me another experience of the ambiguity of life and faith and hope and doubt. Still, I was glad to hear again the story. I was glad to be disturbed. I am glad it is Christmas.

So next year I hope to listen in again to the Cambridge service. Doubtless I will again be comforted and again be shaken.

4. If We Love One Another, God Lives in Us

The daily lectionary for Christmas Day has a passage from the first letter of John. It is a passage about love, perhaps the most profound in all of Holy Scripture. This little discourse about love has these words, "If we love one another, God lives in us" (1 John 4:12).

Our Christmas celebration is of the coming of God in lowliness, in poverty, to lead us home. Jesus is Emmanuel, God with us, God living with us. John tells us what it means when God lives with us: it means that we love each other. I suppose this has been obvious to many, but it struck me with added import this Christmas morning. Anything without love is as nothing, "a noisy gong, a clanging cymbal," as Paul says in that other passage about love.

This is interesting, for so much of all I do is not marked by love, is not infused with God. It remains a deep longing to know God living, love present, in all I do. I hope, as a community, this may be our corporate desire: to be a community of love, to be where God lives.

5. A Disturbing Sign

I have been teaching winter classes. On my way to the university, I pass a little church with a prominent sign. The church diligently changes the sign to fit with the season (interspersed with "Friday Fish Fry," "Chicken Barbecue," and "Food Giveaway").

After Christmas, the sign read, "Jesus is born. Come and learn about him." I have found it profoundly disturbing, and each morning as I pass it causes me to ponder.

Why such a sign has disturbed me, I am not quite sure. But I will try a little self-analysis. (I think my being disturbed is more about me than about this little church of faithful souls.) So here goes . . .

When Christians announce at Christmas "Christ is born" they are making a spiritual rather than historical statement. Of course, it refers back to events two thousand years ago, but our record of those events is scant. If the announcement was of historical interest, it would only read, "Jesus *was* born."

"Christ *is* born" is a profound statement about spiritual realities and mystical union and inner divinity and discoveries of love. (Theologians among us notice the difference between "Jesus was born" and "Christ is born." There is something important here about the Jesus of history and the Christ of faith.)

"Come and learn about him" disturbed me even more. I'm not sure that learning about Jesus is a very helpful idea. I can learn about weather patterns. I can learn about the habits of polar bears. I can learn about the development of mining in Pennsylvania. All very useful in its own way, I suppose. But not exactly life changing! That Christ is born is a spiritual reality that calls us to follow, to experience, to know, to be, to become.

I have pondered what I would have rather seen on the sign. Here's a few contenders:

Christ is born! Be a follower!

Christ is born! Experience love!

Christ is born! Look inside.

That being said, I'm not big into church notice boards and probably would not have one!

6. Post-Christmas Reflections

So now it's all over. Too much shopping, too much food . . . and immediately the sales. Advent turned into frantic activity when, traditionally, it ought to be a time of reflection. Christmas ends with the same frantic opening of presents (to be exchanged in the sales) and the twelve days cease to be.

But turn things around. Post-Christmas is now a time of reflection. It's time to ease back, measure the year past and consider the year to come.

For me, it has been a period of thinking through incarnation; the central mystery of faith as the divine uniting with the human; the transcendent becoming immanent; humanity enlivened by divinity. Incarnation is ultimately sacramental, the created making known the uncreated; humanity through which divinity is glimpsed.

And this year for me the wonder is that all are called to this; to be the daughters and sons of God in whose lives love, kindness, justice, and peace are glimpsed.

May I be as Christ to those I meet. May I be a sacrament. May I, too, be one with the divine, one with ultimate reality.

7. The Holy Land

In the Christmas season—the season of peace and goodwill—one of the prayers in our *Way of Living* (Fitz-Gibbon and Fitz-Gibbbon, 2006) is for "Rulers, especially in the Holy Land." So my mind has been there, each day in our morning prayers, as Jane and I have said the Office. It has been a strange juxtaposition as I have enjoyed the joy and rest of Christmas time and at the same time followed news of great distress in Israel/Palestine. The Bethlehem of Christmas cards and Christmas cribs seems far different to the Bethlehem in the midst of conflict and great unrest.

Many issues have intersected for me this week. Here are some of them:

- On December 28, we remembered the Holy Innocents, when Herod killed baby boys in ancient Judea.
- Hamas rockets fired into Israel killing four people. Pictures of damaged buildings.
- Israeli fighter-bombers killing 400 people in Gaza; 100 who were civilians. Pictures of maimed children; little girls aged five and seven, like my granddaughters, with tears and great fear in their eyes.
- A former student of mine is in Israel. She is Jewish and is part of a peace movement there. She wrote to me and asked for prayers for peace. I wrote back and asked if she is safe. She told me, yes; the nearest rockets had exploded half an hour south of where she is. That is the distance from our home in Ithaca to the university in Cortland where I teach.
- A keffiyeh from Bethlehem bought for me by a friend who is a minister and who this past fall went to the West Bank to work with Palestinians on the olive harvest. Israeli settlers have often harassed these poor Palestinian farmers at harvest time. The presence of internationals helps prevent that. I have worn my keffiyeh this week in solidarity with Palestinian children—it has become a kind of sacrament for me.
- The scriptures in the Daily Office that talk often of the promise of the land made by God to ancient Israel. Stories of battles for the land and of ancient peoples being dispossessed, all in God's name. The ancient stories repeated as justification for intense violence.

I have tried to make sense of all this without much success. I have been sad. But here are a few thoughts.

My commitment to love and nonviolence leads me to condemn all acts of violence whether by state actors or by non-state groups and individuals. I believe that violence is always a failure to love.

In my prayers and imagination, I have tried to put myself in the place of those in the conflict. I can imagine some of the fear of the southern Israelis in range of rocket attacks. The chances of being killed by those rockets are very slim. Yet, the fear remains and is very real. In the 1970s, 1980s, and early 1990s, the IRA regularly and randomly bombed English towns. Several times, we were very close. Once we were on a train when a bomb had been planted at the next station. My brother and his baby son were evacuated from the center of Manchester before the IRA destroyed a whole shopping mall. Jane's sister was a regular visitor to a pub in Birmingham where twenty-one people were killed. The town center of Warrington, where Jane and I were married, was destroyed. Little children were killed as they shopped with their parents. The fear of those random attacks is very real, even though the chance of becoming a victim is rare. Nonetheless, you carry on with your everyday business. I think it will be like that in southern Israel.

Yet, I cannot imagine the fear of living on the Gaza strip where literally thousands of tons of bombs have been dropped in a week. That fear is real terror. Terrorism—the deliberate production of that kind of fear—is loathsome.

As a pacifist, I do not think the just war tradition is sufficient. Yet, it has been a necessary attempt to limit war. It tells us when wars can be fought and by whom, how they may be fought, and how to end wars in a just manner. Proportionality is a major tenet. Defenders may only fight wars with the same amount of force used against them. It must also be the least amount of force necessary. It seems clear to me that four deaths compared to four hundred is a disproportionate use of force. State terror is as sinful as any other kind of terror.

I have tried, and will continue to try, to be faithful to my former student's request. I pray for peace. I pray for the victims of violence. I pray for the children who will be traumatized and radicalized by their experiences.

FOURTEEN

EPIPHANY

1. The Democratization of Mysticism

The season of Epiphany—the unveiling, the coming of the light. This motif of unveiling, revealing, enlightening is not merely theoretical, but is to be entered into in our experience. Today I want to take a tangential look at mysticism: the experience of God.

While there is great similarity between the mystical traditions of East and West, mysticism is difficult to categorize. There has never been a church of mystics only, as if mysticism could be institutionalized, for institution and mysticism are contrary (though, perhaps, the Quakers come close). Most mystics have not claimed to be mystics but have been termed so by others. In Ernst Troeltsch's sociological typology (1992), mysticism is the third religious type and is least important historically. He spends most time differntiating the church and the sect.

The church is that kind of religion into which one is born and which provides the rituals and life passages. The church gives a religious legitimation to society. The sect is that kind of religion one joins as an adult and is characterized by disdain for the world and a radical commitment to the sect's aims. According to Troeltsch, mysticism is the religion of the individual who avoids the compromise of the church and the radicalism of the sect. Yet, mystics have been found not only as isolated individuals but also in both church and sect types of religion.

In the Lindisfarne Community, we look in the direction of the church type (with our apostolic succession and links to the great tradition through it), in the direction of the sect type (with our dissent and radicalism), but we most closely resemble that type of religion Troeltsch terms mysticism.

What characterizes the mystic? W.R. Inge, who remains a trustworthy authority on Western mysticism, gave twenty-six classical definitions of mysticism in his *Christian Mysticism* (1899) and added several more in his *Mysticism in Religion* (1947). He found consensus amongst the scholars with one exception: the mystics divide over the value of ordinary consciousness and the visible world. Some mistrust the material world; others recognize the sensible as being symbolic of ultimate reality. Yet, even given this difference, spiritual experience (what Otto calls the numinous) the unity of all things and a profound sense of love are the stock-in-trade of the mystic.

Ursula King's contemporary definition summarizes what many think and falls on the side of the sacramental (the sensible world as mediator of the ultimate).

> A mystic is a person who is deeply aware of the powerful presence of the divine Spirit: someone who seeks, above all, the knowledge and love of God and who experiences to an extraordinary degree the profoundly personal encounter with the energy of the divine life. Mystics often perceive the presence of God throughout the world of nature and in all that is alive, leading to a transfiguration of the ordinary all around them.
>
> (2001, 3)

Yet, this definition suggests that the mystical experience is found in few people. It is the province of the rare human being who has some direct contact with God to an extraordinary degree. Here I tend to disagree. Dorothee Soelle (theologian and mystic who taught at Union Seminary in the 1980s) used the term "democratizing the concept of mysticism" (2001). She says we are all mystics, or are so potentially. Far from being an esoteric experience of the very few, the mystical experience can be the normal experience of all who seek after God.

What is the heart of the mystical experience? It is the movement of the self toward the Other, where the self becomes self-forgetful (loses itself) and becomes focused on the Other in love.

2. Ways of Enlightenment

Epiphany is the season of light, enlightenment, the coming of God to us. I want to suggest there are four ways of enlightenment, each interconnected with the other and each, in its own way, sacramental. In the words of Ursula King, we are speaking of the:

> Interpenetration of spirit and matter, where matter itself becomes a vehicle for Spirit, a sacrament.

It may be possible for a human being to have an unmediated experience of the divine presence. However, if so, I think such experience would be quite rare. There is a long tradition that for the human spirit to gaze unmediated on pure light, goodness, or beauty would be to die. The human frame is not presently equipped for the experience. There is the Jewish story of Moses who wanted to see divine glory, and who was given a glimpse of the "back parts" of God. The full view was too intense. It is a very beautiful little story. There are, of course, other stories where great saints and adepts have been given the glimpse of God (Mother Julian of Norwich's visions, come to mind). However, we know of them because they are rare and, therefore, worthy of recording and remembering over the centuries.

The route to enlightenment for you and me—the route to seeing—will most often be sacramental. It is a mediated experience of the transcendent through the immanent. God will show herself to us in tangential ways, not altogether clearly, in ways open to various interpretations. We hear the voice speak, and others ask if it thundered. We awake from a dream of heaven, and we wonder what we had for dinner the night before! There will always be ambiguity.

The experience comes to us also through mindfulness. Here is opportunity to find God each moment of each day, for those with eyes to see. It requires the discipline of awareness. To be mindful at all times. To be present in each moment, not to be locked into the past, with its troubled memories, and not anxious of the future with its uncertainties.

The experience of divinity also comes through sacred texts. We are fortunate to have the record and wrestling of many good people who have been on the same quest toward enlightenment. Their quest is found in the sacred texts of many traditions. It is why we read the scriptures daily as part of the Daily Office. Yet, we take these holy texts as they are—a finite and very human (therefore, imperfect) reaching beyond. They are the wrestling of sometimes very troubled souls facing the same issues we face in our ordinary humdrum lives. The answers and insights they offer will not always satisfy us. Their inordinate outbursts will trouble us. That is to the good. There are no quick fixes. As they struggled, we struggle too.

We experience God, then, through reasoned interpretation. Texts, of all kinds, need careful interpretation. There is no such thing as an uninterpreted text. This issue is magnified when the texts, through long use and untold benefit, have become sacred. The text cannot stand alone as a guide. This is quite a radical idea, for we have been used to thinking that all we need to do with people is give them a copy of our preferred holy book, and all will be well. Sacred texts need a framework of interpretation to make sense. Otherwise the text can make no sense, or even worse, bad sense. That is why in many traditions a high value is placed on the spiritual discipline of study. It is true for us in the Lindisfarne Community for those reading for holy orders.

Finally, we experience the divine through the mediation of the Spirit of God, the divine energy, the *qi*. Spirit is what bishop theologian J.V. Taylor called the "go-between God" (2010). Spirit is not a completely unmediated experience of the "Godhead beyond God" (as Eckhart would have it). Yet, Spirit brings us closer. For Christians, Jesus is an archetype—a human being filled with divine Spirit. Spirit for Christians is God in the face of Jesus Christ. The mystery of spirit is also the experience of Spirit in people. Christians have become so familiar with the term "the body of Christ" that its power is often lost. Christ as light comes to us not only in an inner mystical way, but is embodied in people of flesh and blood. People become a sacrament of divine presence. Christ is in all. Spirit is in all. Divine energy is in all. May we find the light.

3. Am I Enlightened?

The people who walked in darkness have seen a great light; those who lived in a land of deep darkness-on them light has shined. (Isaiah 9:2)

The people who sat in darkness have seen a great light, and for those who sat in the region and shadow of death light has dawned. (Matthew 4:16)

In religious language, there are a number of motifs that speak of the human telos, the goal to which human beings are moving. The motifs are expressed as metaphors—"it's a bit like this." This is not literal language, but more than literal. It takes the form of "from" and "to":

> From slavery to freedom . . . the telos is freedom
> From death to life . . . the telos is birth, being born into new life
> From suffering to peace . . . the telos is perfect peace
> From illness to healing . . . the telos is wholeness, completeness
> From darkness to light . . . the telos is enlightenment

There are more, but these suffice. The form of "from" and "to" suggest a few things. Human life is not as it could or should be; we know there is a lack. Human life is not static; there is movement from something toward something else. There is a promise and hope; things will be different.

There is within us a longing for this other thing. We long to be free, to know the fullness of life, to know perfect peace, to be whole, to see things as they really are. Even when unaware, the longing is in an inarticulate ache, a restlessness. I am tempted to say that that this longing is the root and substance of the religious impulse. It is the spark of divinity deep in all of us reaching out for Ultimate Reality.

In this season of Epiphany, we focus on light, on enlightenment. In my musings, I wondered, "Am I enlightened? Do I truly see?"

My tentative answer is, "yes, and no." I do not think I am enlightened. Yet, I do think that I have had moments of enlightenment. There have been occasions when it is almost like the veil has been removed and for the briefest of times I see with great clarity. And then it is gone.

Sometimes these moments are like daydreams, when the everyday world recedes and I find myself in some other place where all is clear. It may be sitting reading, or driving the car to work, or even in the shower.

Sometimes the moments of enlightenment are in my dreams while sleeping. At a recent retreat, the main speaker, a psychoanalyst, talked to us about dreams. I asked him why it was that sometimes in my dreams I have such clarity of insight, only to be lost on wakening. The insight remains for the briefest of moments and then it is gone. Did I really see that clearly? His opinion was, yes, it was a true glimpse of reality. A glimpse. Nothing more; but, nothing less. A glimpse of reality.

It is these briefest of glimpses, moments of enlightenment, that give us hope that we are in movement toward the fullness of enlightenment.

Yet, there is another way to think of it. Enlightenment may come in two ways. The first is like the switching on a light. Here we are in darkness; the light is turned on and the darkness is no more. I think the brief moments of enlightenment are like that. When the light comes, the darkness goes and we see. Of course, if we have been in the dark a long time, the light itself is blinding and even in the light we do not see. It takes time for eyes used to darkness to adjust.

The other way of enlightenment is the gradual rising of the sun.

Last week we had opportunity to leave home in the darkness for an early appointment in another city. As we drove in the darkness, gradually dawn came. It was a cloudy day, so we did not see the sun rise. Yet the light came. The light came in imperceptible increments. It was difficult to say when the day had broken. It is equally hard to say at what point enlightenment happens. It is very gradual. I see more clearly now than I did a moment before. Yet, there is nothing spectacular; no great event you could put your finger on. If I compare what I see now, with what I saw before, it is more.

However, I will not be dogmatic about what I think I see. As the light begins to dawn, shadows play tricks on the eyes. Dawn and dusk are the most difficult times to drive. There is sight, but it is far from perfect. One of the greatest problems with religion (and it can be very dangerous for others) is when someone gets the beginning of enlightenment and proclaims that they now see clearly. It is the arrogance of the spiritually immature. The world is full of it and is a more violent place because of it.

When I look back on my early years as a minister, I cringe at the arrogance of my spiritual immaturity; the dogmas I confidently proclaimed; the things I thought I saw clearly and insisted that others see too. The shadows played tricks, but I was unaware and people suffered. Nonetheless, enlightenment awaits! Humility is needed with the little we think we see now.

FIFTEEN

LENT

1. The Desert

A few general Lenten thoughts and the image of the desert.

The desert is literally a place of deprivation, something left waste. Little grows in the desert. There is no civilization. The desert offers meagre fare. Hence, the image of the desert has become a powerful metaphor for aspects of life when we find ourselves in a place of deprivation. There are times when the desert seeks us out . . . illness, life changes, the loss of a loved one, the loss of a job, and depression (the deprivation of meaning, of well-being) are all desert experiences.

The desert became a potent symbol in early Christianity. John the Baptizer chose the life of the desert. Jesus sought the desert before beginning his ministry where he wrestled with his own inner demons. After around 250 CE there was a movement we now call the desert mothers and fathers. The desert mystics intentionally left society to find a physical desert to practice their spirituality. The early Irish monastics often sought out a barren island as their home, such as Skellig Michael where they lived in stone-built huts.

When "desert experiences" are often so painful, why choose the image of desert as an image of spiritual life?

Human nature (as with all animal nature) may be said to be a bundle of needs. Psychologist Abraham Maslow pointed this out in 1943, and his view is respected still. Those needs, when largely met, are not a problem to us. But needs are closely related to desires. Desires have often been termed "the passions." A great deal of philosophy and spirituality over the centuries has tried to deal with the passions. The passions left unruly dominate human life, and always bring suffering in their wake. The desert has been found to be a way to help deal with problematic passions.

There has been an unhealthy fear of the passions. Desires and passions have often been socially constructed as feminine, with rationality constructed as masculine. And everyone knows that reason is preferable to emotion. In patriarchal cultures this has been one more way of denigrating the feminine and women generally. Yet, I cannot conceive of an understanding of love without desire. In fact, desire is the beginning of love. To eradicate desire from human life would be to deny love. Not a happy solution! I am not convinced that all desires or all passions are a problem. Yet, some are. The mystics entered the desert to conquer problematic desires.

Buddhism has a very useful insight. Suffering come from desire, desire can be conquered. The eightfold path is one way to do that. Here is the path:

Wisdom
    (1) Right view
    (2) Right intention
Ethical conduct
    (3) Right speech
    (4) Right action
    (5) Right livelihood
Mental discipline
    (6) Right effort
    (7) Right mindfulness
    (8) Right concentration

This noble eightfold path is said to be the way to deal with the troublesome desires that cause suffering. These all have their equivalents in Christianity, though there is no reason why Christians cannot simply follow the eightfold path. There is no incompatibility.

Historically, in the mystical tradition of spirituality, there are times when we seek the desert. Lent is such a time. It is the desert experience that helps us come to terms effectively with need, desire, passion. That is what the "what are you giving up for Lent?" question is all about. In Lent we have a deliberate time when we can take stock, see whether the needs, desires and passions of life have mastery over us, or whether we have mastery over desire. How often we choose to fast (to deny ourselves something for a specific period) only to find an immediate and desperate craving for that thing?

Regular retreat is also helpful. Retreats are desert places. It need not be a long retreat. A period each day of quietness and emptying is a retreat. These are the little deserts that we enter each day, to remind us that the demands of need and desire do not have the final say.

2. The Grubbiness of Torture

Today is Palm Sunday, the final Sunday of preparation before Easter. One of the alternative readings in the lectionary is to read the whole of the torture and crucifixion narrative. We choose to do that each Palm Sunday. It is not an edifying experience. We read for a while and then have a period of meditation. Then read again. Then meditate again. Today I was struck with the grubbiness and inhumanity of torture.

In the mail last week, we received spam containing a "woman's devotional." It was daily readings for women about beauty. So I read a little. The daily reading I came across talked about the beauty of the cross of Jesus. It said that true beauty was not what you look like outwardly, but rather true beauty was Jesus being crucified. I felt sick. There is nothing of beauty, or honor, or glory in the inhumanity of someone torturing and cruelly abusing the body of another.

At this time of year, there is that other silliness that says Jesus suffered more than any other human being ever could or has suffered. I read this week in the London Times the story of a man who survived recently two months of torture in Syria. The story was very difficult to read, and the man suffered horribly. I will not repeat here the details of the torture he endured. Suffice it to say that it was excruciatingly painful and repeated day after day. The world is in outcry at the abuses of government power in Syria, and rightly so. Torture and execution is, and always has been, a grubby and shameful thing.

Thankfully, though the news and entertainment industries lead us to think that violence and torture are on the increase, this is not the case. I read recently Steven Pinker's *The Better Angel's of Our Nature*. Pinker argues persuasively that violence, war, and torture have been in decline for a long time. If this seems counterintuitive, get his book. Only a few centuries ago, torture was accepted by most in society as a helpful tool in the arsenal of government. Torture and execution were public spectacle, enjoyed by the crowds as a spectator sport. The equivalent would be watching on prime time television gruesome tortures and executions, just for the fun of it. Such an idea now turns our stomachs.

Pinker roots the change in Enlightenment reason from the seventeenth century onward. It is too long and involved a thesis to consider here. My own gloss on his thesis is that the better Enlightenment sensibilities were themselves rooted in the tradition of humanity that grew in the Jewish wisdom and prophetic traditions, of which Jesus was an exemplar. (A tradition mirrored in the East in the Buddha, the Dao, Confucius and the Baghavad Gita.) It has been the growing realization that violence, war, and torture are not the glory of humanity, but its shame. In its place is humaneness, tolerance, kindness, and forgiveness—in short love. Human relationships are better as loving relationships than as hateful and harmful ones. It has taken a long time for us to begin to realize this. Collectively we have a long way to go. My conviction is that loving nonviolence is a way of living whose time has come.

For those of us who are Christians, where does it leave the crucifixion of Jesus? Not something of beauty. Not the silliness that his torture and execution was any different to the suffering of millions of others. It leaves us (following Renee Girard) with the notion that in Jesus is the end of torture, executions, scapegoating and sacrificing. It is not, as in some traditional theology, that causing the pain of others is pleasing to God—as if God delights in the torture and death of any. I have long been convinced that if the death of Jesus has cosmic meaning, it is that God suffers with those who suffer—that because God suffers in and with us we ought to work toward the end of suffering.

SIXTEEN

EASTER

1. Easter Thoughts

Some Lents are better than others are. This year, for some reason, Lent has been a struggle for me. I have not been as focused as at other times. I have not felt as centered. It began well with Ash Wednesday and a beautiful service at the motherhouse here in Ithaca. There were the usual elements of fasting and preparation, yet with no particular sense of importance this year. I think I was feeling bad that it had not been a better Lent.

Then, on Maundy Thursday, there was a very sweet sense of God's presence. On Good Friday, we ended the liturgy in darkness and silence. And expectation.

Then, today, Holy Saturday, Jane and I spent the afternoon in the garden. We cleared away the debris of the winter; moving leaves, revealing life. Life was everywhere. I felt overwhelmed. Then revelation came. Lent is preparation for life. I think I had always seen Lent as preparation for death. But no, death had been there during the winter months. There was no need to prepare for death. It was upon us. Today, in the garden we made way for life. It is perhaps obvious, but it came new to me today: the Lenten weeks prepare us for life . . . unstoppable, irrepressible, overabundant life.

Christ is risen. Alleluia!

2. The Same But Different

In Christian tradition, there is a fruitful tension in seeing Jesus as the same but different. By that I mean the same but different to every other human being. The tension is very real and the weight has tended to shift from one to the other in different movements and at different times. On balance, I think the tradition has sided with the "different" understanding of Jesus. Because Jesus is different to us, Jesus can save us. He is different to us because he was born of a virgin. He is different to us because he worked all those miracles and walked on water. He is different to us because he rose from the dead.

I want to think about the sameness. This has been more of a minority tradition, but still a strong one. Jesus is the same as all other people and this gives us hope. If Jesus is so different to us, then as an example he is not very useful. "It was OK for Jesus, because he wasn't like us. He didn't know how we struggle with the things we struggle with." Yet, the sameness means that we can be like Jesus. I think this was something of the feeling of charismatic theology, which said Jesus did not do miracles because he was the unique Son of God, but because he was a human being (like us) empowered by God. If Jesus, as a human being like us, could heal the sick, then we too empowered by God can heal the sick.

This is the Easter season when we focus on the resurrection of Jesus. If Jesus is so different that the resurrection is seen as unique, then it helps us little. However, if, in sameness to us, the resurrection of Jesus awaits us all, then there is much to be glad about. If the story of Jesus rising is the hope of the world, then all who die rise in the same way. Death is not the end, not the finality of everything, but rather a gateway to something new. Those we love who have passed before us have risen as Christ has risen. I think that is the meaning of the *pericope* that says when Jesus died and rose; the graves released their occupants. Just like Jesus, the dead are raised. They too continue to be.

There is a second way of looking at the same but different theme in terms of the resurrection. It is a central idea in Christianity, but it is full of mystery. It is very difficult to understand what the resurrection is about. It perplexed the early Christians who strongly affirmed it, yet found it difficult to get their heads around. They expressed it in narrative form in the Easter stories, but the stories have inconsistencies, ideas difficult to grasp. Jesus appears but is not really known. He speaks but his voice is somehow strange. He appears and disappears, yet seems to have substance as he eats fish.

One way to look at the stories is to say that in resurrection Jesus is the same, but different. Jesus is clearly a continuing self, a person who continues after death, the person after death forming a continuing narrative with the person before death. Yet, the person after death is different than the person of flesh and blood. A continuing self, the same but different. That is a meaning of resurrection and it is an idea full of hope.

The Psalmist wondered: "Do you work wonders for the dead? Will those who have died stand and give you thanks? Will your loving-kindness be declared in the grave? Your faithfulness in the land of destruction? Will your wonders be known in the dark? Or your righteousness in the country where all is forgotten?" (Psalm 88:11-13)

That wondering is common to all people at some time. What happens when we die? Is there something or nothing? The popular BBC science fiction series *Torchwood* touches on life and death a great deal. One of its main characters dies and is brought back to life, only to live in some shadow half-life. He is asked what it is like to die. His answer is that there is nothing. You die and there is nothing. In some respects that is a hopeful idea. If there is nothing, then you do not feel anything good or bad. Death, then, is not to be feared. No heaven or hell. No continuing self. Just nothing.

The Christian story tells it differently. What happens when we die? Just like Jesus we continue. Differently, but continue as the same self, with the same memories, the same experiences passed through that shape and make us the people we are. Yet the sting is removed, the poison taken away, the suffering ended. The scars are there in hand and side, but they no longer afflict. The same, but different.

3. A Natural Theology of Easter

A cloudless sky. Spring birdsong. White, pink, red, and yellow blossoms on the trees. Sitting in the hottub taking it all in. A perfect Easter Sunday morning. In years past, I have been mildly disappointed to awaken on Easter morning to an overcast sky—or one year (our first in the United States) to a six-inch blanket of freshly fallen snow! The Easter season is the season of life, of spring, of newness.

Around the world today congregations will echo with the refrain "Christ is Risen!" I will gladly join the refrain. But what is it we celebrate? Not the mere resuscitation of a corpse. Something much more profound than that. I will celebrate something fundamental about the nature of the universe. There is *something* rather the *nothing*.

Death is nothing—literally no-thing. Death is the absence of life, the ceasing to be, the void, the absence of consciousness. When push comes to shove, is the universe we inhabit a universe of absence, or of presence? Of death (no-thing) or life (some-thing)? My money is on life! Christ is risen! Death is not the final word, for out of death comes new life.

Of course, I can't prove this. Nothing or something? Toss a coin? Heads is something, tails is nothing. Or is there something a little less haphazard?

While the "big" question is outside the realm of proof, its answer is not merely a lottery. We move into the realm of plausibility based upon our experiences of life, and by our observations of life. (The deck is already loaded—it is experiences of *life*, observations of *life*, rather than death that is our subject.) Nature points in a certain direction.

I am a fan of the seasons—fall, winter, spring, and summer. I love each in its own way. I love the distinctiveness. I love that each contains the season to come. In the fall, you get the occasional deep chill that promises winter is coming. In the middle of winter, if you look closely you will see the beginning of buds on the trees. Spring surprises us with the occasional June day of summer warmth and scents. In the middle of summer, you notice a few leaves turning. There is always *something*, always change. The darkest night contains the beginnings of morning. These are nature's clues.

All is connected. When I "shuffle off this mortal coil"—from Hamlet. How much the quaintness of the English language owes to Shakespeare!—which I undoubtedly will, likely as not my body will be buried. In a short while, as my body decomposes it will bring nourishment to the soil, and through the soil to everything that grows. That which grows will be consumed by others, and nourish them until they too return to the earth. Earth, plants, animals, people—we are all of the same stuff. There is something rather than nothing, and we are an organic and intimate part of that something. Interconnected. In interbeing.

So much for bodies. But we are more than bodies. We are conscious beings—bodies and souls, or bodies, souls and spirits. We feel, and know, and experience, and sense. Descartes reached for something important with his *cogito ergo sum*—I think, therefore, I am. Consciousness is that which cannot be doubted. That I am conscious of my thoughts, my wondering, my doubting all that can be doubted, *that* is foundational. And like material reality that goes on and on, and changes, and transforms, and becomes, so too does consciousness. For if consciousness, like the body, is something rather than nothing, then something wins the day.

Christ is risen! For Christ is not nothing, but something. And if Christ is something rather than nothing, then all those who have lived and died are also something rather than nothing. For nothing has no existence. Existence is reality. If nothing has no existence, and that which exists is the real, then nothing is unreal.

But how do we *know* that there is something rather than nothing? Here we are beyond the realms of proof. There are certain "basic beliefs" that we hold because we can do no other. These basic beliefs come from our culture, from common sense, from intuition, from great minds. Of course, they can, and should, from time to time be challenged and questioned and examined. That there is existence rather than nonexistence makes sense of life and experience.

On this Easter Sunday morning I celebrate that Christ is risen. Christ is risen indeed!

4. Easter Lectionary Reflections

Exegetical comments:

(1) The Luke-Acts tradition is, like all the gospels, a "making sense" of the Christ event—the coming of one who was life and love, who was killed and is now risen, present with those who confess the name.

(2) However, the event needs some explanation, some framework to understand, some matrix within which to live.

(3) There was great expectation and joy as one came from God, who seemed to make everything right, whom to know was life.

(4) Then, he was taken away and unjustly and brutally executed. All the hope, expectation, and longing were shattered in the events of a night and a day.

(5) Death shattered. Hope renewed. A new power, as the presence is now within—the Spirit of Jesus no longer an external friend, but an internal presence. [In the Johannine tradition, there is a different

account of Pentecost. The risen Jesus breathes on the disciples on the night of resurrection, the Spirit is within from the day of resurrection. In the Lukan tradition, there is a period of waiting and preparation.]

(6) In this first flush of astonishing presence and power, it is assumed that the coming reign of God will be soon. If Christ has come in the Spirit of Jesus, then surely the longed-for consummation of all things is near. But no. Time passes and the Messiah does not return. How are we to explain this?

(7) In the lectionary today there are two streams of interpretation. In the Lukan stream, in the gospel the explanation is that when the inner empowering happens, it is for the purpose of taking the good news of God's love in Christ to all the nations. It is implicit, that when this gospel has been heard and received by all that the consummation will come. In the Acts, the mission of Jesus continues in the healing of the lame with sign and symbol that the work continues. This will continue in the name of Jesus until the restoration of all things. This universal restoration is yet future, and Acts leaves us with the job only beginning as the gospel of Jesus is brought to Rome.

(8) In the Johannine tradition, emphasis is on inner transformation from sin to life and love, knowing that one day as God's children we will see God and be like God, though we do not know what that will be like. [There are some things difficult to understand parts of John, like "those who have been born of God do not sin." It raises important and difficult questions such as what is sin, what is to be born of God, which I cannot now stay with.]

Reflections: What are we to make of this?

(1)   Common to them all is a looking forward, a message of hope.

(2)   In Luke, the hope is that all nations will find the forgiveness of God in Jesus through a change of heart and mind.

(3)   In Acts, the hope is one of universal restoration when all shall be made well.

(4)   In John's letter, the hope is transformation into the image of God in Jesus.

(5)   Key words are: forgiveness, restoration and transformation, and these are close to the heart of the message of Jesus.

(6) We, and the entire world, are in process. The process is toward a fulfillment of goodness and love and justice, when all will be made well.

(7) It takes trust to believe such. Trust that in God, all shall be well, and that is given to us in the resurrection of Jesus.

(8) This side of death all is not made well. In the world there is so much injustice, suffering, wrong that is not well at the time of death. That is why death is such an enemy. Death seems to rob us of justice. Death seems to end love. Death interrupts goodness.

(9) The gospel of Jesus tells us that there is life through death. Death is part of the process through which life eventually triumphs. [Sitting in the garden in spring, look around you is a sign. Death is swallowed up in life.]

(10) It is sometimes hard to trust. In the midst of aging, illness, failing senses, can we trust that all shall be well? That is the message of Easter.

5. Choose Life

Today is Easter Sunday. Jane is in Arkansas visiting the family—first time seeing our grandson Kieran! I am home alone. Not quite—two foster kids and two pugs. I have spent the day in quietness and reading, sitting on the deck enjoying a beautiful spring day. I am thankful for life and the signs of new life all around. The pugs and I took a slow walk around the yard. Lots of life breaking out, where there was deep snow only a couple of weeks ago.

I finished a Jonathan Saffron Foer's *Eating Animals* (2009). It's a book we are reading in my class "Animals and Ethics." I did not learn much new information (I have been teaching animal rights for ten years), but I was profoundly moved again. Moved to tears, I have to admit. Foer's book is less philosophical and more journalistic than the other books we read in my class. For that reason, it will have a much wider general readership. It deserves to be read. By everyone.

The enormity of animal cruelty and suffering at the hands of human beings is extravagant. Most of it is related to the food we eat and the way we produce it. Our culture sees our animal cousins as mere products to be consumed, and not as companions to share God's good earth.

The Easter story is a retelling of the story that suffering, cruelty and death are not the final words. Life—beautiful, vibrant, fresh—springs forth from the hopelessness of devastation.

Easter reminds us to side with life. The way we eat sides with life or death. Choose life!

> The wolf and the lamb shall feed together, the lion shall eat straw like the ox . . . They shall not hurt or destroy on all my holy mountain, says God (Isaiah 16:25)

SEVENTEEN

PENTECOST

1. A Non-Exclusive Way of Seeing

Today in the cycle of the church's year we celebrate the feast of Pentecost. The calendar is a yearly reminder of God's work in the world. We begin with the promise of Messiah in Advent. God is revealed to the world in Christ at Christmas and Epiphany Then at Easter time God is shown in suffering love, and life from death. At Pentecost we celebrate the ongoing work of God in Christ through the Spirit. In this telling, the cycle is thoroughly Trinitarian.

Today my question is: What does it mean for God in Christ to be present in the world through the Spirit? My answer is that it means a non-exclusive seeing of God in all people, in all things, and in multifarious ways. The Spirit of God is present everywhere.

I have not always thought this. I was taught, and believed it to be true, that the Spirit of God was only present in a few. Let's call them "the elect," as we did in my Calvinist formation. The Spirit was not for the world but for a select remnant. One of the sad outcomes of such a view was a "them and us" mentality. Further, despite its connection with a belief in the sovereignty of God, in practice it is a very narrow vision of God in the world. Most of the world is outside the Spirit of God.

It's all a question of seeing. It needs a new way of looking. What if the feast of Pentecost tells us that the Spirit of God is loosed in the world; loosed in the entire world; that God in the Spirit is present to all, and in all, if only we could see it?

Rephrasing it: To find the Spirit in all is to find Christ in all is to find God in all. All the goodness in the world comes from God. There is more goodness in the world than badness. Wherever we find goodness, there we find the Spirit of God.

This week, I was reading a student's paper. The student said something like this: "For every act of kindness in the world, I wager you could find ten atrocities." In a way, this is an empirical wager. Theoretically, we could count all the acts of kindness and all the atrocities and see how many there are. Practically, that is impossible. But I think that the student was not making such an empirical claim. She was asserting a way of seeing life. It is a way that sees life in a very pessimistic way.

I did have opportunity to talk with her about this. My response was this. For every atrocity in the world, I wager there are thousands of acts of kindness and goodness—every kind word, every act of generosity, every fulfillment of duty, and every gentle and loving touch. Sadly the media, which is so pervasive in shaping thought, tells us mostly only the bad.

The Spirit of God is loosed in the world as goodness. In the multifarious acts of goodness, we find the Spirit. Paul helps us in 1 Corinthians 12, where he says: "There are varieties of gifts, but the same Spirit; there are varieties of service but the same Lord; there are varieties of activities, but it is the same God who activates all of them in everyone." All these good gifts, services and activities present ion the world come from the same Spirit, Lord and God. (Notice Paul is here also very Trinitarian.)

So, to celebrate Pentecost is to celebrate the working of the Spirit of God in goodness in all. It is an expansive, non-exclusive way of seeing.

WORKS CITED

American Psychiatric Association. (1994) *Diagnostic and Statistical Manual of Mental Disorders* (*DSM-IV*). Fourth Edition. Washington, D.C.

Aristotle. (1962) *Nicomachean Ethics*. Translated by Martin Oswald. Indianapolis, Ind.: Bobbs-Merrill.

Augustine, Saint, Bishop of Hippo. (1952) *The Confessions*. Translated by E. B. Pusey, Maruc Dods, and others. Chicago: Encyclopaedia Britannica.

Beatie, Tina. (2008) *The New Atheists: The Twilight of Reason and the War on Religion*. Maryknoll: Orbis.

Beer, Francis. (1998) *Julian of Norwich: Revelations, Motherhood of God*. Cambridge: D.S. Brewer.

Bellah, Robert N. (1985) *Habits of the Heart: Individualism and Commitment in American Life*. Early, Calif.: University of California Press.

Bethge, Eberhard. (1970) *Dietrich Bonhoeffer: A Biography*. Minneapolis: Fortress Press.

Borg, Marcus. (2008) *Jesus: Uncovering the Life Teaching, and Relevance of a Religious Revolutionary*. New York: Harper Collins.

Bruce, F.F. (2000) *Paul: Apostle of the Free Spirit*. Grand Rapids: Eerdmans.

Buber, Martin. (1923) *Ich und Du*. Leipzig, Insel-Verlag.

—. (1937) *I and Thou*. New York, Charles Scribner's Sons.

Circle of Courage Philosophy. http://www.reclaiming.com/content/about-circle-of-*courage* (accessed 30 August 2012).

The Cloud of Unknowing. (2002) Translated by A.C. Spearing. New York: Penguin.

Donne, John. (1959) *Devotions upon Emergent Occasions* (Meditation XVII, 1624). Ann Arbor: University of Michigan Press.

Dunn, James. (1997) *Jesus and the Spirit: A Study of the Religious and Charismatic Experience of Jesus and the First Christians as Reflected in the New Testament.* Grand Rapids: Wm. B. Eerdmans.

Epictetus. (2008) *Discourses and Selected Writings.* New York: Penguin.

Fiorenza, Elizabeth Schüssler. (2001) *Wisdom Ways: Introducing Feminist Biblical Interpretation.* Maryknoll: Orbis.

Fitz-Gibbon, Andrew. (2000) *In the World, But Not of the World: Christian Social Thinking at the End of the Twentieth Century.* Lanham and Oxford: Lexington Books.

—. (2011) "Unity and Love for All" in *Call to Compassion: Religion and Animal Advocacy.* Edited by Lisa Kemmerer and Anthony Nocella II. New York: Lantern Books.

—. (2012) Adam Hochschild, "To End All Wars: A Story of Loyalty and Rebellion, 1914-1918." Book Review. *Journal for Peace and Justice Studies,* vol. 22, no. 1, pp. 144-147.

—. (2012) *Love as a Guide to Morals.* Amsterdam: Rodopi.

—, and Jane Fitz-Gibbon. (1995) *The Kiss of Intimacy.* Crowborough: Monarch.

—. (1997) *Prophetic Lifestyle and the Celtic Way.* Crowborough: Monarch.

—. (2006) *A Way of Living: A Worship, Prayer and Liturgy Resource for the Lindisfarne Community.* Philadelphia: XLibris.

Fletcher, Joseph. (1966) *Situation Ethics: The New Mora*lity. Philadelphia: Westminster Pr.

Foer, Jonathan Saffron. (2009) *Eating Animals.* New York: Little, Brown, and Company.

Foucault, Michel. (1977) *Discipline and Punish: The Birth of the Prison* (French original: *Surveiller et punir: Naissance de la prison*). Translated by Alan Sheridan. New York: Pantheon Books.

Freud, Sigmund. (2005) *Civilization and Its Discontents.* New York: W.W. Norton.

Hanh, Thich Nhat. (1995) *Living Buddha, Living Christ.* New York: Riverhead Books.

Hick, John. (2004) *The Fifth Dimension: An Exploration of the Spiritual Realm.* New York: One World.

Hill, Christopher. (1980) *The Century of Revolution 1603-1714.* New York: W.W. Norton.

Hochschild, Adam. (2011) *To End All Wars: A Story of Loyalty and Rebellion 1914-1918.* New York: Mariner Books.

Hume, David. (1969) *A Treatise of Human Nature.* New York: Penguin.

Huxley, Aldous. (2009) *The Perennial Philosophy: An Interpretation of the Great Mystics, East and West.* New York: Harper Collins.

Inge, W.R. (1899) *Christian Mysticism: Considered in Eight Lectures Delivered Before the University of Salford.* New York: Charles Scribner's Sons.

—. (1947) *Mysticism in Religion.* London: Hutchinson.

James, William. (1982) *Varieties of Religious Experience.* New York: Penguin.

Jantzen, Grace M. (1999) *Becoming Divine: Towards a Feminist Philosophy of Religion.* Bloomington and Indianapolis: Indiana University Press.

Kant, Immanuel. (1964) *Groundwork of the Metaphysics of Morals.* Translated by H. J. Paton. New York: Harper & Row.

Kierkegaard, Søren. (1954) *Fear and Trembling and The Sickness unto Death.* Garden City, N.Y.: Doubleday.

King, Ursula. (2001) *Christian Mystics: Their Lives and Legacies Throughout the Ages.* Mahwah: Hidden Spring.

Knitter, Paul F. (2009) *Without Buddha I Could Not Be a Christian.* New York: Oneworld Publications.

Laing, R. D. (1960) *The Divided Self.* London: Penguin.

Leech, Kenneth. (1980) *Soul Friend: An Invitation to Spiritual Direction.* San Francisco: Harper Collins.

Lewis, C. S. (1960) *The Four Loves.* New York: Harcourt Brace.

—. (2004) *The Chronicles of Narnia.* New York: Harper Collins (original 1949).

MacIntyre, Alasdair. (1981) *After Virtue.* London: Duckworth.

Marx, Karl, and Friedrich Engels. (1967) *The Communist Manifesto.* Translated by Samuel Moore. London: Penguin.

Moore, G. E. (1903) *Principia Ethica.* Cambridge: At the University Press.

Moss, H. St. L. B. (1998). *The Birth of the Middle Ages 395-814.* Translated by D. J. A. Matthew. London: Folio Society.

Niebuhr, H. Richard. (1951) *Christ and Culture.* New York: Harper.

Nietzsche, Friedrich Wilhelm. (1886). *Beyond Good and Evil.* Waiheke Island: Floating Press.

—. (1887). *The Genealogy of Morals.* New York: Boni and Liveright.

Otto, Rudolf. (1950) *The Idea of the Holy: An Inquiry into the Non-Rational Factor in the Idea of the Divine and Its Relation to the Rational.* Translated by John W. Harvey. London: Oxford University Press.

Philips, Adam, and Barbara Taylor. (2009) *On Kindness.* New York: Farrar, Straus, and Giroux.

Pinker, Steven. (2011) *The Better Angels of Our Nature: Why Violence Has Declined.* New York: Viking.

Plato. (1937*) The Apology, Phaedo, and Crito of Plato.* Edited by Charles William Eliot, Benjamin Jowett, and others. New York: P. F. Collier & Son.

Putnam, Robert D. (2001) *Bowling Alone: The Collapse and Revival of American Community.* New York: Touchstone.

Raine, Andy and John Skinner. (1994) *Celtic Daily Prayer.* London: Marshall Pickering.

—. (1995) *Celtic Night Prayer.* London: Marshall Pickering.

Simmer-Brown, Judith. (1999) "Commitment and Openness: A Contemplative Approach to Pluralism" in *The Heart of Learning: Spirituality in Education.* Edited by Steven Glazer (New York: Tarcher/Penguin).

Singer, Irving. (2009) *Meaning in Life: The Creation of Value.* Boston: MIT Press.

—. (2009). *Meaning in Life: The Pursuit of Love.* Boston: MIT Press.

—. (2009). *Meaning in Life: The Harmony of Nature and Spirit.* Boston: MIT Press.

Smith, Adam. (1982) *The Wealth of Nations.* New York: Penguin.

Soelle, Dorothee. (2001) *The Silent Cry: Mysticism and Resistance.* Minneapolis: Fortress.

Taylor, John V. (2010) *The Go-Between God.* London: SCM Press.

Tillich, Paul. (2011) *Dynamics of Faith.* San Francisco: Harper Collins.

Toulson, Shirley. (1993) *The Celtic Year: A Celebration of Celtic Christian Saints, Sites, and Festivals.* Rockport, Mass.: Element Books.

Troeltsch, Ernst. (1992) *The Social Teaching of the Christian Churches* (2 Vols). Translated by Olive Wyon. Louisville: Westminster/John Knox Press.

Wells, H.G. (2008) *The Time Machine.* New York: W.W. Norton.

Wilhelm, Richard. (1997) *The I Ching or Book of Changes.* Princeton, N.J.: University of Princeton.

Wisdom Stories. "Finger Pointing at the Moon." http://www.storiesofwisdom.com/finger-pointing-at-the-moon/ (accessed 30 August 2012).

Zhuangzi. (1996) *The Book of Chuang Tzu.* Translated by Martin Palmer, Elizabeth Breuilly, Chang Wai Ming and Jay Ramsay. New York: Arkana.

ABOUT THE AUTHOR

ANDREW FITZ-GIBBON, bishop-abbot of the Lindisfarne Community, was an accredited minister with the Baptist Union of Great Britain and Ireland, serving from 1981-1999. Presently, he is Associate Professor of Philosophy, Chair of the Philosophy Department, and Director of the Center for Ethics, Peace and Social Justice, at the State University of New York College at Cortland, where he has taught since 2000. He earned his PhD from Newcastle University, United Kingdom. His academic interests are in the areas of ethics, nonviolence, love, mysticism and community. He is the author, co-author, or editor of ten books, numerous book chapters and articles in peer-reviewed journals such as *Social Philosophy Today, The Journal for Peace and Justice Studies, The Acorn,* and *Philosophical Practice.* Currently, he is the President of Concerned Philosophers for Peace. He is an Associate Editor, VIBS, Editions Rodopi, B.V., where he edits the Social Philosophy Series. He is a fellow of the American Philosophical Practitioners Association, certified in client counseling.

Printed in Great Britain
by Amazon.co.uk, Ltd.,
Marston Gate.